The Queen, The Chairman and I

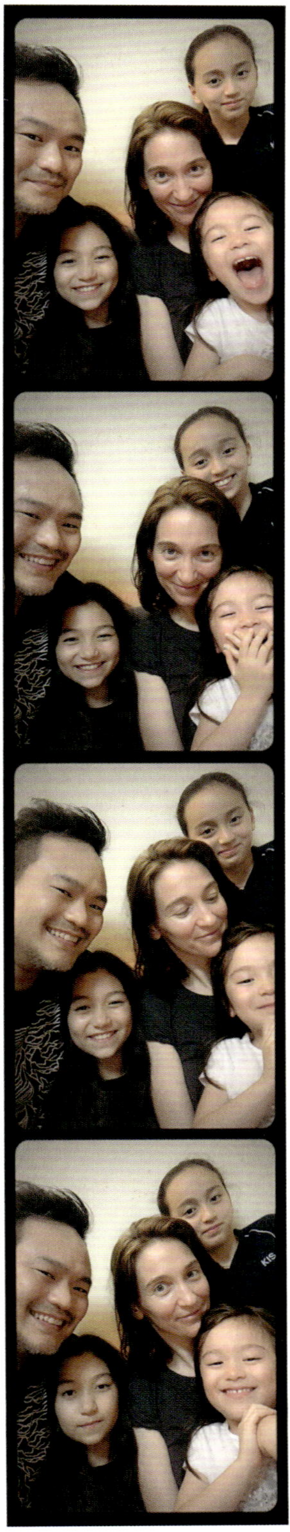

女皇, 主席與我

唐景鋒

The Queen, The Chairman and I

Kurt Tong

Dewi Lewis Publishing

Lianzhou Museum of Photography

「世界總是在變化。我們必須審視自己的內心，尋找那些不變的東西，
比如忠誠、我們共同的過往以及對彼此的愛。透過這些東西，
過去的真相才得以永遠延續。」

－羅納德・巴斯－

這個項目從我為女兒們寫的故事書開始。1977年，也就是中國政府與英國政府就香港前途問題展開談判的五年前，我在香港出生。我們港人有著與國內同胞很不一樣的身份背景，畢竟我在學校裡唱的國歌是《天佑女王》。我一直知道我最後會定居英國。我父親在英國唸書，他總和我說，在一九九七年香港回歸中國後，我們也許再不會回去。

可最後他還是回香港了。事實上，他從來未真正離開過。另一方面，我被送到英國上學，娶了一個蘇格蘭女孩，並在這裡組建了家庭。在三種不同的文化中長大，有一個問題一直縈繞在我的腦海裡。我到底算不算中國人，我究竟是誰？

我父親的祖父是一名甲板水手，1911年清朝滅亡後，為了能在相對穩定的英國殖民地找到更好的工作，從上海移民來到了香港。我母親的家族曾是中國南方地區的大地主。他們離開大陸來到了香港，很可能因此逃過了之後的一劫。兩年來，我一直在追溯我的家族歷史，借此了解兩位近代史上極其重要的領導人是如何影響了我的家庭。這個系列透過同等重要的新照片、老照片和文字，以我對家族往事的追憶為主題，把我與過去的香港重新聯繫起來，人性化地看待讓我的家族由香港最終落腳到英國這一過程之中所發生的一連串政治和社會事件。

在創作的過程中，我發現這些私人故事總是能夠引起人們對自身的家庭歷史展開談論，不論他們來自哪裡，或有著什麼樣的種族背景。這本書的故事雖然發生在香港，但裡面涉及到許多共同的話題，包括家庭、分離、移民、殖民主義和多元文化主義等等。

"The world is always changing. We have to look inside ourselves to find what stays the same, such as loyalty, our shared history and love for each other. In them, the truth of the past lives on."

– Ronald Bass –

My project began with a storybook I made for my daughters.

I was born in the city of Hong Kong in 1977, five years before China wanted it back. Us 'honkies' have an identity that's very different to those of China, after all, I sang 'God Save Our Queen' as my national anthem at school. I always knew I was going to live in England. My father had studied there; he had always told me that when Hong Kong went back to China in 1997, we would not be going back.

But go back he did. In fact, he never really left. I, on the other hand, got sent to school in England, married a Scottish girl and started a family there before moving back again to Hong Kong. Having grown up between three different cultures, one question is always at the back of my mind. How Chinese am I, or indeed, who am I?

My father's grandfather was a deckhand. He came to Hong Kong from Shanghai after the fall of the Empire in 1911, lured by better job prospects in the relatively stable British colony. My mother's family were big landlords in Southern China. They came to Hong Kong, probably escaping certain death. For two years, I traced back the history of my family in a bid to find out how two of the most influential people in history affected my family. Paying equal importance to new photographs, found photographs and writing, the work reconnects me with the Hong Kong of the past through the recollection of my extended family, humanizing the political and social upheaval that brought my family to Hong Kong and then eventually to the United Kingdom.

I have found that the personal stories always prompt people to talk about their own family history, no matter where they are from or what ethnic background they are. Although set in Hong Kong the book deals with many different issues – family, displacement, migration, colonialism and multiculturalism.

800 years ago, long before the Tong and Leung Clans settled in what would become Tong's Bay, the surrounding area was a banyan tree forest. One day, a fisherman noticed that this particular tree resembled the Buddha, Siddhārtha. Local villagers began praying and carried out offerings around the tree. Later, the Tong's temple was built in front of the tree. Both the temple and the tree survived the Cultural Revolution and still stand today.

八百年前，早在唐氏和梁氏家族在現今的唐家灣定居之前，這邊原本被一片榕樹林包圍。某一天，有漁夫在去海邊的路上註意到這棵看起來很像佛陀悉達多的樹。當地的村民們開始對著樹祈禱，並在樹的周圍獻祭。後來，唐氏宗祠選址在該樹前面並至今依然屹立不倒 。

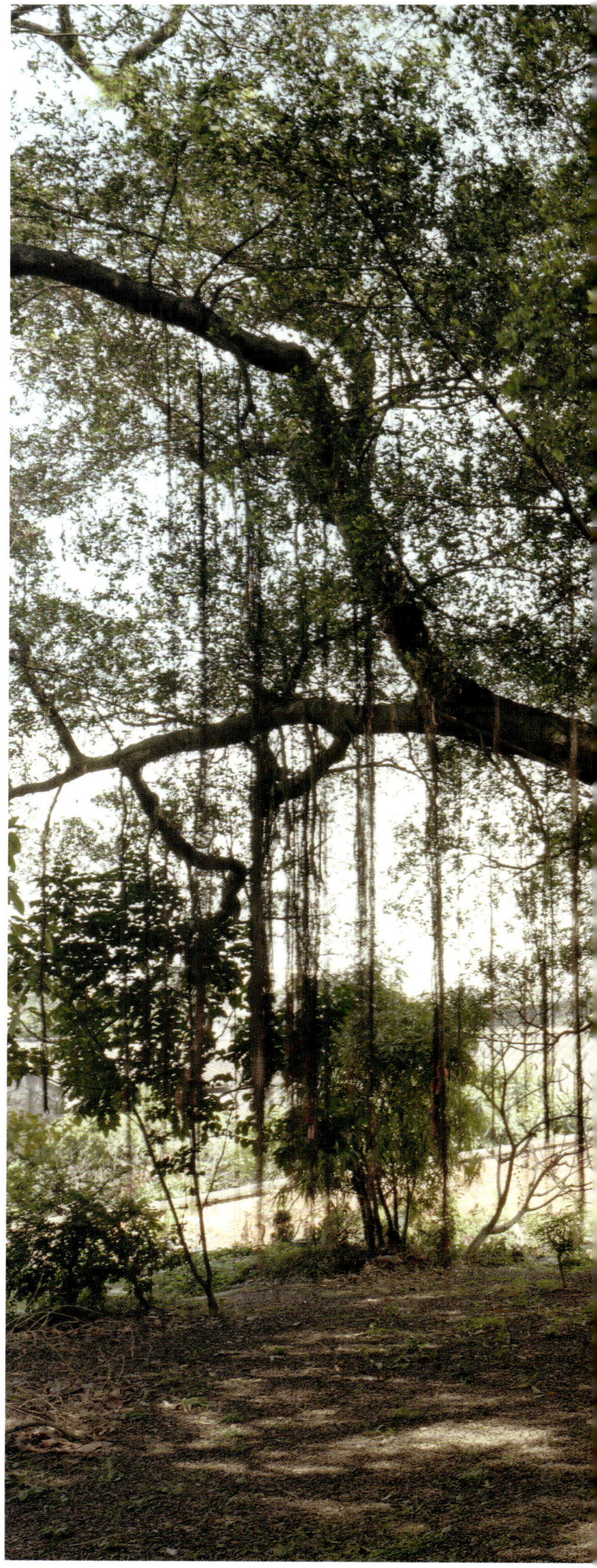

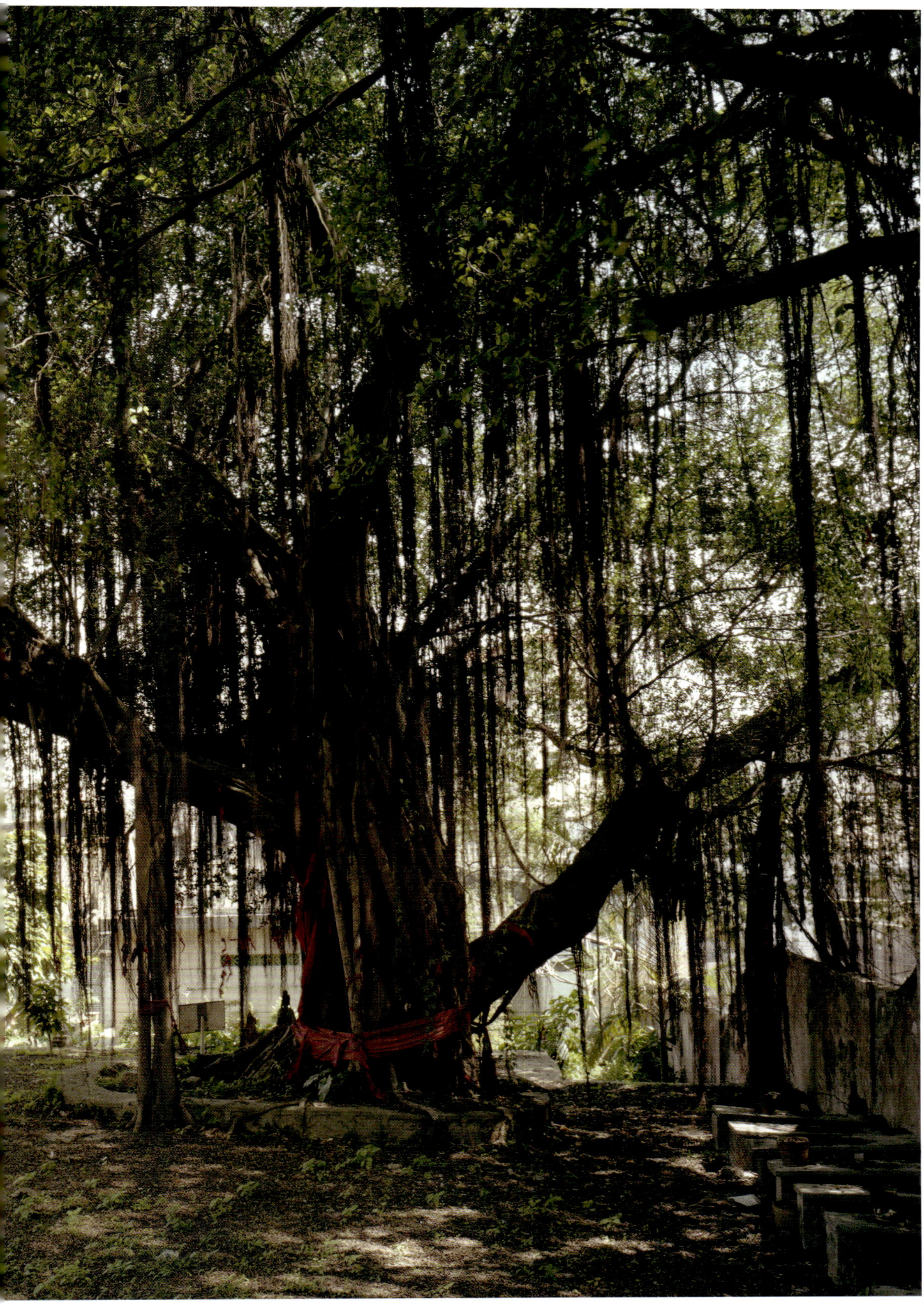

I 賓南
Bunnan

Bunnan was born in Shanghai in 1903. His family were economic migrants, originally from a village called Tangjaiwan (Tong's Bay) in Guangdong. His grandfather set up opium pipes for paying customers in an opium den. He died at the age of 27. His father worked as a deckhand and was often away for months at a time. His mother was a strict woman and clearly didn't like the other woman in the photo whom she scratched out.

賓南1903年出生於上海。他的家庭原籍廣東省唐家灣鎮，後來因為經濟原因移居到了上海。他的祖父在鴉片館里為顧客準備抽鴉片所需的工具，二十七歲便去世了。他的父親是一名水手，經常出海，一次便離開好幾個月。他母親是一名嚴厲的女人，從被她劃花的照片中可以看出她顯然並不喜歡照片中的另一個女人。

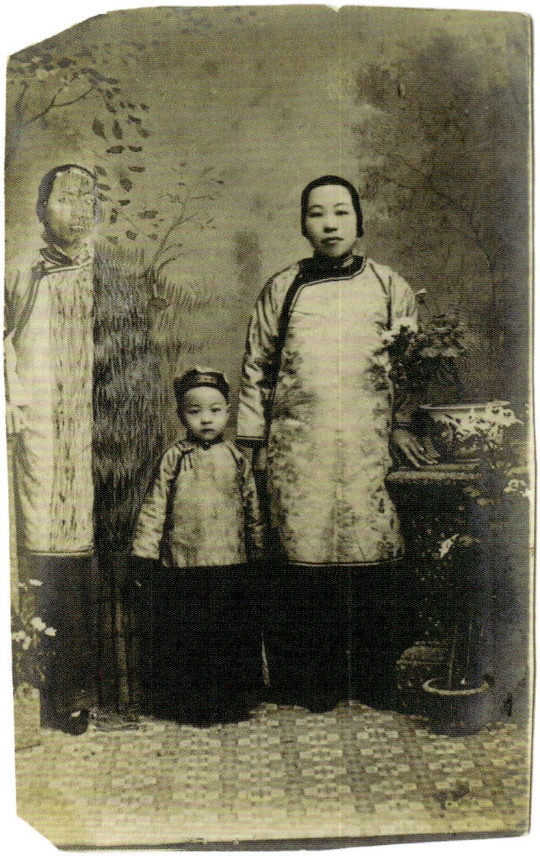

An altar for worshipping the Tong Ancestors stands inside an abandoned house in Tong's Bay.

唐家灣鎮一間已被廢棄的房屋，屋內供奉著唐家祖先的靈位。

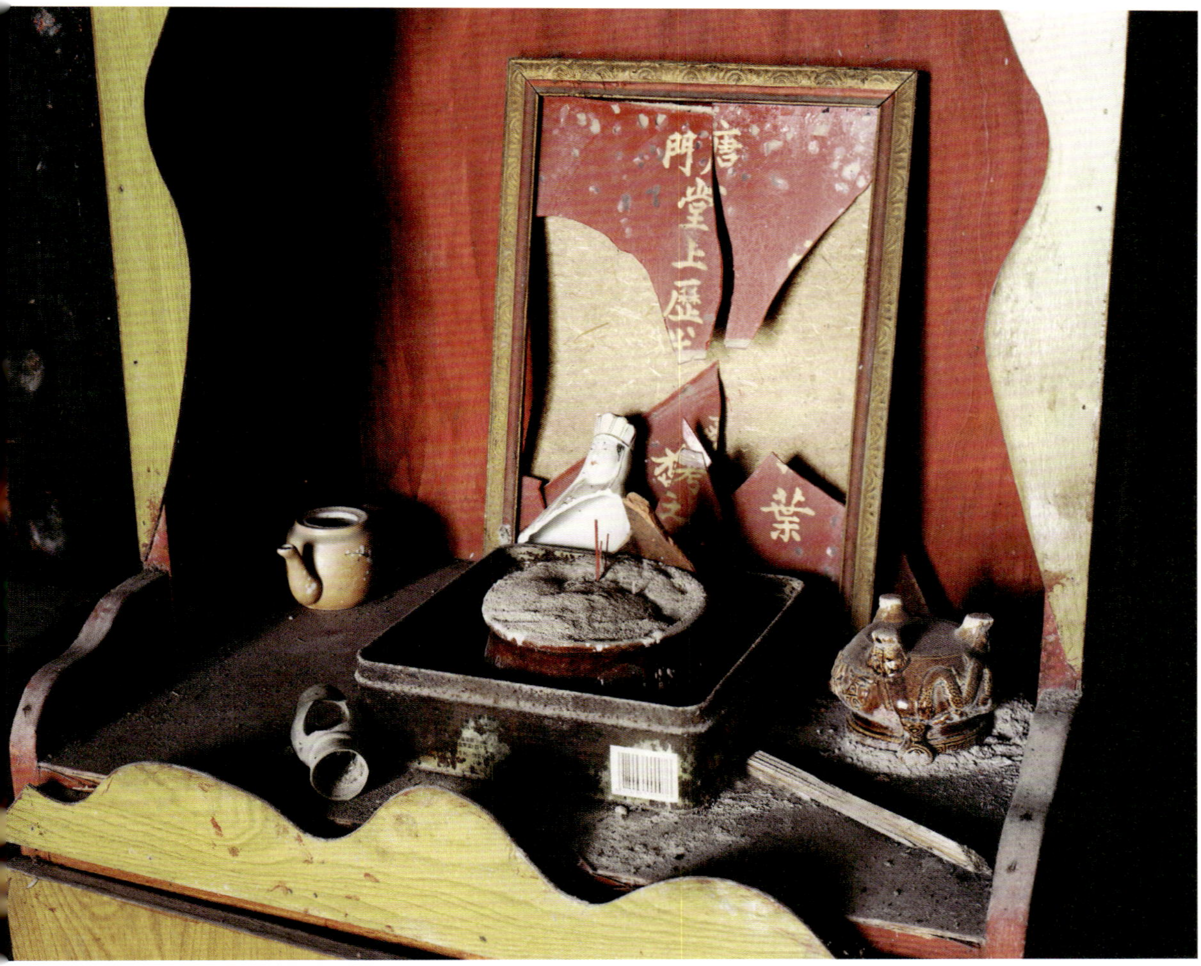

Bunnan's father moved his family to Hong Kong in 1911 after the fall of the Imperial empire. He continued to work as a deckhand on whatever ship he could and was away for months at a time. Addicted to opium he would spend his time, whenever the ship docked, smoking the same drug that had killed his father.

賓南的父親在1911年清朝滅亡後，舉家遷往香港。他繼續從事著水手工作，一次便會離家好幾個月。他是個癮君子，船一靠岸就去吸鴉片，這一曾奪去他父親生命的毒品。

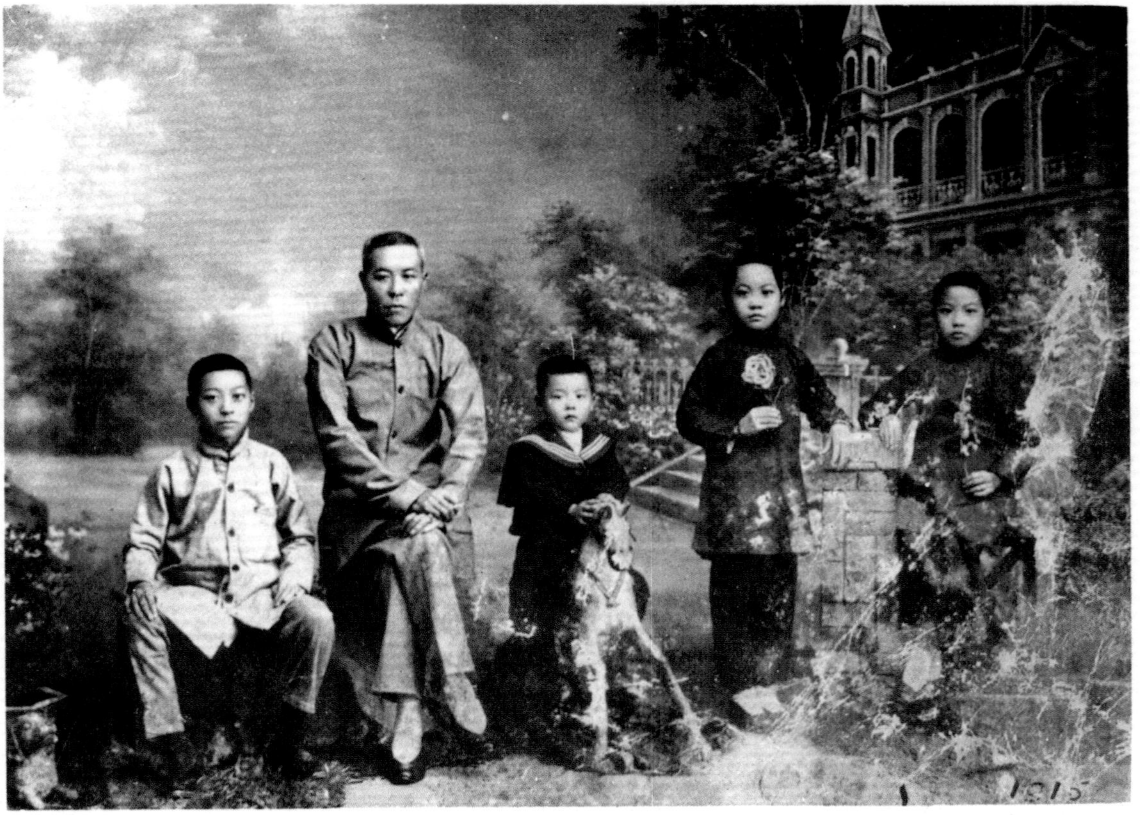

After graduating from high school, Bunnan got a job at Jardine Matheson Holdings, one of the biggest British founded Far East Trading companies in Hong Kong and rumoured to have made its fortune in the trading of opium in the nineteenth century. Bunnan worked in the imports and exports department, trading a variety of commodities, with tea and silk being the most profitable goods.

高中畢業後，賓南在香港最大的英資洋行怡和集團找了一份工作。怡和洋行早年參與對中國貿易，主要從事鴉片買賣。賓南在進出口部工作，經營各種商品的貿易，其中茶葉和絲綢是利潤最高的商品。

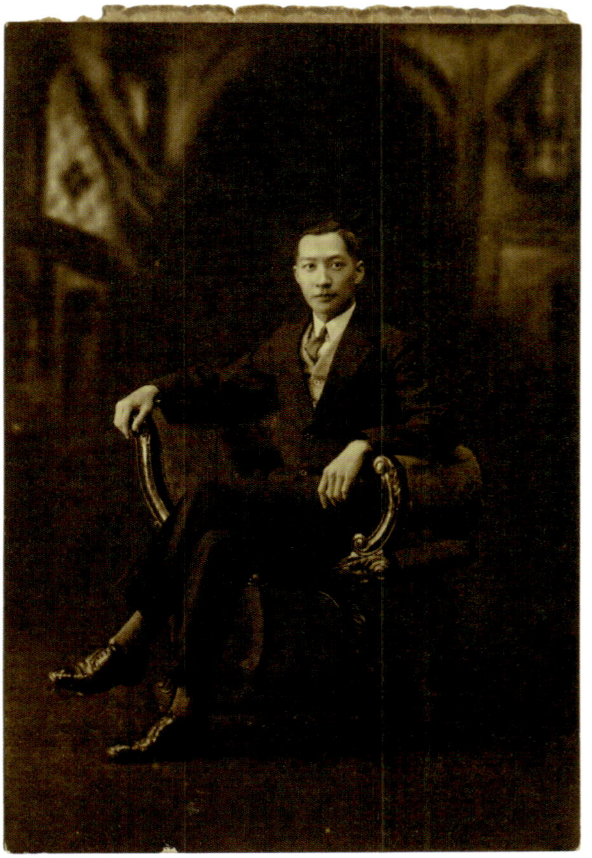

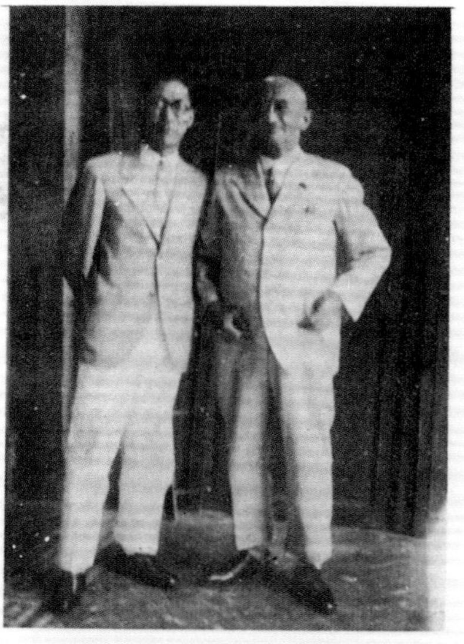

After seven years of working at Jardine, Bunnan felt confident that he had learnt everything he needed to, in 1935, started his own trading company with two German traders. They imported goods such as rare earth metal, animal skins and tea from China and exported them abroad. After the liberation of China in 1949, merchants with money came to Hong Kong in droves and opened factories here. The company started exporting these goods.

在怡和工作了七年後，賓南對自己所學到的一切充滿信心，隨後於1935年與兩個德國商人創辦了自己的貿易公司。他們從中國進口稀土金屬、獸皮、茶葉等商品並出口到國外。1949年建國以後，富商們成群結隊來到香港，在這裡開設工廠。賓南的公司開始出口這些商品。

Hong Kong means 'fragrant port' in Chinese. It was the name given to a small settlement on the southern shores of the island, one of the first points of contact between the British and the local fishermen. Fragrant incense was stored around the harbour, giving the port its name. After the Treaty of Nanking, the entire island was then referred to as Hong Kong and the British began developing Victoria Harbour on the northern shores on the island.

香港，意為「帶有香味的港口」，原為香港島南面的一個小村落（現稱香港仔），是英國人與本地漁民最先接觸的地方之一，港口一開始因被用作存放香料而得名。《南京條約》簽訂後，整個島嶼被稱為香港，英國人開始在北岸發展維多利亞港。

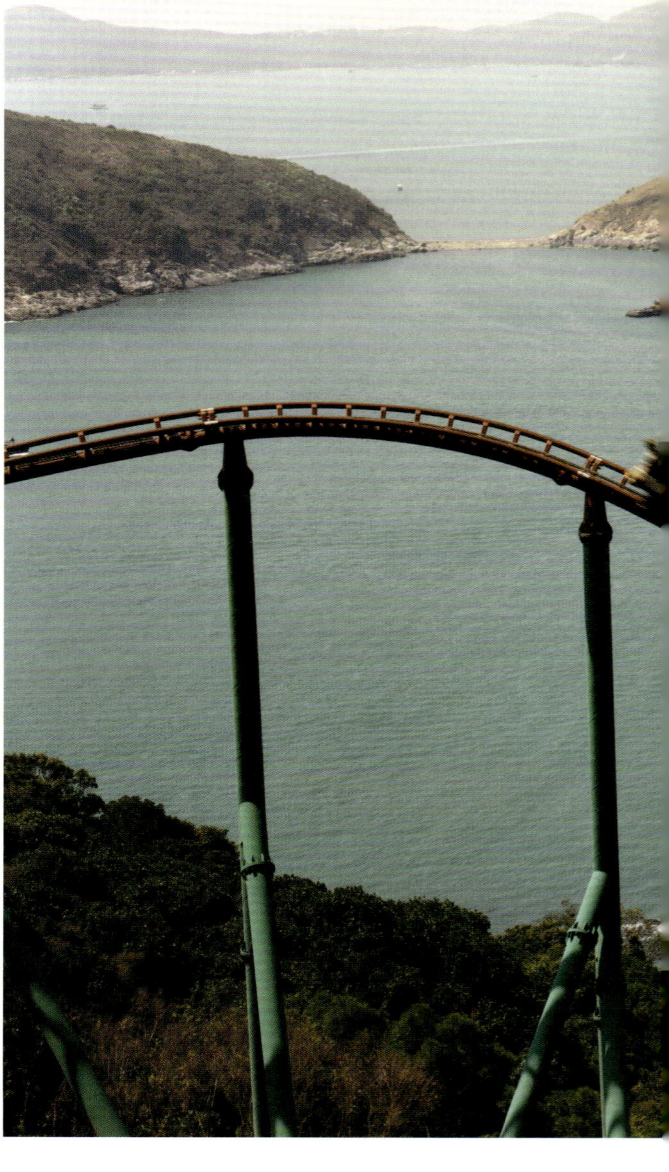

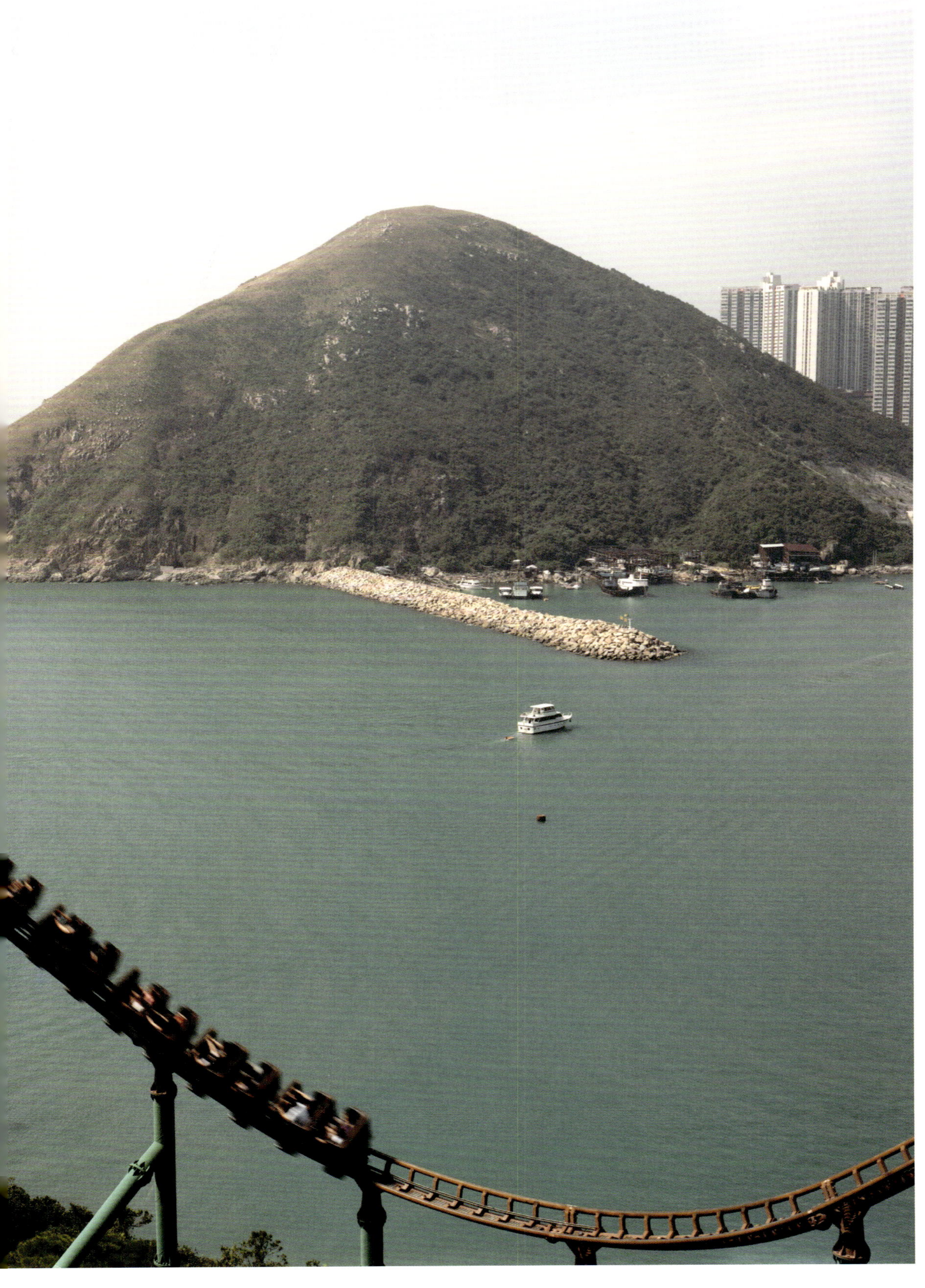

II 仲錫
Chung Zak

Chung Zak was born in 1908 to one of the wealthiest families in Guangzhou, South China. The Wong family tree can be traced back 27 generations through records kept at the Wong's temple. They were one of the biggest landlords in the city and also owned a chain of pawn shops. Taken in 1880, the image shows Chung Zak's father (far left), grand-uncle (sixth from the right) along with other important members of the family posing with two German traders. What they traded, however, can't be traced in the records.

仲錫1908年出生於中國南方城市廣州，他們家是最富有的家庭之一。黃家的族譜可追溯到二十七代之前，並被安放於黃氏宗祠之內。他們是當地最大的地主之一，經營連鎖當舖。這張照片攝於1880年，合照內有仲錫的父親（最左）、三叔（從右邊數起第六個）以及其他重要家庭成員，另外還有兩名德國商人。然而，他們當時具體的交易內容卻無法從記錄中找到。

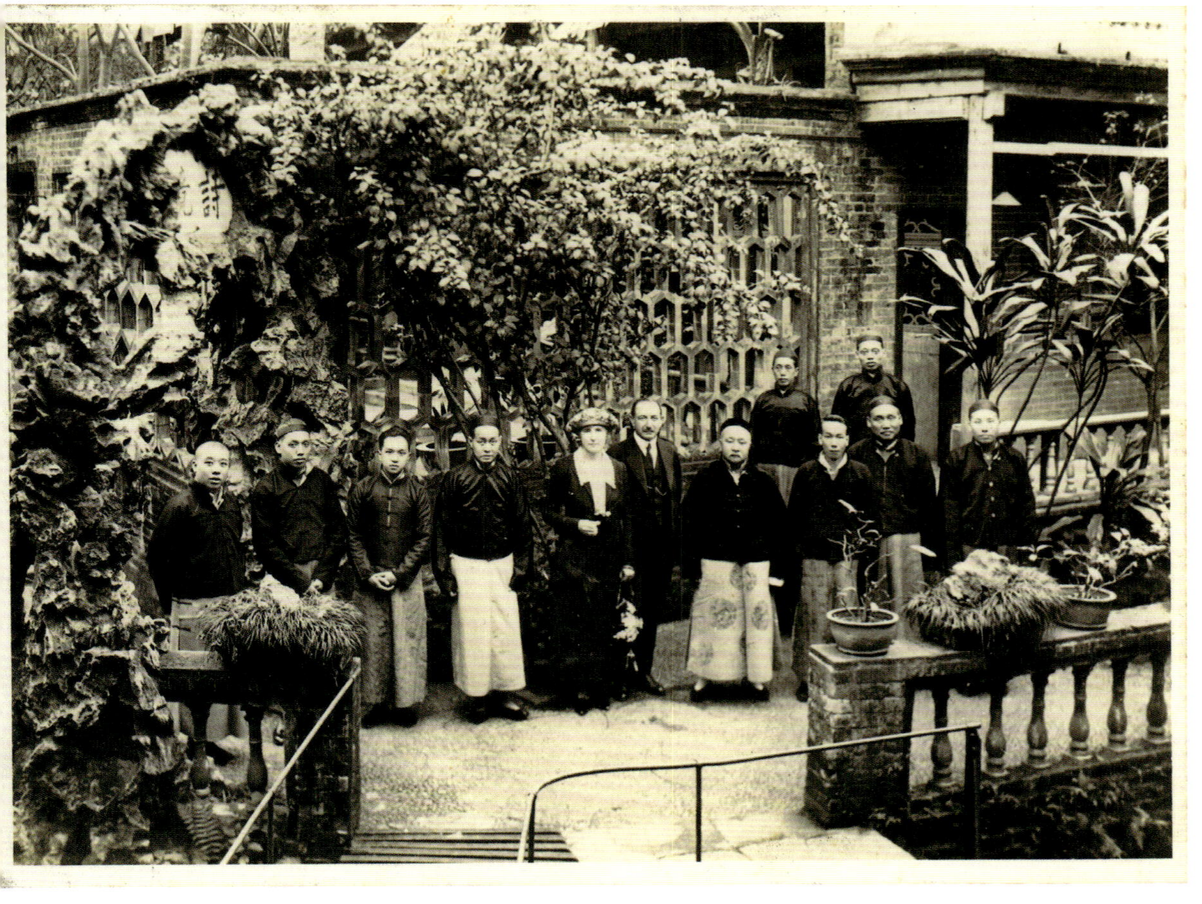

Land Deed, circa 1600

Wong's mansion took up a whole block, and was one of the biggest houses in West Guangzhou. Male descendents were allocated sections of the house when they married and continued to live within the house; male cousins were considered brothers. Daughters would be matched up with a suitable family at an early age and once they were married out, they were no longer considered part of the family.

地契，十七世紀

黃家大宅佔地足有一整條街之長，是廣州西城最大的一棟住宅。男性子孫在婚後被分配到數個房間，並繼續住在房子裡，堂兄弟之間也以兄弟相稱。女性從小便與門當戶對的家庭訂婚，一旦嫁出去之後就不再被視為家庭的一部分。

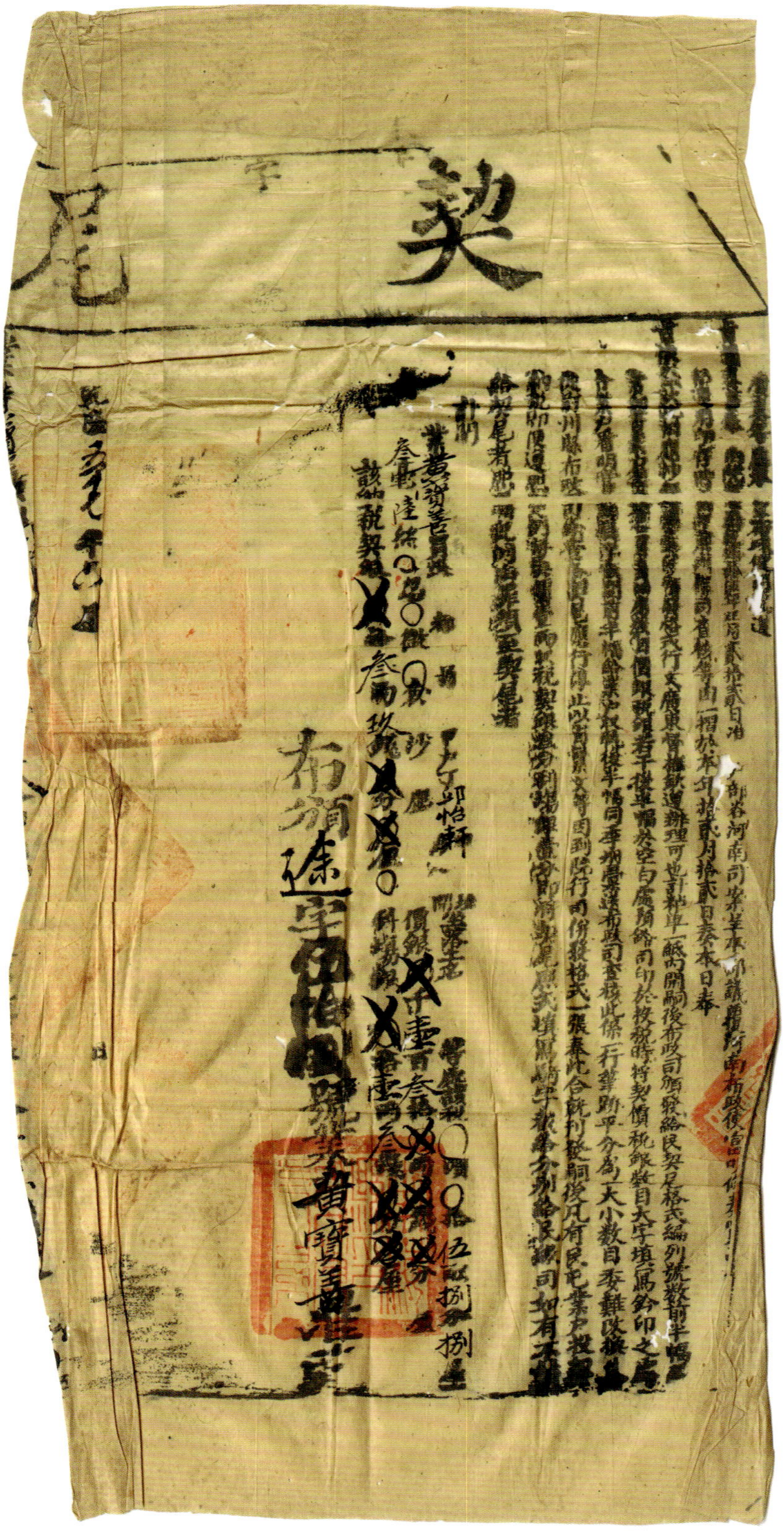
契
尾
布政司

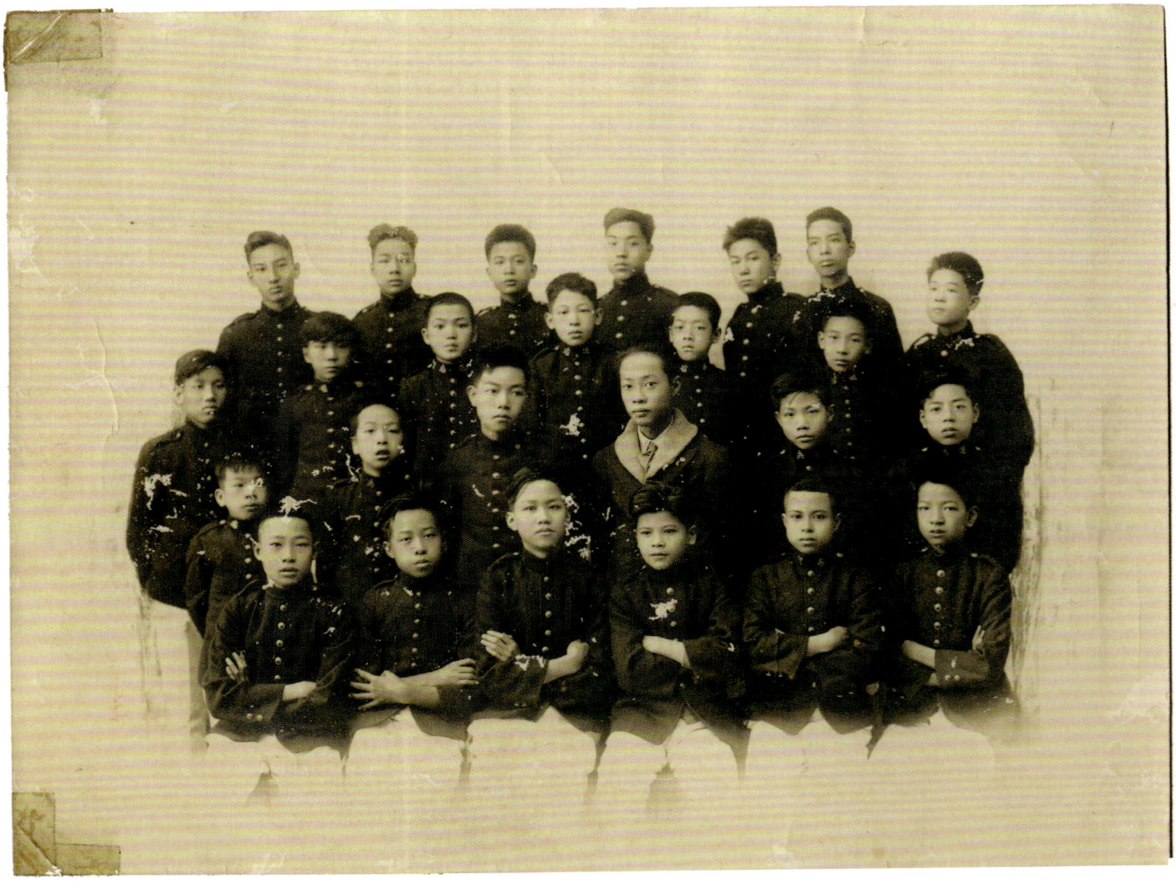

Chung Zak went to one of the finest schools in Guangzhou, followed by an education at a top university in Shanghai. Through connections that the Wong family had in the city, after university he was able to get a government job.

仲錫就讀廣州最好的學校之一，並隨後在上海一所頂尖大學唸書。大學畢業後，仲錫通過家人的關係在南京找到一份政府部門的工作。

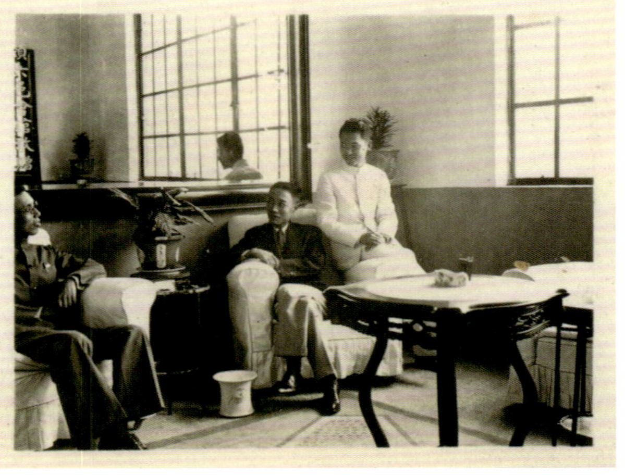

After losing the first opium war in 1841, the Qing government agreed to make Hong Kong Island a crown colony, ceding it to the British Queen "in perpetuity to provide British traders with a harbour where they could unload their goods". Lord Palmerston, the British Foreign Secretary at the time, was less than impressed, calling Hong Kong "a barren rock with scarcely a house upon it". Hong Kong remained a British colony for the following 156 years.

1841年第一次鴉片戰爭落敗後，清政府被迫將香港割讓給英國，讓英國商人可以在港口卸貨。然而，當時的英國外交大臣帕默斯頓勳爵對此結果並不以為然，稱香港為「一片貧瘠的岩石，幾乎沒有房屋」。就這樣，香港在未來的一百五十六年間成為了英國的殖民地。

III 盲婚啞嫁
Blind wedding, mute marriage

Bunnan's marriage was arranged through a matchmaker. After a match had been found, a picture was sent to the prospective wife. For the photoshoot, he dragged along his ugly friend so as to make himself look better.

賓南的婚事是通過一名媒人安排的。在找到一名合適的對像後，媒人把他的照片寄給了未來的妻子。為了照片的拍攝效果，他讓一位長得不怎麼好看的朋友一同合影，好讓自己看起來更英俊一些。

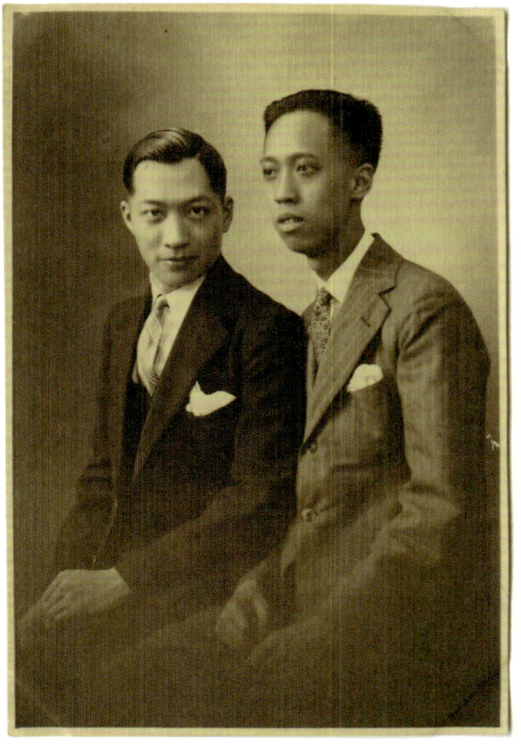

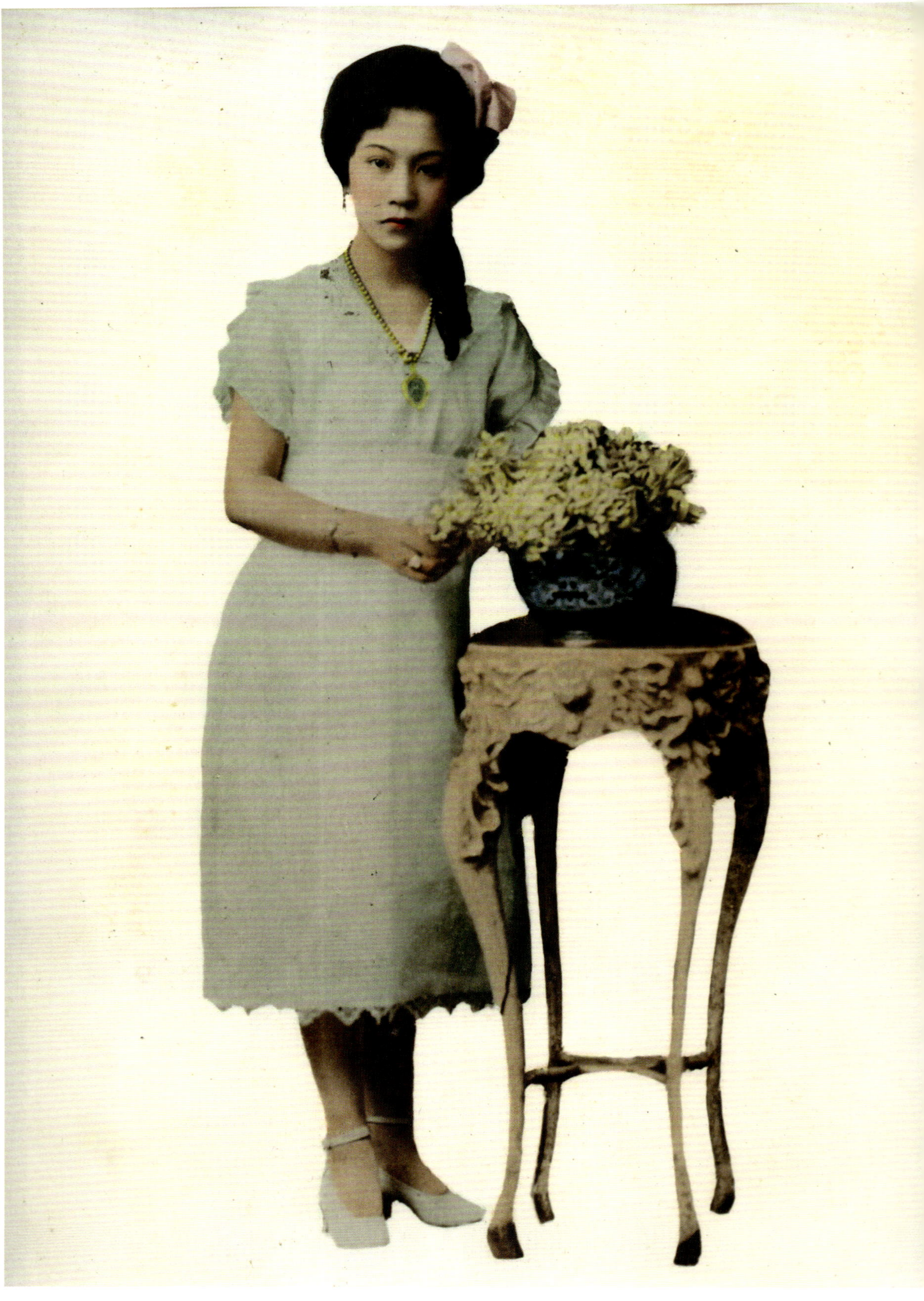

Shook Ying, born in 1911, was the daughter of a Chinese trader based in the Philippines. She sent in this image as her matchmaking picture, hoping to find a good husband. She initially thought the unattractive man on the right was to be her husband and commented that, "well, as long as he is hard working and ambitious."

陳淑英，1911年出生，是菲律賓一名中國商人的女兒。她把這張照片作為相親照，希望能找到一個好丈夫。她起初以為右邊那個沒什麼魅力的男士將會是她的對象，並說：「好吧，只要他滿怀大志並足夠努力工作。」

Bunnan and Shook Ying were married through a traditional Chinese tea ceremony.

賓南和淑英通過傳統的中國茶禮結婚。

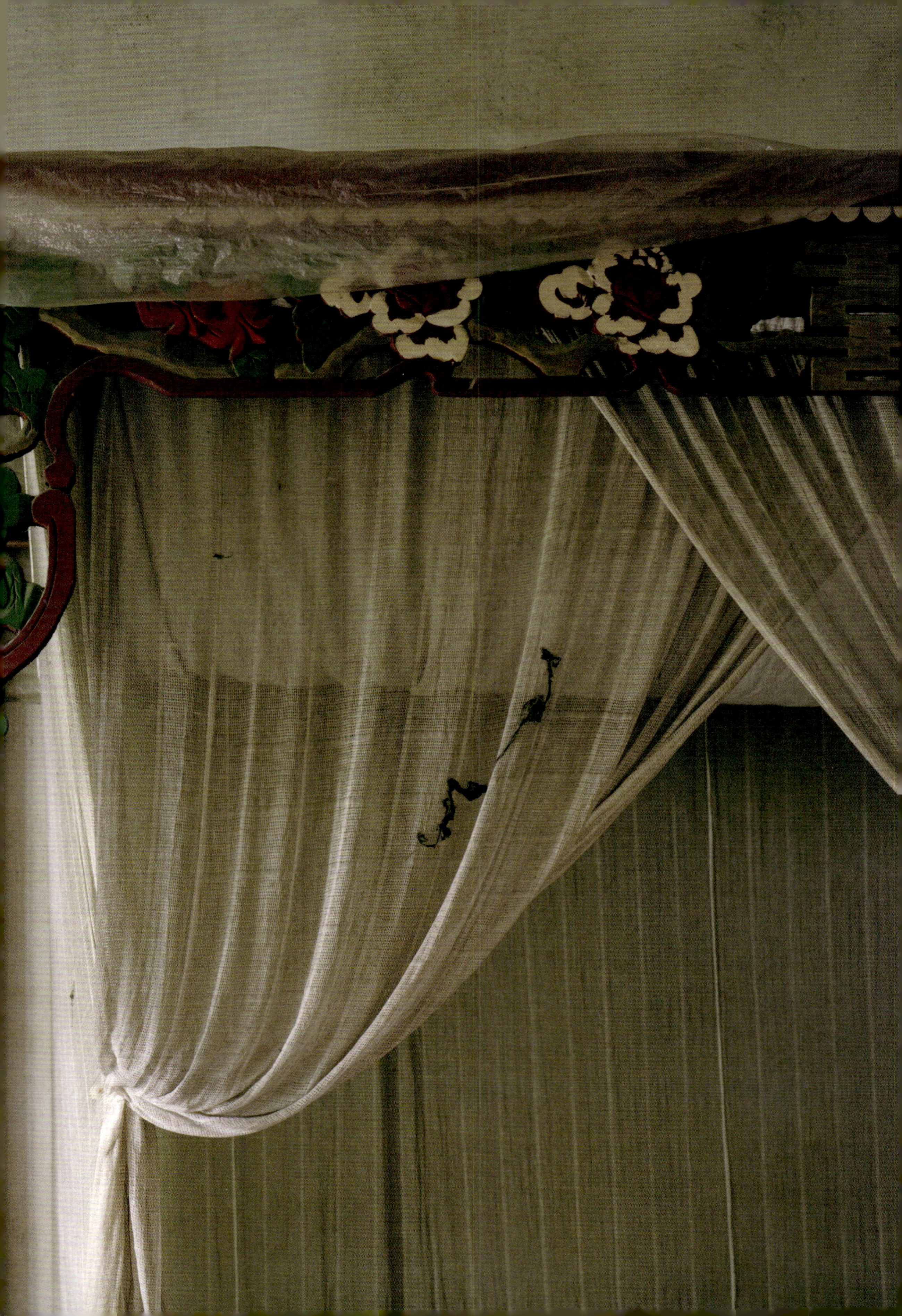

A year after they married, Shook Ying gave birth to a daughter, the first of their thirteen children.

結婚一年後，淑英生了一個女兒，她是這對夫妻十三個孩子中的老大。

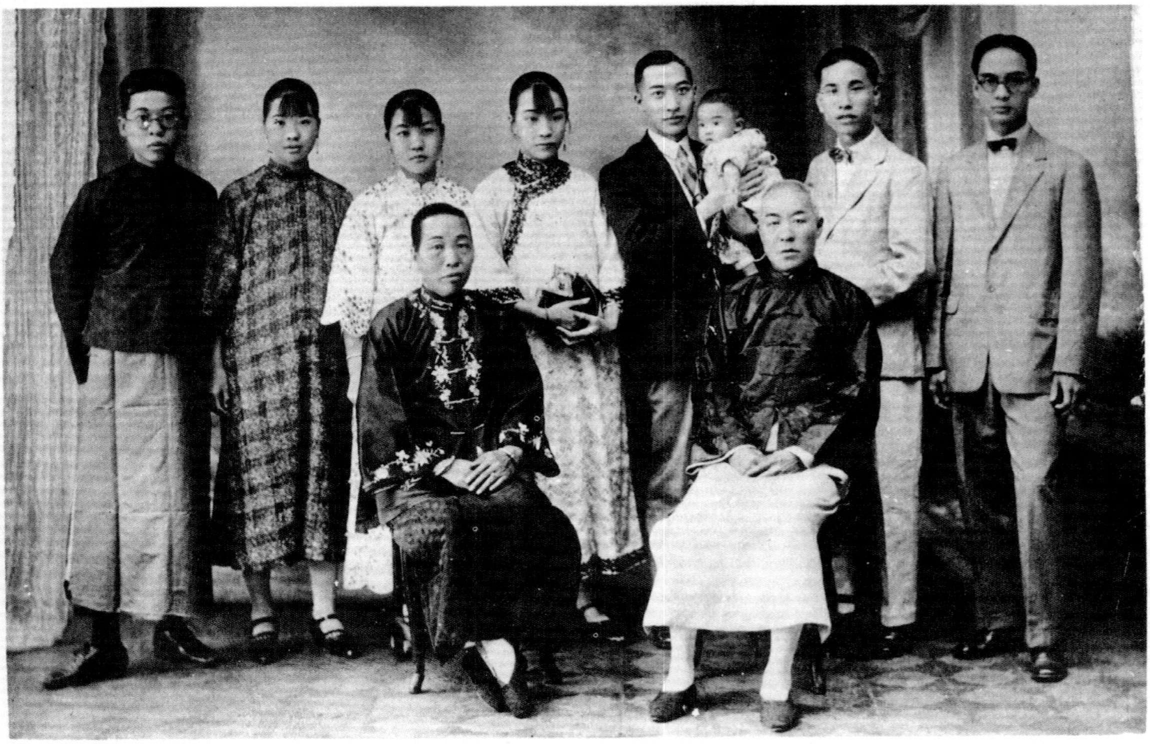

IV 花花公子
The young man with many flowers

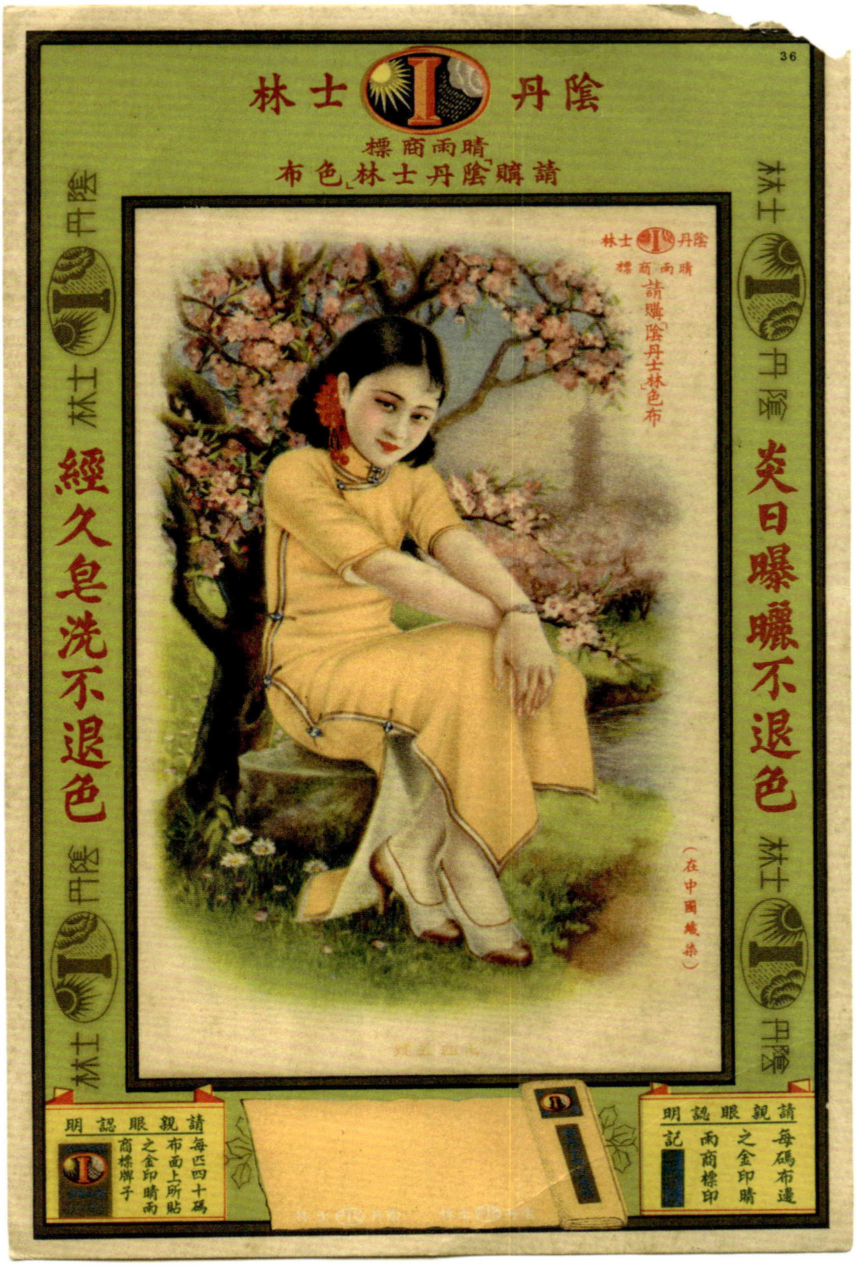
36
陰丹士林
晴雨商標
請購「陰丹士林」色布
經久皂洗不退色
炎日曝曬不退色
（在中國織染）
請親眼認明
每疋四十碼布面上所貼之金印晴雨商標牌子
請親眼認明
每碼布邊之金印晴雨商標印記

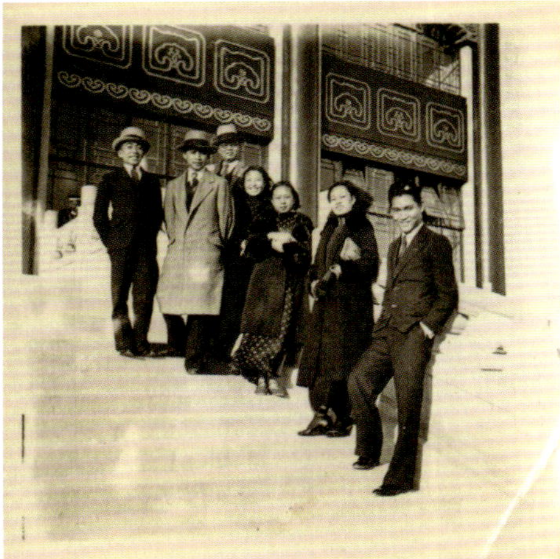

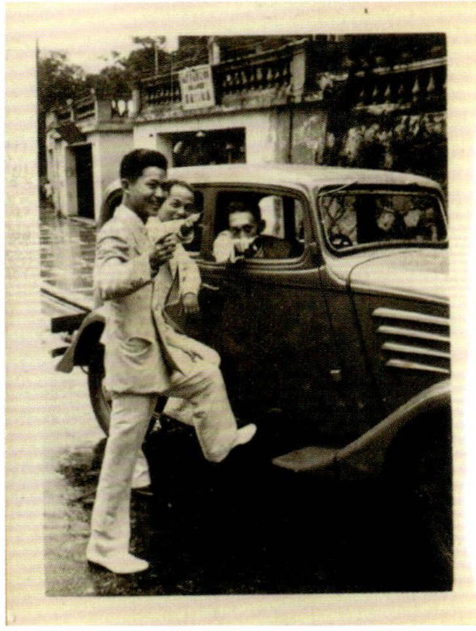

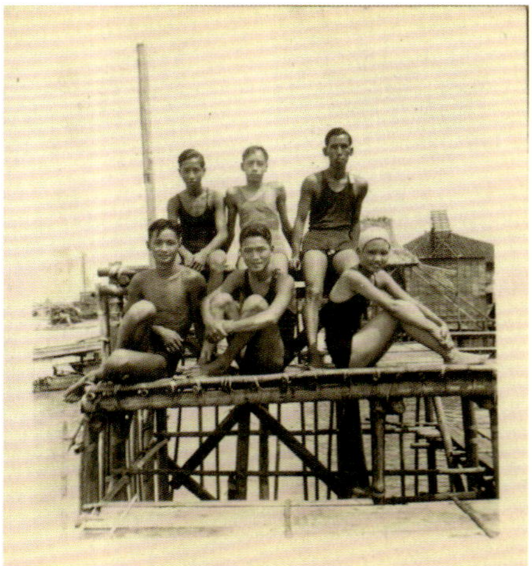

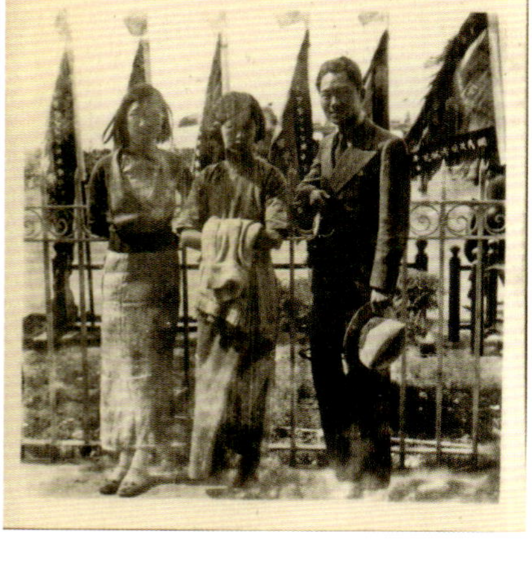

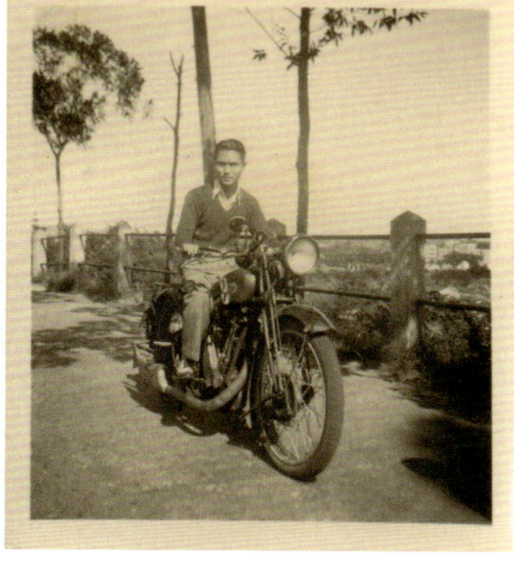

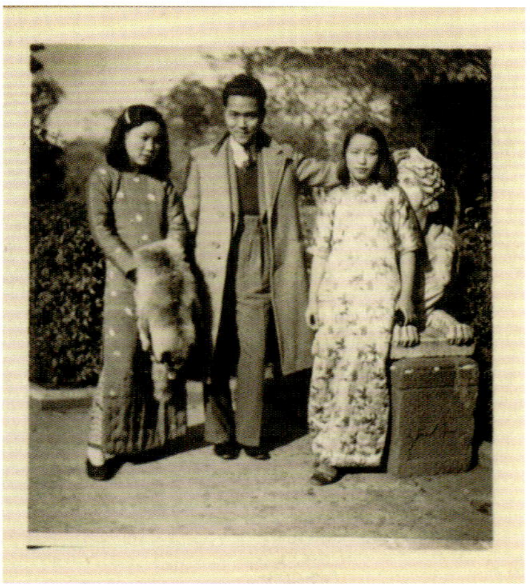
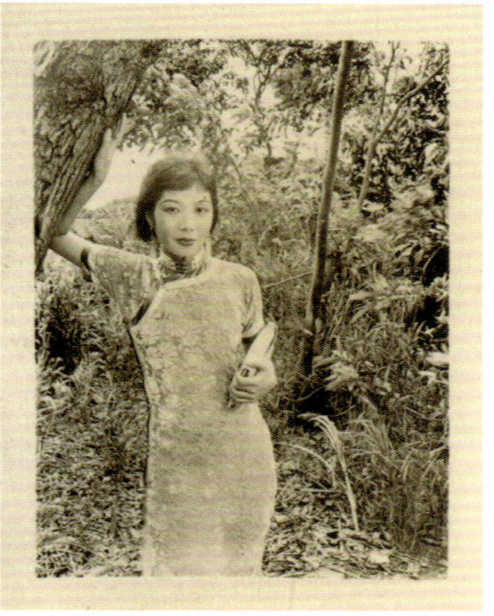
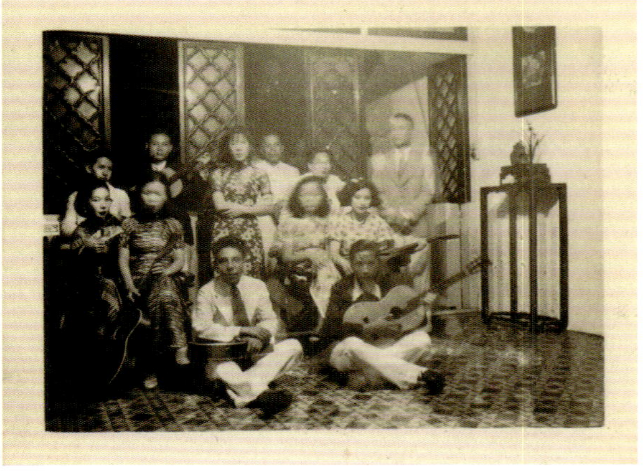
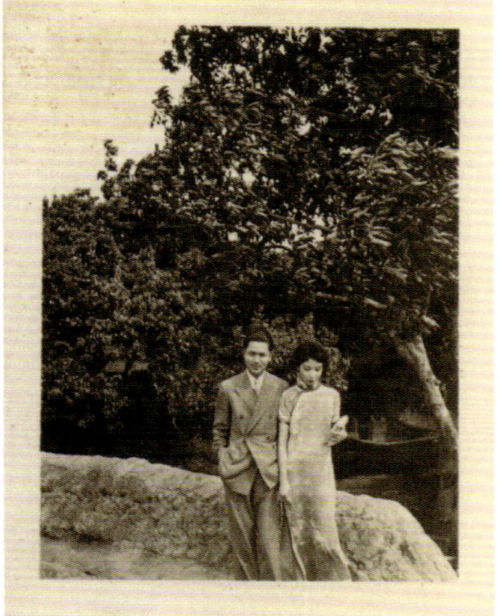
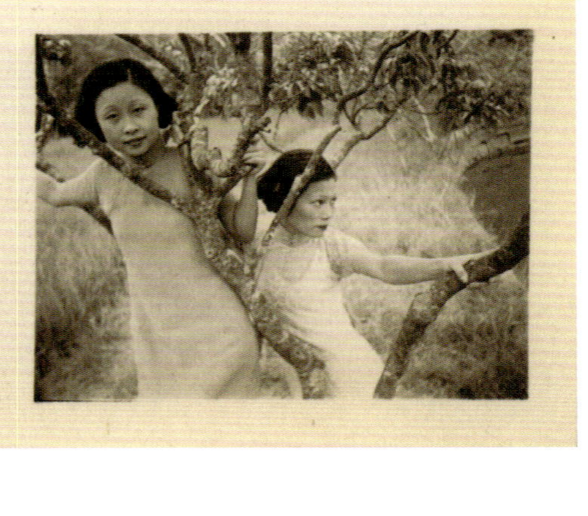

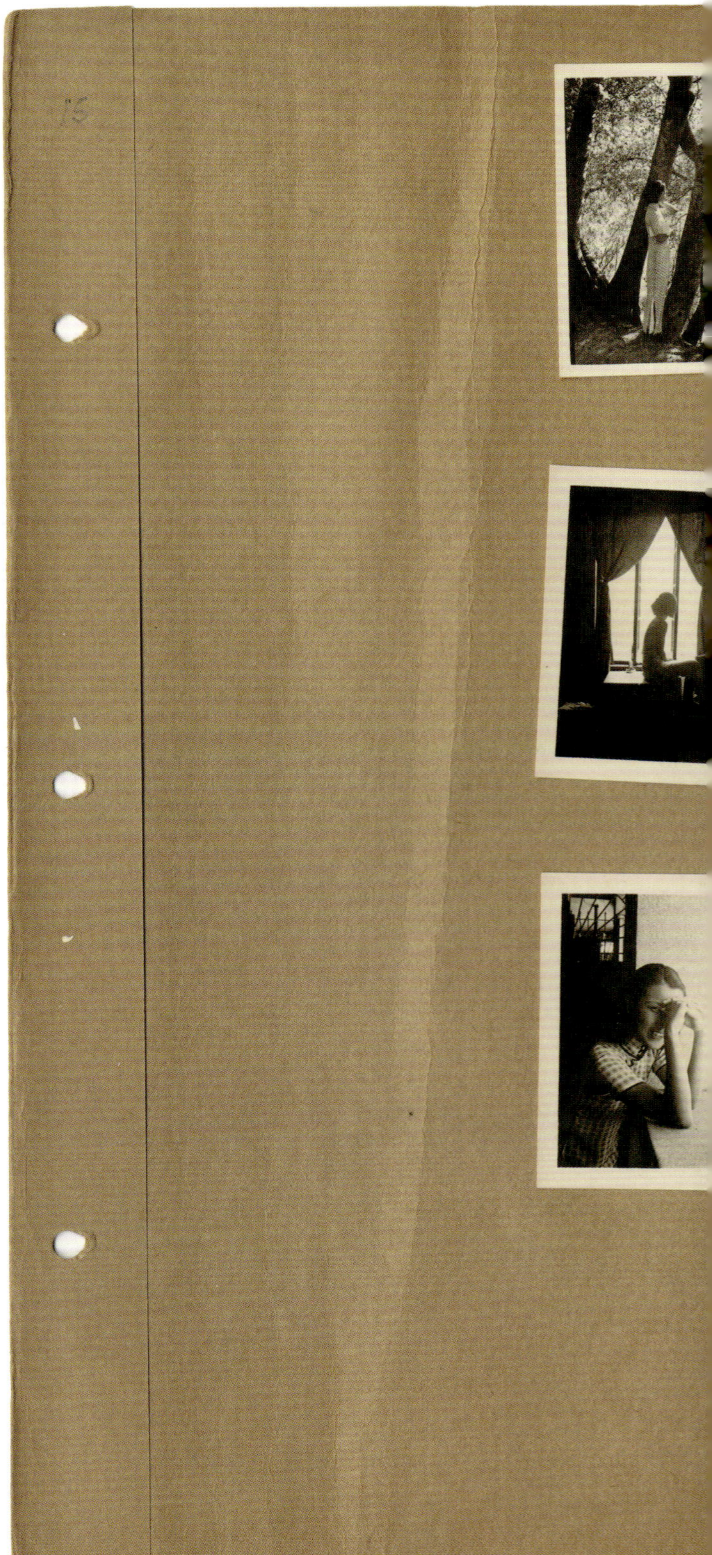

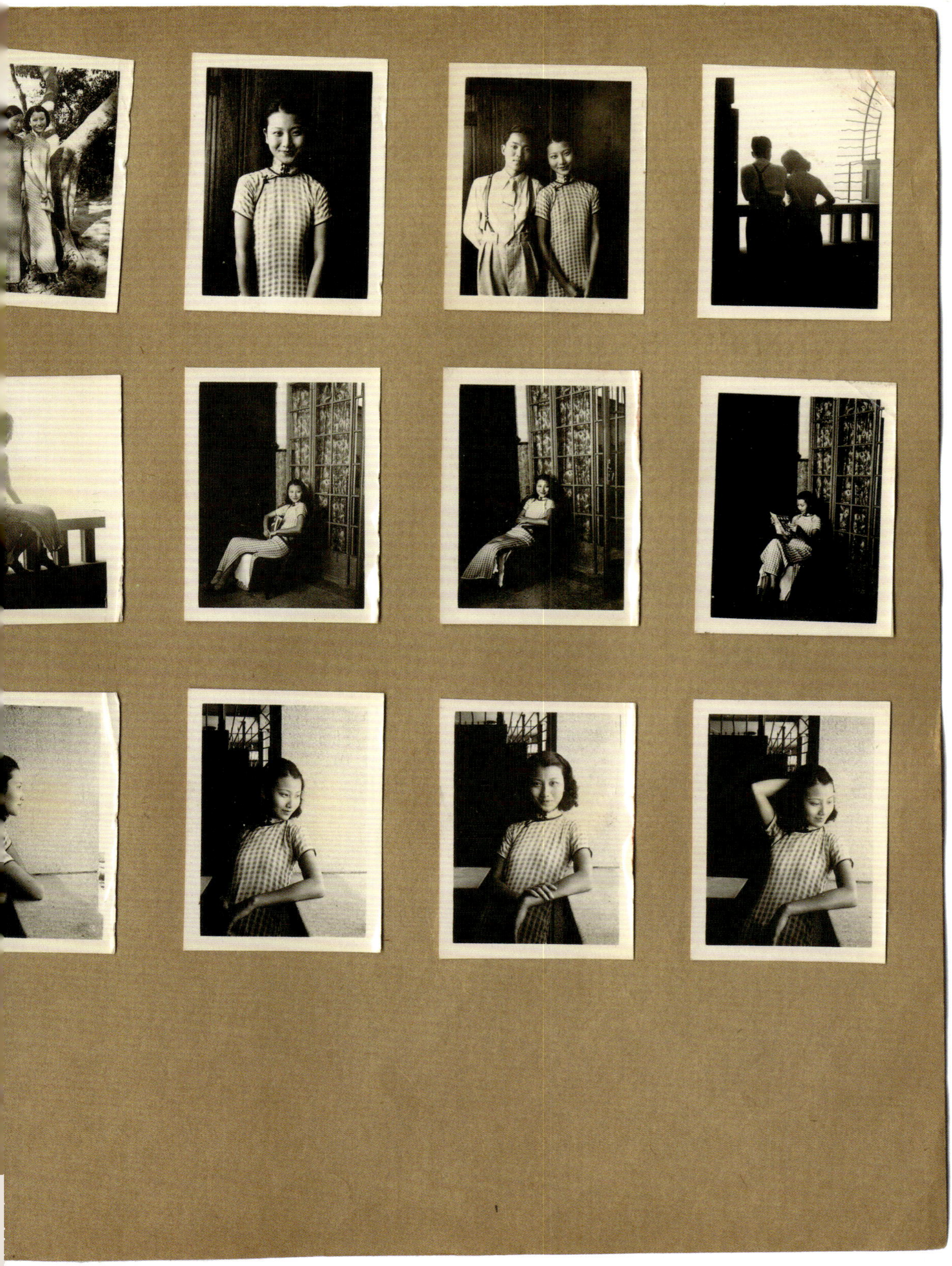

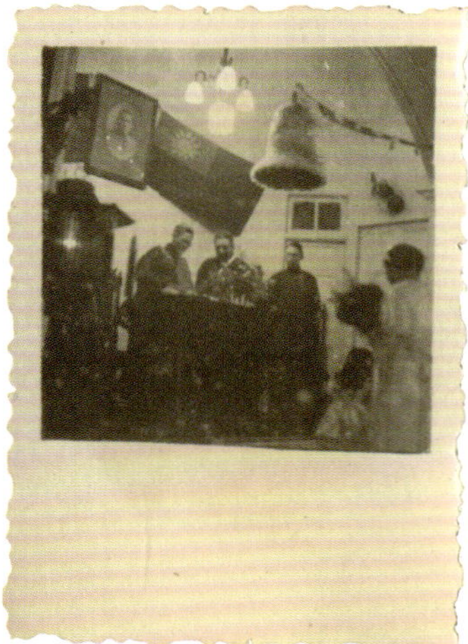

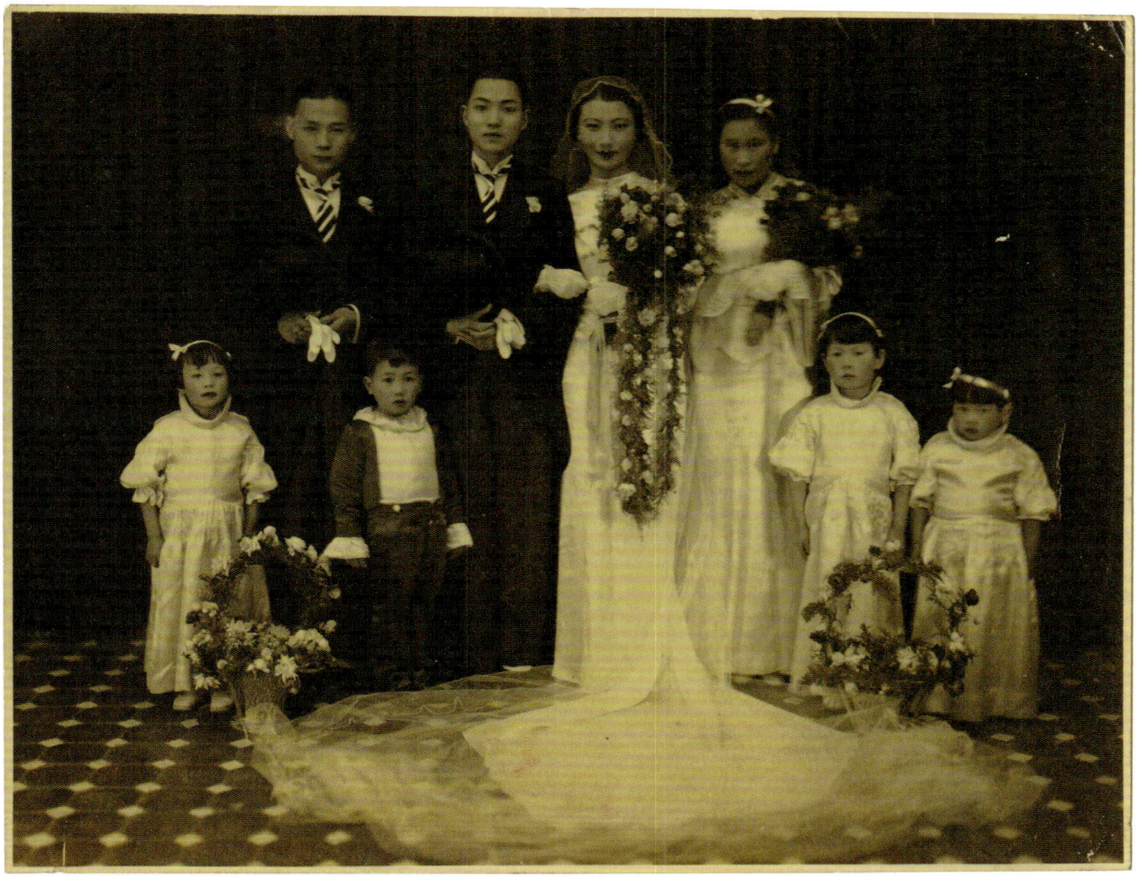

Chung Zak, a keen ballroom dancer, met Yun Nan on the dance floor and quickly fell in love. They married in both a Western style ceremony, and in a traditional Chinese one. There are very conflicting versions of what kind of family Yun Nan came from. There are documents suggesting that her grandfather was a government official, but there are also rumours that, for money, she accompanied men on the dance floor in social ballrooms. It is also rumoured that Chung Zak's father, furious at this, desperately tried to stop the wedding.

仲錫對交際舞有著濃厚的興趣，他在舞廳裡遇見苑蘭並很快就墜入愛河。他們同時舉行了西式和中式婚禮。對於苑蘭來自什麼樣的家庭，說法不一。有文件顯示，她的祖父是一名政府官員，不過也有傳言說，她在社交舞廳以陪男子跳舞為職業，為此仲錫的父親非常生氣，曾拼命想阻止婚禮。

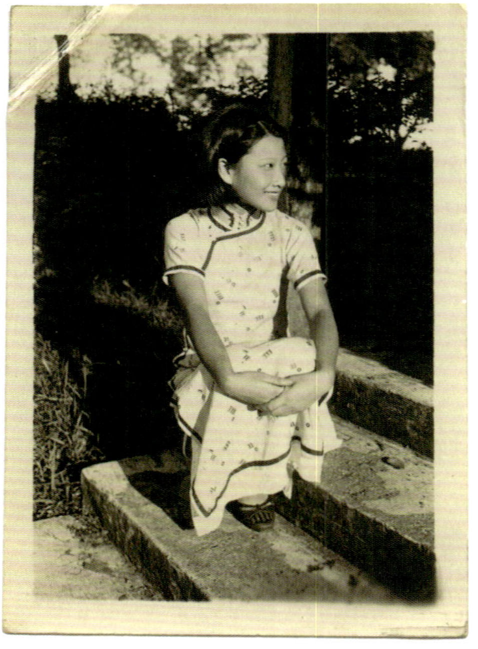

In the late 1930s, Chung Zak's father put up a block of flats opposite the old family home. It was the first building in the whole district to be built with concrete. It was given to his two sons. Befitting their social lifestyle, Chung Zak and his wife converted the top floor into a dancefloor.

仲錫的父親於上世紀三十年代末在老房子的對面建了一棟公寓樓，並交給了他的兩個兒子。這是當時全區第一幢混凝土建築物。仲錫夫婦出於對社交生活的熱愛，把頂層改成了舞池。

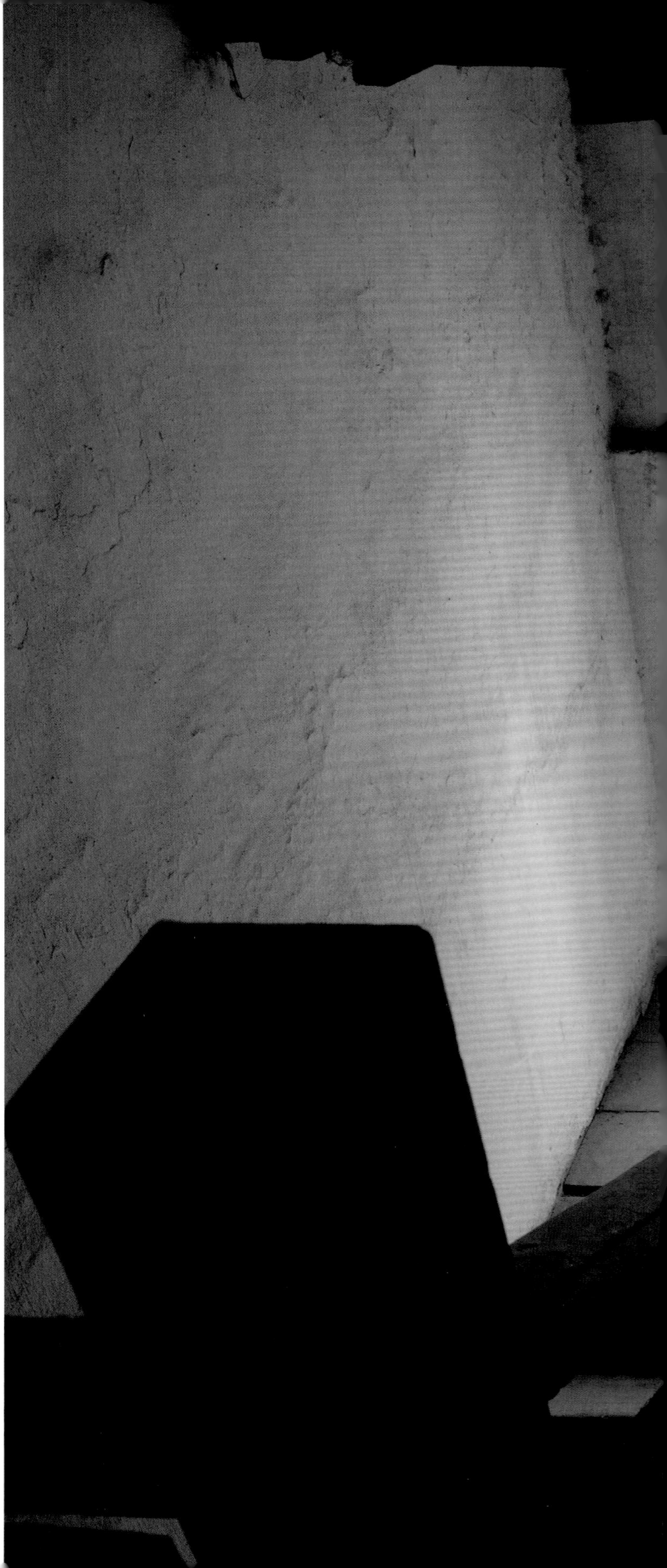

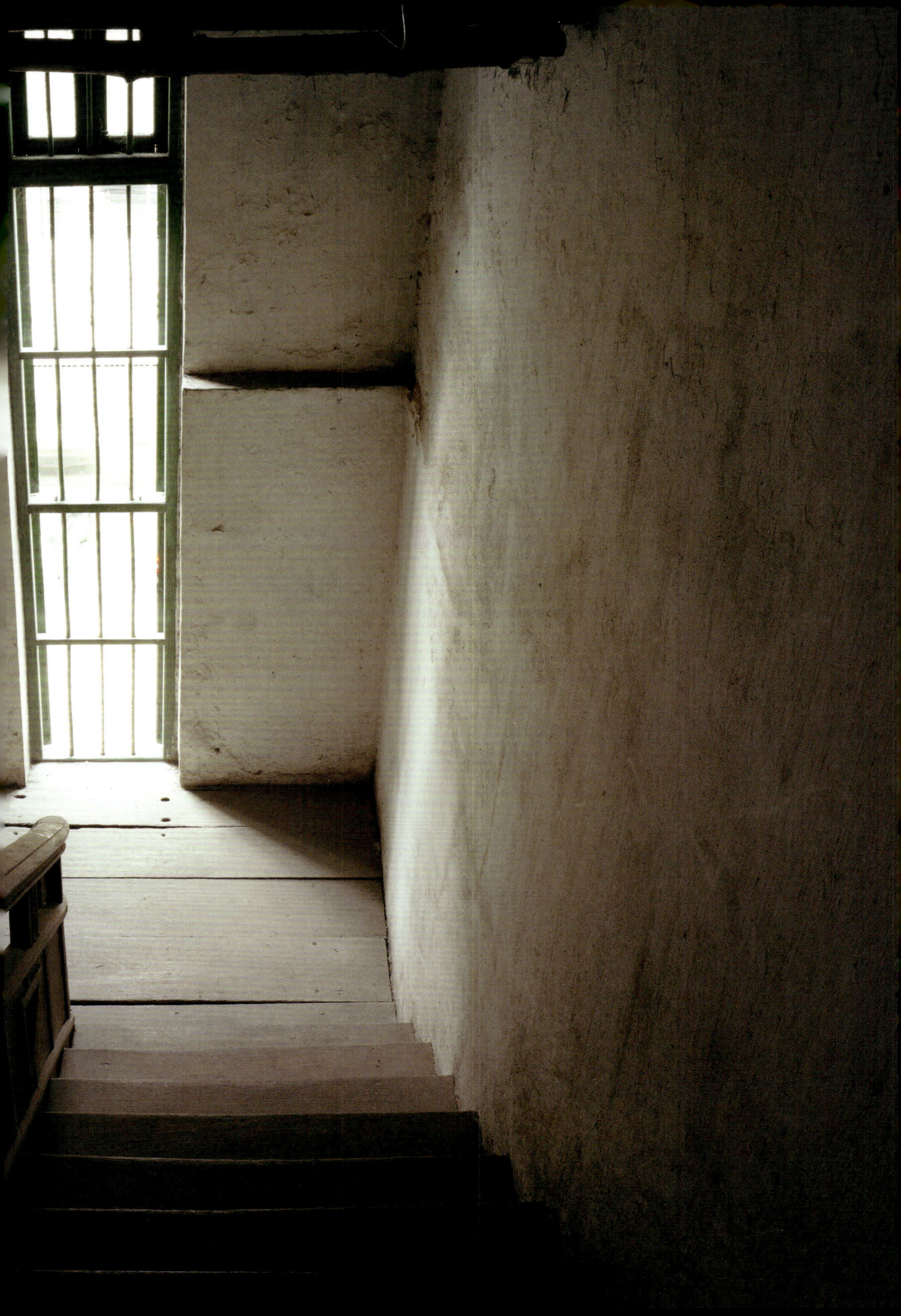

Their first child, a boy called Woon Yin, was born in 1936.

他們的第一個孩子，一名叫煥延的男孩，出生於1936年。

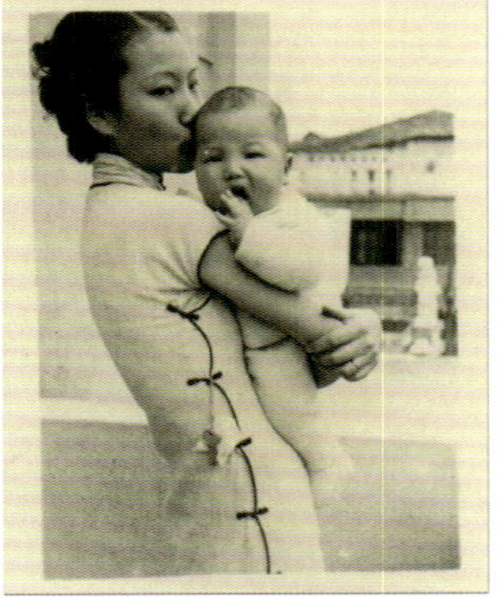

V 日本鬼子
Japanese Devils

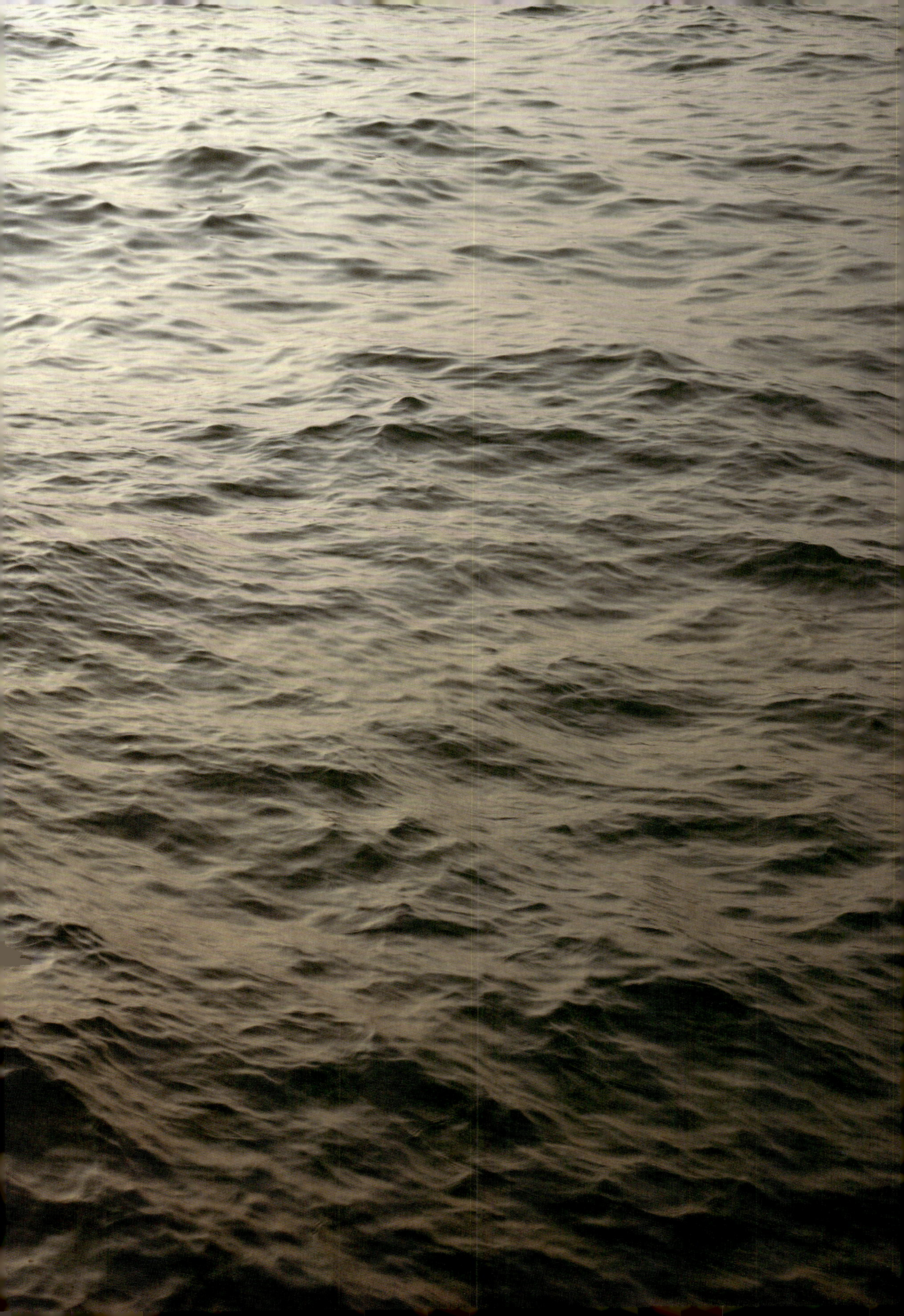

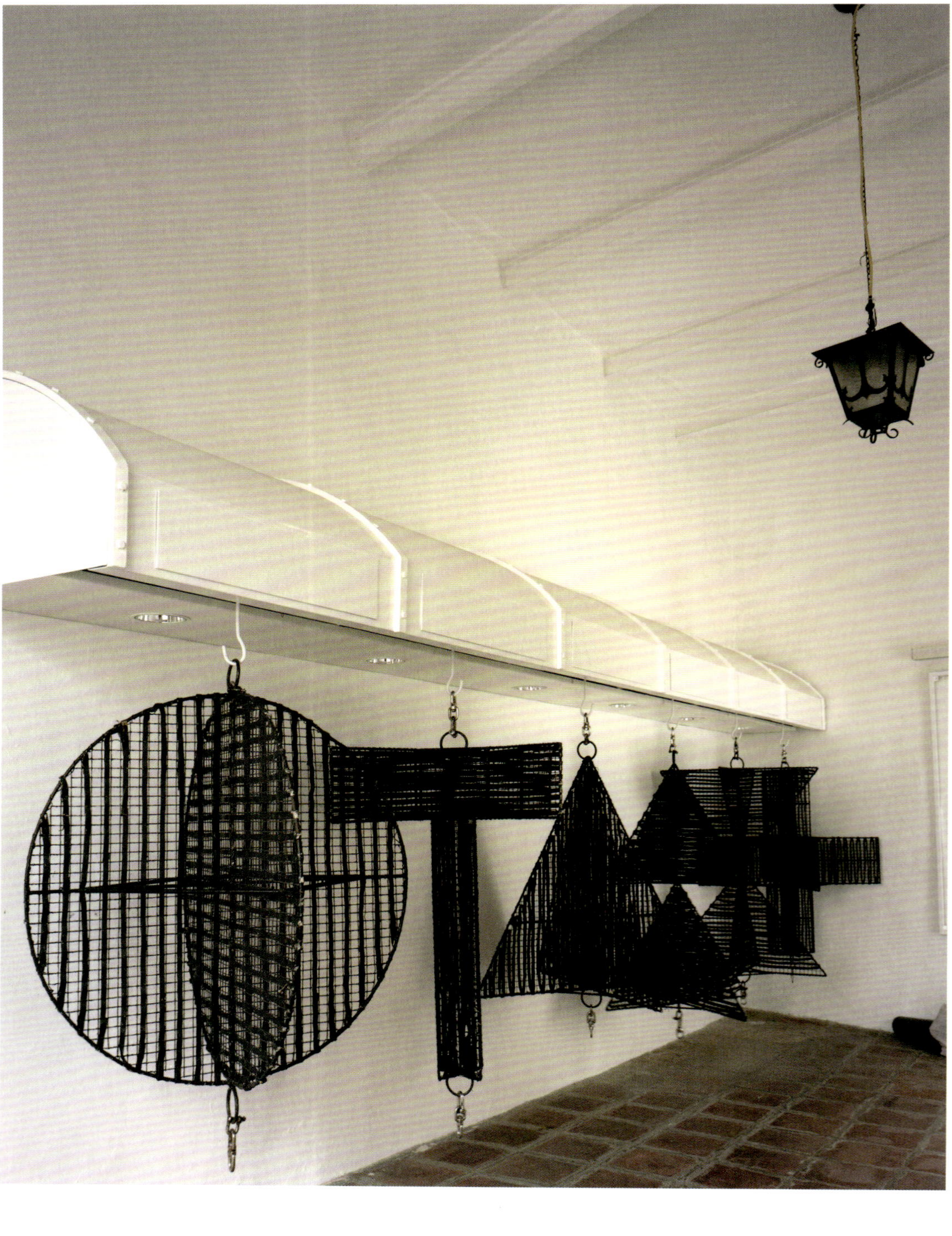

During the Japanese occupation of Hong Kong, trading in Bunnan's company came to a halt. The family of thirteen were only able to survive thanks to insurance money that had been received after a vessel carrying his stock sank during a typhoon on the way to England, just prior to the fall of Hong Kong.

在日本佔領香港期間，賓南的貿易生意一度中斷。在香港淪陷前夕，一艘載有他的貨物的船隻在前往英國途中遭遇颱風沉沒，一家十三口所幸得以依靠保險金度日。

Bunnan took his family to Macau to seek refuge. On their way to join him, his sister and her family were on board a civilian ferry when it was sunk by the Americans, who believed there were firearms on board. Everyone was killed. Fearing that she would take the news badly, his mother was never told about her death. For the next 25 years, until her death, she believed her daughter had emigrated to the USA. Bunnan regularly sent her letters and money in his sister's name.

賓南帶著家人到澳門避難。在前往的路上，他姐姐一家所在的渡船被美國人擊沉了，只因懷疑船上藏有槍支。船上所有的人都因此喪命。因擔心母親無法接受這個壞消息，賓南一直沒有將姐姐的死訊告知她。在此後直到母親離世的二十五年間，她一直以為女兒已經移居了美國。因賓南常以姐姐的名義給母親寫信和寄錢。

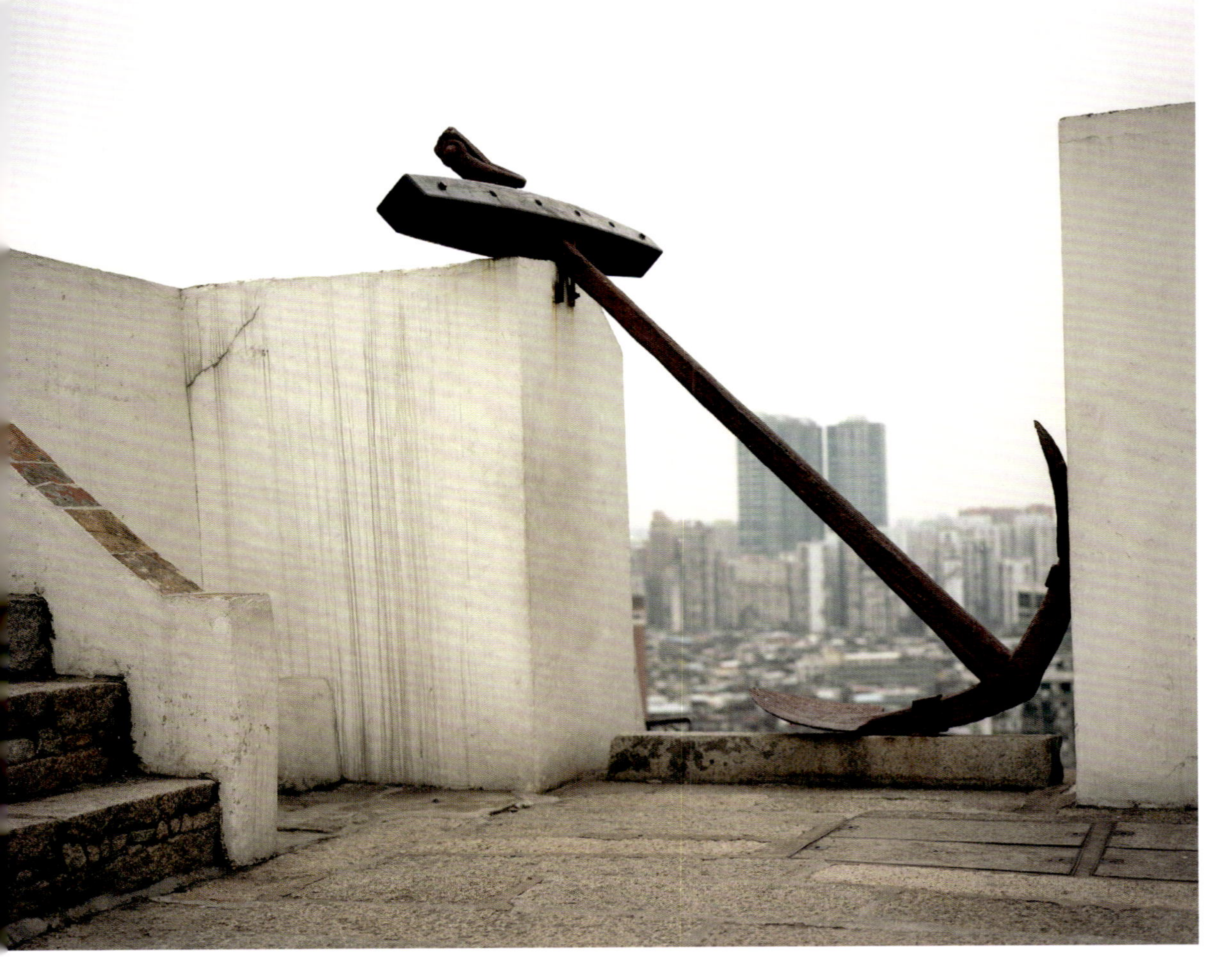

When World War II broke out, one of Bunnan's two German partners decided to return to the fatherland to fight for the Nazi Party. The other partner, disagreed with Hitler's ideology, and left for Macau, a Portuguese colony. Neither returned to Hong Kong after the war ended, both presumed dead. As a result, Bunnan ended up with the company to himself.

二戰爆發後，賓南的其中一個德國生意夥伴決定回國為納粹黨效命。另一個夥伴對希特勒的意識形態持反對態度，決定前往葡萄牙殖民地澳門。兩人在戰爭結束後都沒有返回香港，很有可能已經不在世上。最後賓南只能獨自經營公司。

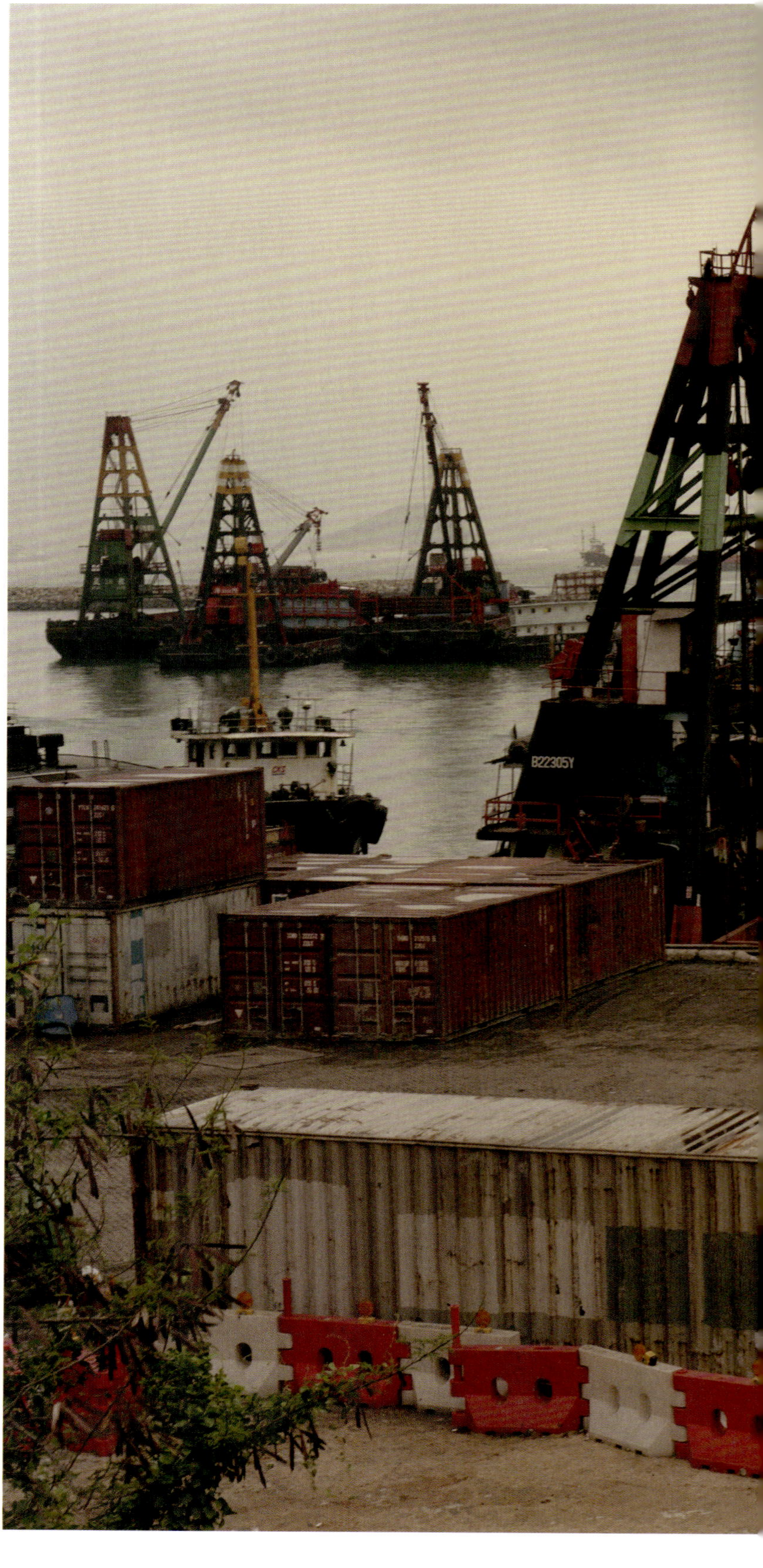

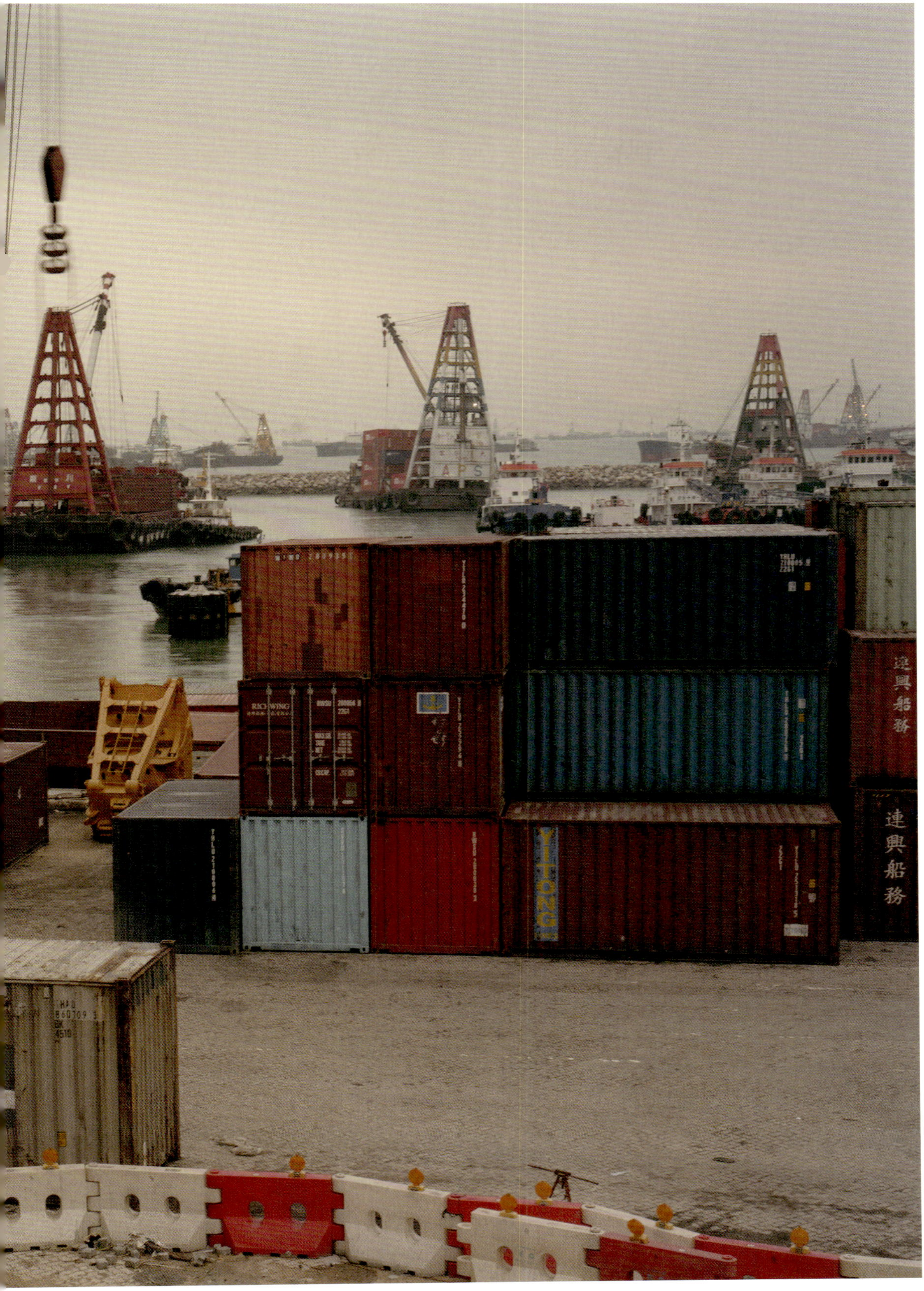
YITONG
連興船務
連興船務

Prior to the occupation of Hong Kong by the Japanese, Bunnan would welcome his third son, Tai Ching in May 1940, a month after his second son had been born.

在日軍佔領香港的前夕，賓南在1940年5月迎來了他的第三個兒子大楨。離他第二個兒子出生僅差了一個月。

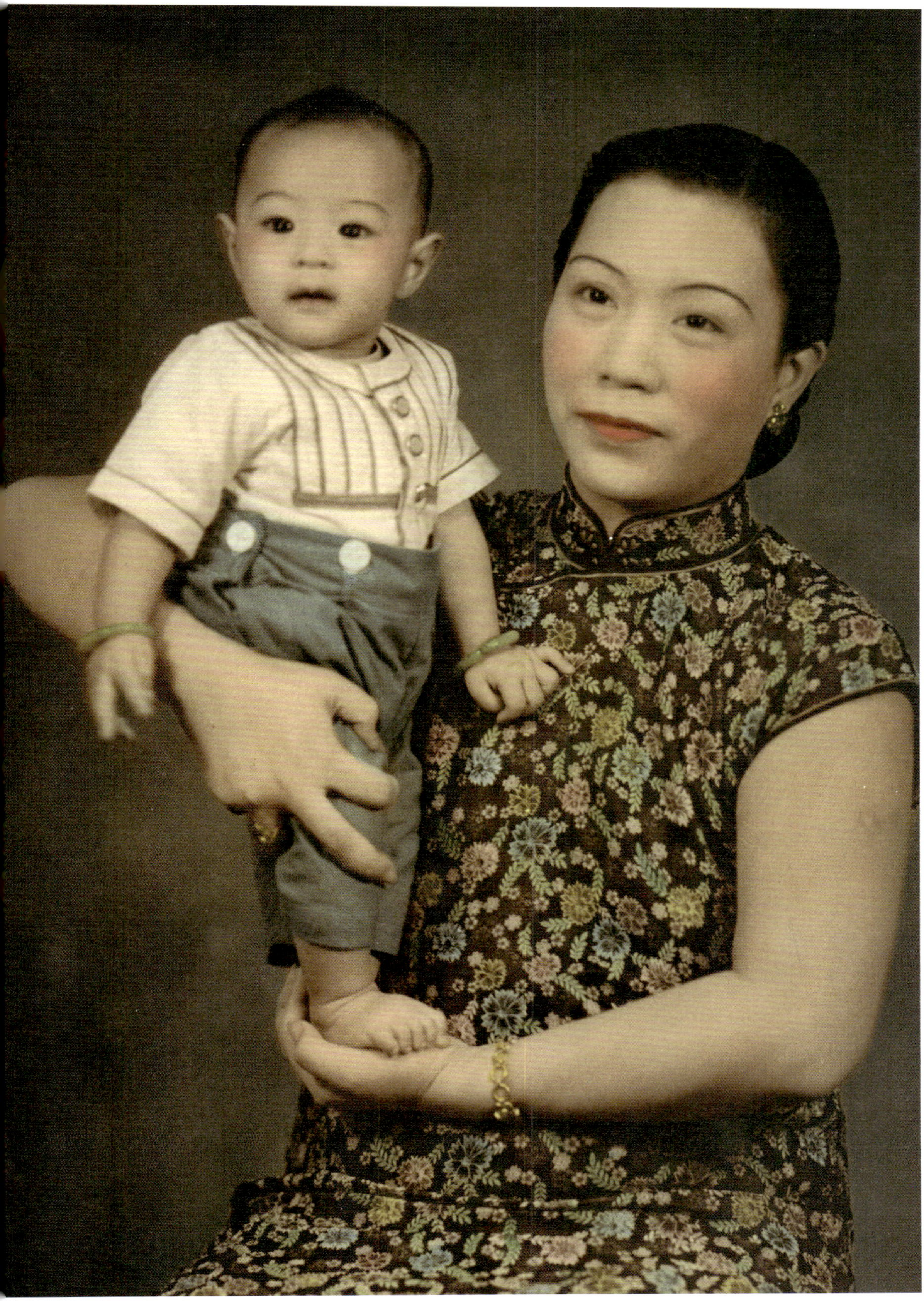

VI 奶媽
Milk mother

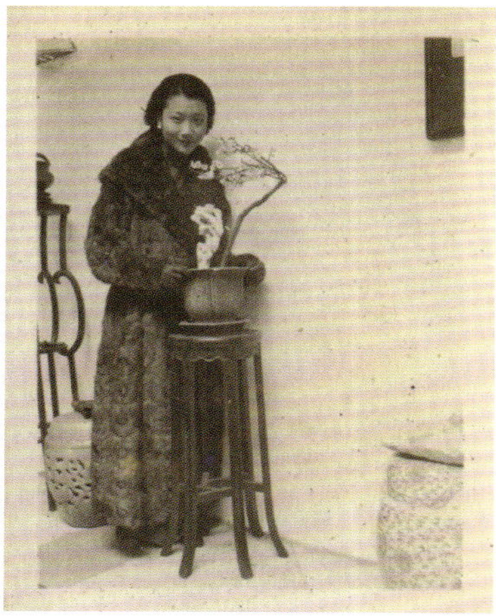

During the Japanese invasion, although their lives were not greatly affected by the ongoing war, Chung Zak and his family moved back to their ancestral home, away from the potential danger of Guangzhou.

日本侵華期間，仲錫一家人搬回了鄉下的老家，遠離當時危險的廣州。生活也因此並未受到戰爭的很大影響。

Their fifth child, a girl called Yip Hang, was born a month before the surrender of the Japanese. She contracted tuberculosis as a child and spent several months in hospital.

他們的第五個孩子，一個叫業恆的小女孩，出生在日本投降前一個月。她小時候得了肺結核，在醫院住了好幾個月。

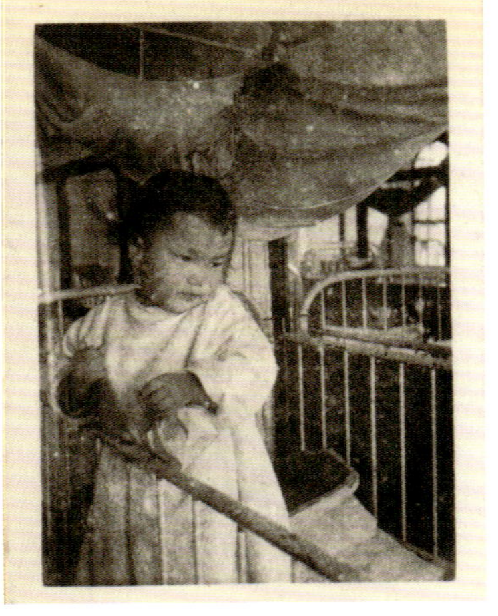

「我殺曬仔女，之後再自殺。」

"I am going to kill all our kids and then commit suicide."

With the birth of each child came three new servants, a maid, a nanny and a wet nurse, who would be in charge of the breastfeeding. As the eldest son, Woon Yin was involved in the interview process for Yip Hang's wet nurse. Each prospective wet nurse was brought into the main hall and asked a series of questions about her health. A small glass would then be given to her to be filled with her milk and tasted by Chun Sak, Yun Nan and Woon Yin.

It wasn't uncommon for the men in the Wong's mansion to have sexual relationships with the maids in the house and this was generally tolerated by their wives. Yun Nan, however, forbade Chung Zak from having extra-marital affairs. Woon Yin, their eldest son overheard a heated argument after she had found out that Chang Zak had been sleeping with one of the wet nurses. Yun Nan threatened to kill the children and commit suicide.

A ten year old Woon Yin, could not understand why his mother would want to kill him.

每個孩子出生後家裡都會請三個新傭人，包括一位女傭、一位保姆和一位負責哺乳的奶媽。作為長子，煥延參與了業恆奶媽的面試過程。每個前來申請工作的奶媽都會被帶到大廳，回答一系列關於她健康狀況的問題。然後她需要把奶水放到一個小杯子裡面，由仲錫、苑蘭和煥延分別品嚐。

在黃氏宅邸裡，男人和女傭發生性關係的情況並不少見，這是他們的妻子普遍能夠容忍的。苑蘭卻禁仲錫有任何婚外情。在發現仲錫和一名奶媽發生關係後，苑蘭和仲錫之間曾發生一場激烈的爭吵，並被他們的大兒子煥延無意聽到。苑蘭揚言要殺死這些孩子們並自殺。

當時只有十歲的煥延並不明白他媽媽為什麼要殺他。

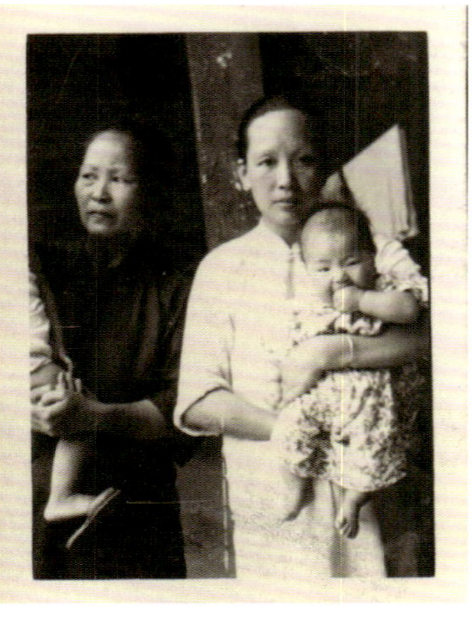

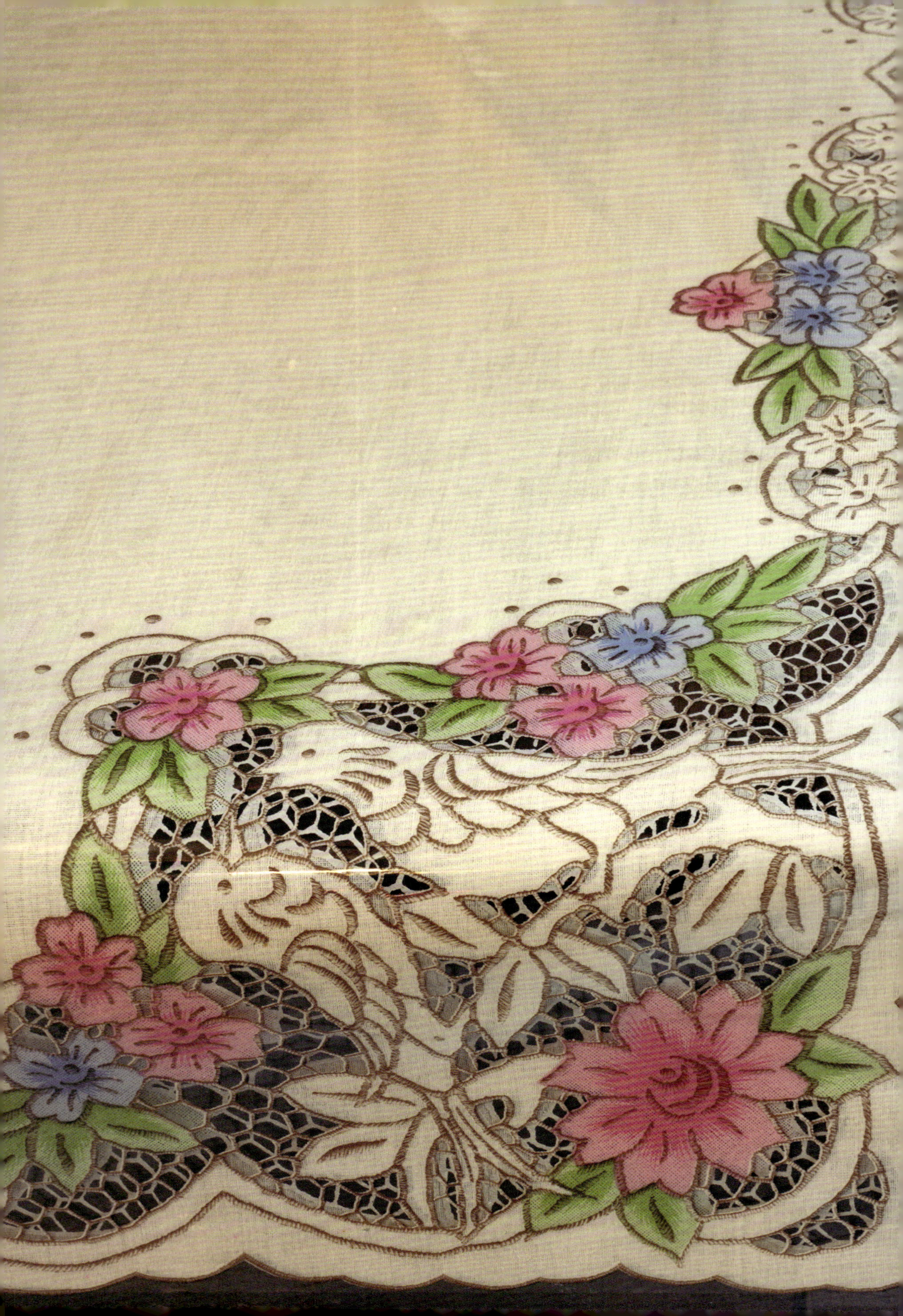

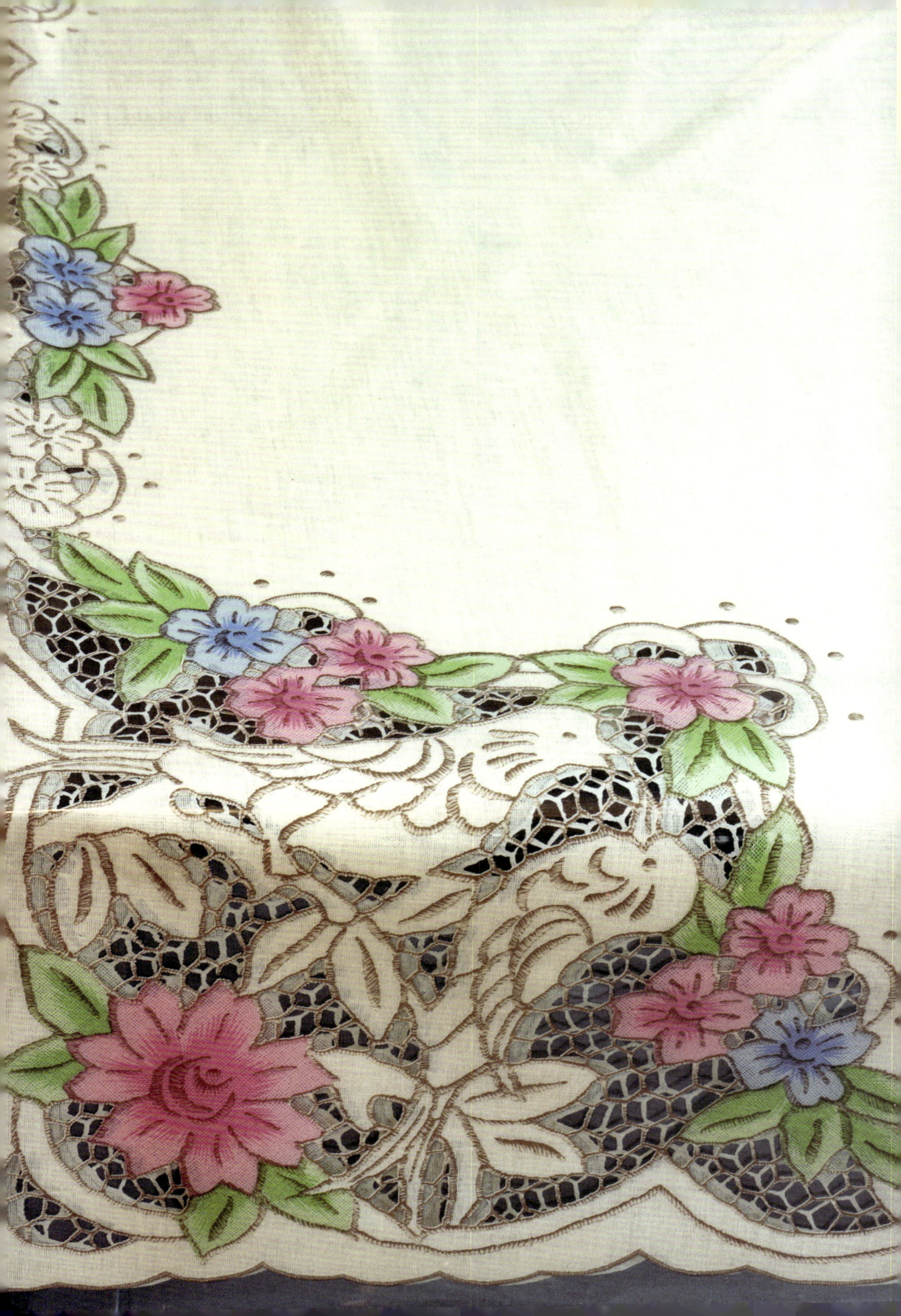

VII 鋼琴與土製炸彈
Piano and homemade bomb

Tong family portrait taken in 1940

Bunnan is fourth from the left on the back row. In front of him just to his right, is his first wife, Shook Ying. To her left, is Bunnan's mistress, Ah Mei. By the time that Tai Ching was born, Shook Ying had given birth to eight children, bearing seven daughters and only one son. She was seen as having failed in her duties as a wife. Ah Mei, Bunnan's secretary and mistress, fell pregnant and gave birth to a son. Had she given birth to a daughter, she probably would have been paid off, but as she had borne him a son she was moved into the family home, even though it was illegal by then to have more than one wife.

Tai Ching, born a month after his half brother, probably kept Shook Yin's status within the family.

唐家的全家福，拍攝於1940年。

賓南站在後排中間位置。他的正前方是他第一任妻子淑英。淑英左邊是賓南的情婦阿美。大楨出生前，淑英共生下八個孩子，其中包括七個女孩和一個男孩。當時的人們認為她未盡作為妻子的責任。阿美原本是賓南的秘書，在和他發生關係後懷孕並生了一個兒子。如果她生的是一個女兒，很有可能只會拿到一筆錢，儘管在那時娶多個妻子是違法的，但由於她給賓南生了一個男孩，被批准搬到家裡住。

大楨比他同父異母的哥哥晚一個月出生，他的出生也保住了淑英在家裡的地位。

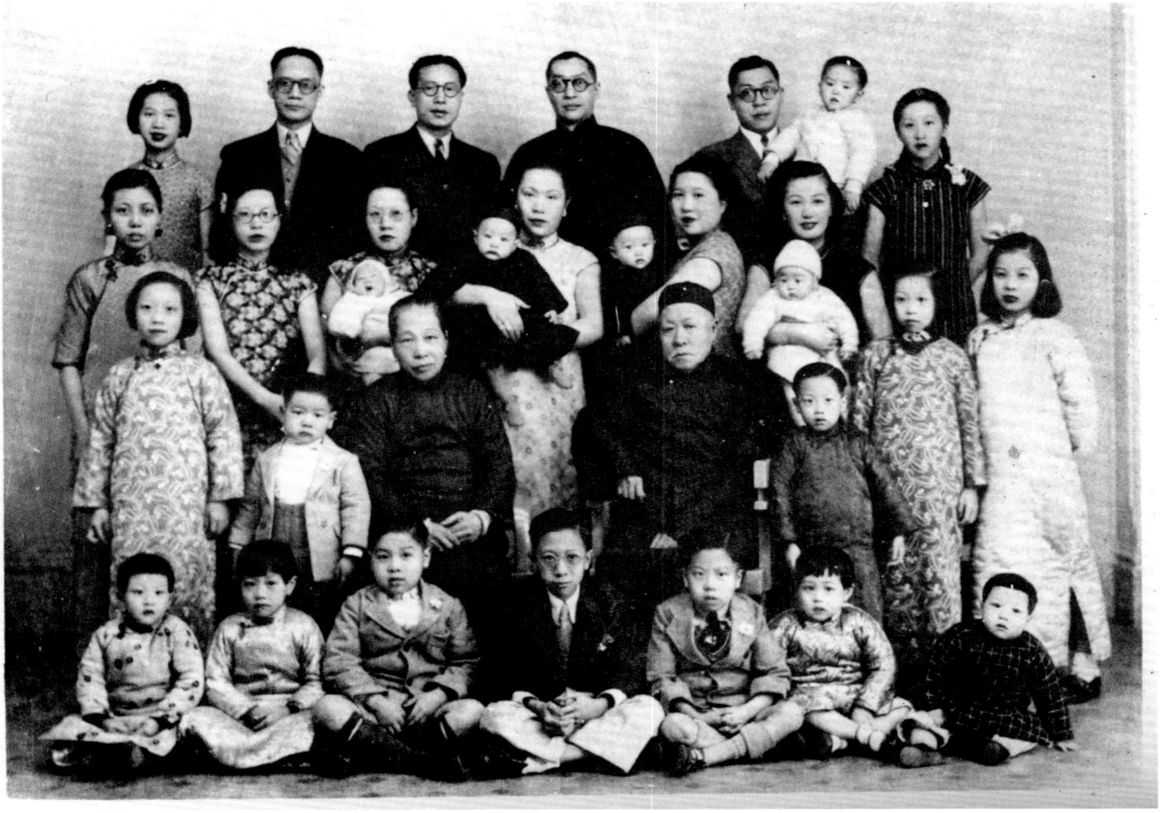

Tai Ching moved here in 1940, not long after he was born. Having gone to Macau towards the end of the Japanese occupation, the family returned, later moving across the street to 84, Robinson Road. In the 1970s, his father put up a twelve storey block of flats in which he still lives with his wife.

"Everything has changed round here, except for that old wall with the trees growing on them. I used to be scared of them; I vaguely remember a dead body hanging from them during the Japanese occupation, perhaps it was only a tale my nanny used to tell me to scare me."

就在大楨出生後的1940年，在日本佔領時期短暫移居澳門後，一家人又再返回香港並搬回於此居住。後來他的父親於上世紀七十年代在街對面的羅便臣道84號建了一棟十二層高的公寓樓，直到如今他仍和妻子一起住在那裡。

「這邊的一切都不同了，除了那面長滿樹的老牆。我以前很怕它們，隱約記得在日本佔領期間，曾有一具屍體掛在了樹上面，當然也有可能這是保姆當時用來嚇我的一個故事。」

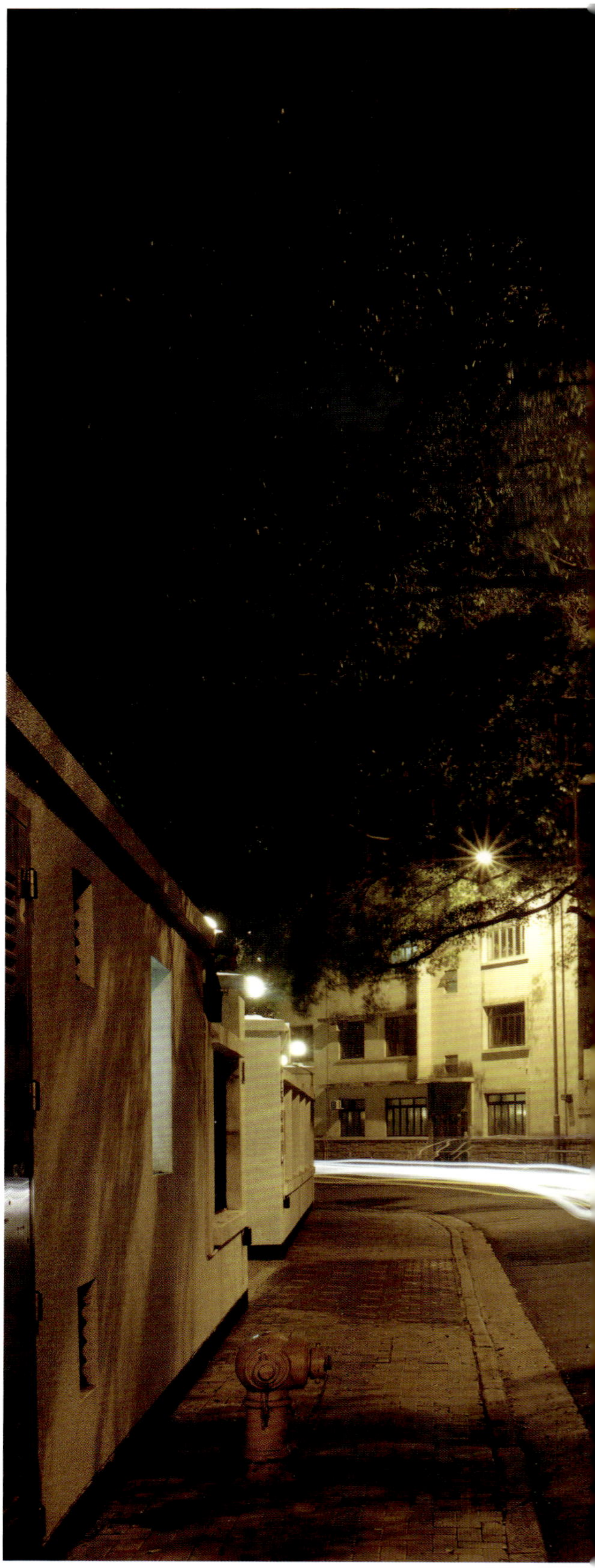

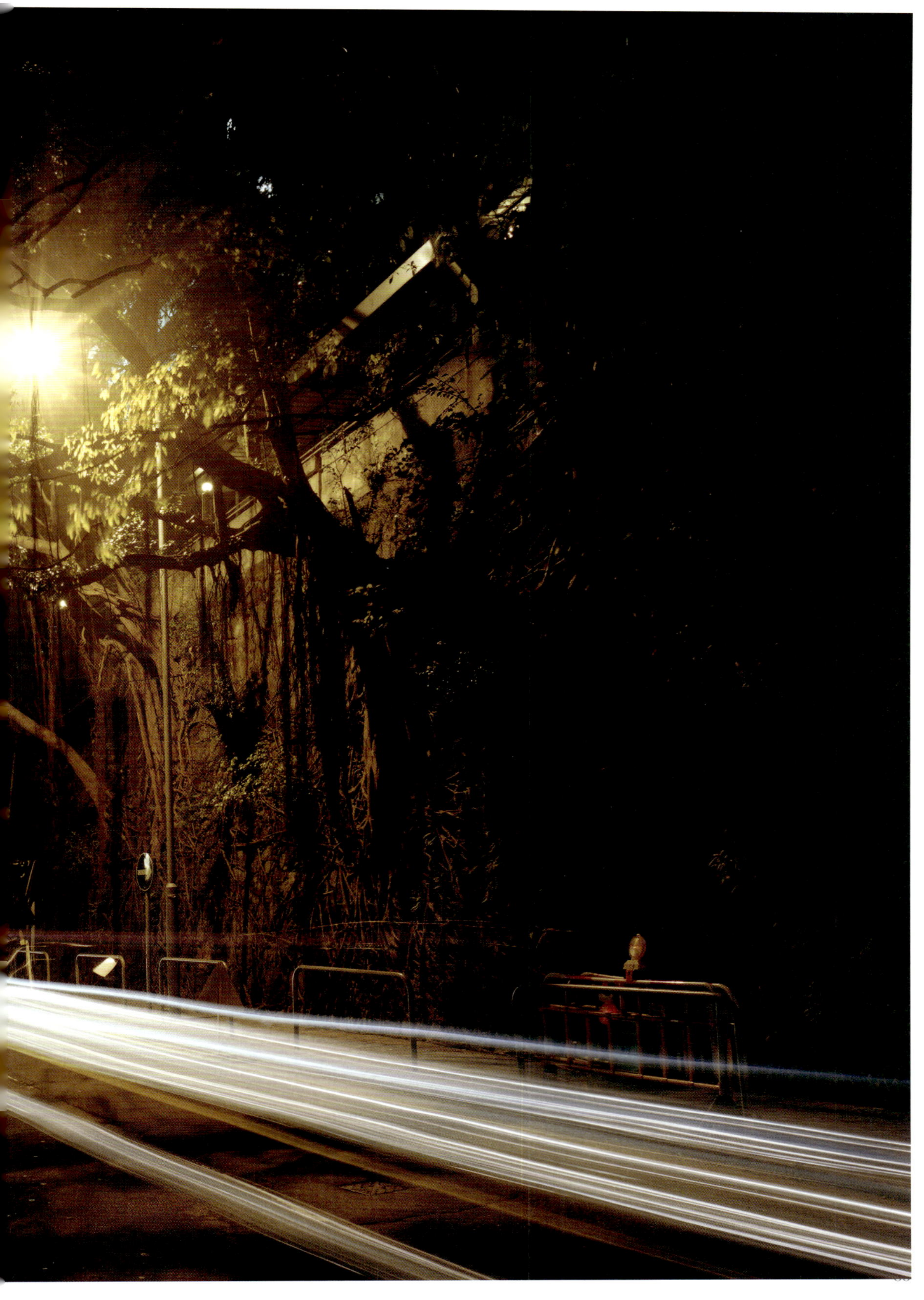

Tai Ching (far right) grew up with eight sisters who often ganged up on him. His elder brother, by twelve years, had no time for him. He was constantly in direct competition with his half brother, with the two wives using them as pawns to gain Bunnan's attention. Several years later, he was joined by a younger brother who became Bunnan's favourite. Growing up, he enjoyed his own company and spent the majority of his time playing the piano left behind by one of Bunnan's German partners.

He also enjoyed making homemade bombs.

大楨（最右邊）和八個姐姐一起長大，她們經常一起欺負他。比他年長十二歲的哥哥並沒有時間陪他。他經常被拿來和同父異母的哥哥作比較，賓南的兩個妻子常常利用他們來吸引賓南的注意。幾年後，他多了一個弟弟，這個弟弟成為了賓南最喜歡的兒子。長大後，他更喜歡自己獨處，大部分時間都在彈賓南的德國生意夥伴留下的鋼琴。

他也喜歡在家裡自製「土炸彈」。

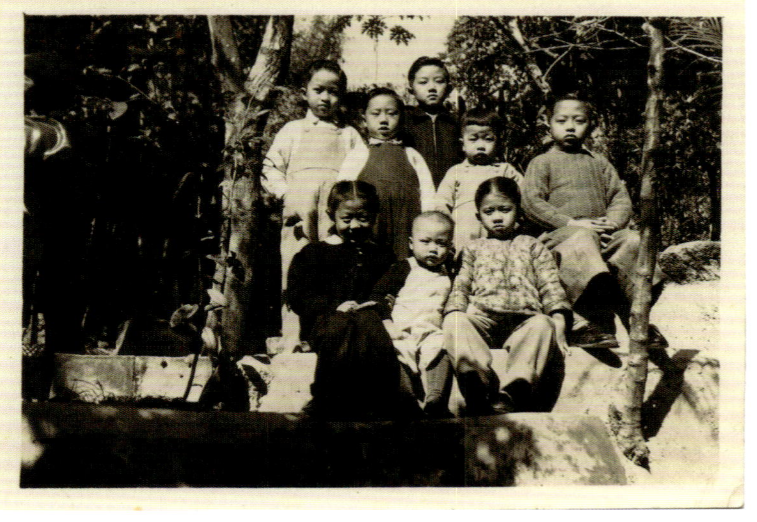

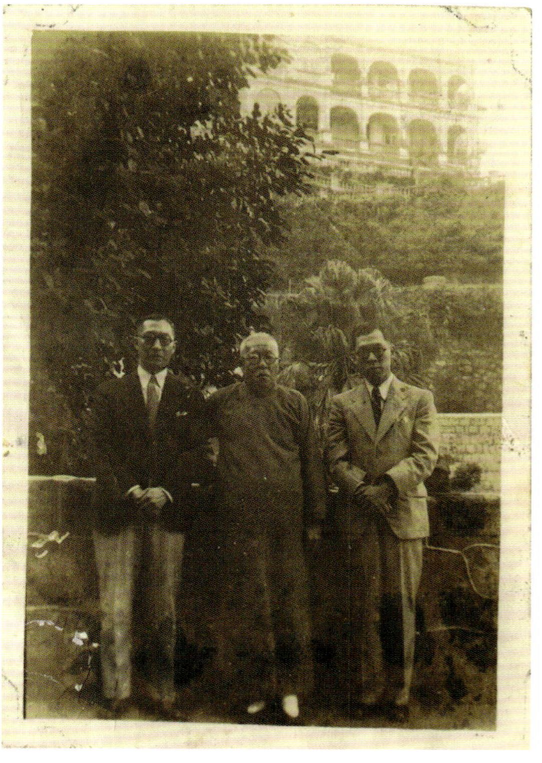

Bunnan was himself a victim of favouritism. Under Japanese occupation, Japanese soldiers would frequently request that a male member of a family report to the local base for questioning. It wasn't uncommon for the men to be beaten up or even killed. His mother would always send Bunnan instead of his younger brother, who was her favourite son.

賓南本人也是偏心的受害者。在日本佔領期間，日本士兵經常要求家庭派出一名男性代表到當地軍營報到問話。這些人被毆打甚至殺害並不少見。而他的母親總是派賓南代替弟弟前往，因為弟弟才是他母親的最愛。

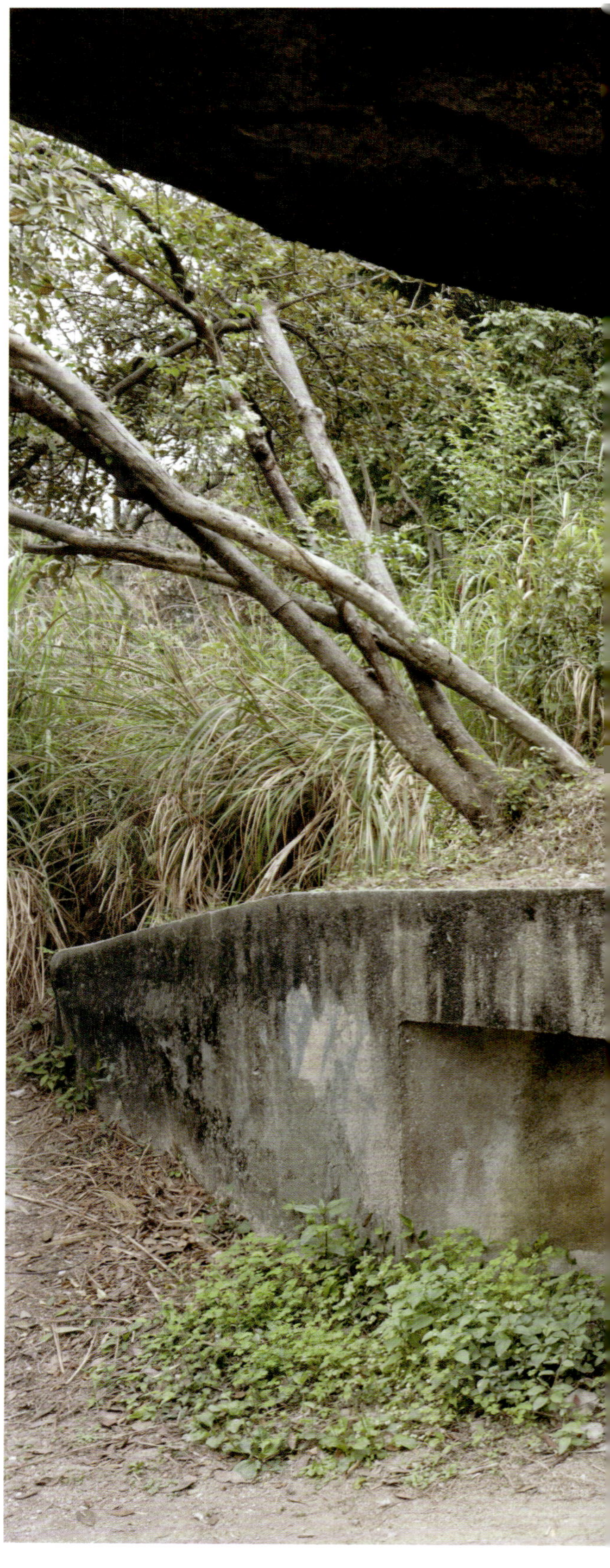

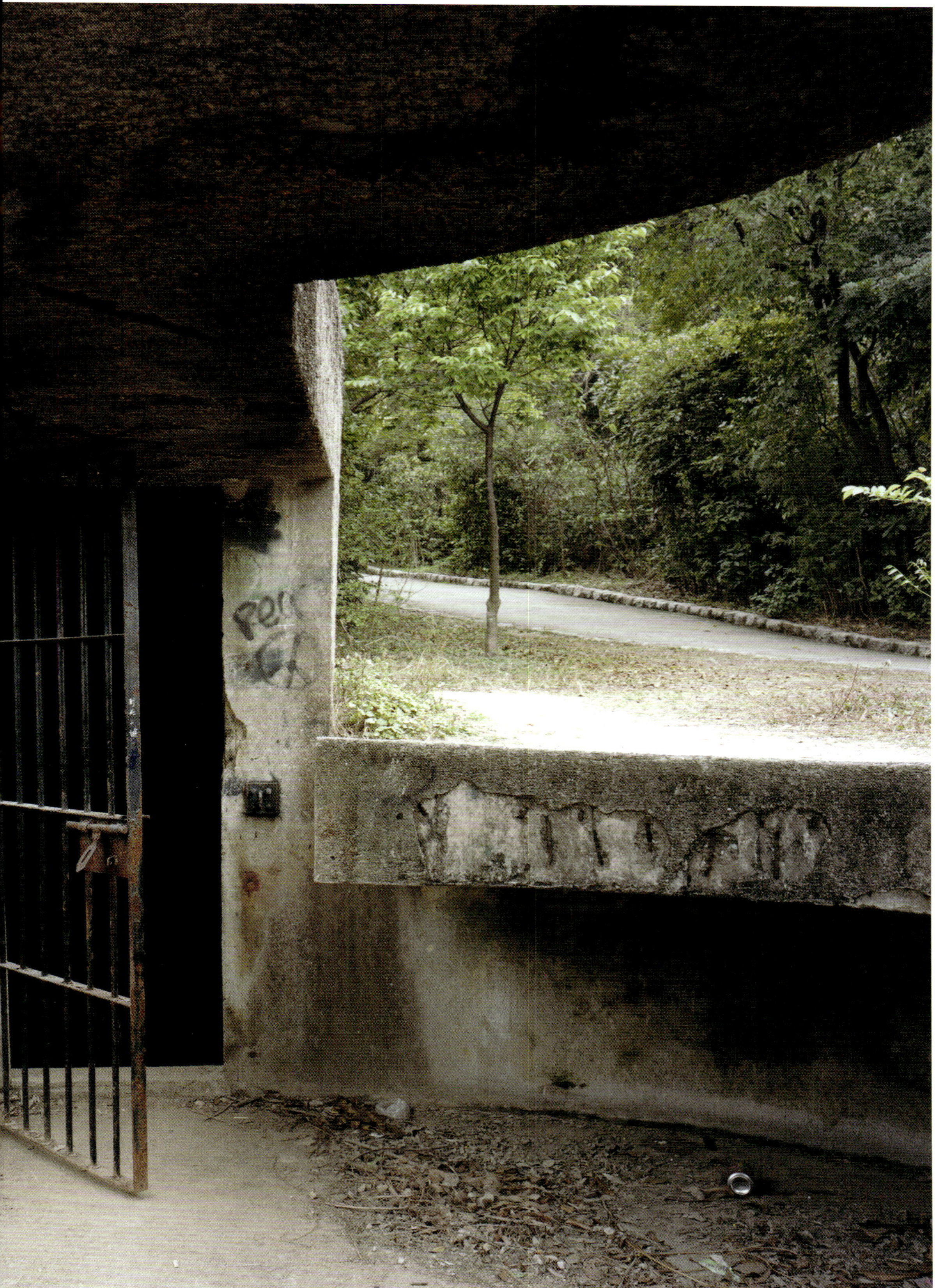

VIII 中國共産黨
Chinese Communist Party

In 1949, Chun Zak sought refuge in Hong Kong. Believing that he would return in a matter of months, rather than taking valuables such as gold bars or antiques, he only took what he saw as daily essentials. With these packed in wooden trunks, and along with 21 servants, he travelled to Hong Kong. He never returned to his family home.

1949年，仲錫去了香港。他相信他幾個月後就會回來，所以並沒有把金條和古董等貴重物品帶上，只把一些日用必需品裝在幾個木箱子裡，和二十一名僕人一同前往。

他從此再也沒有回到廣州的家裡。

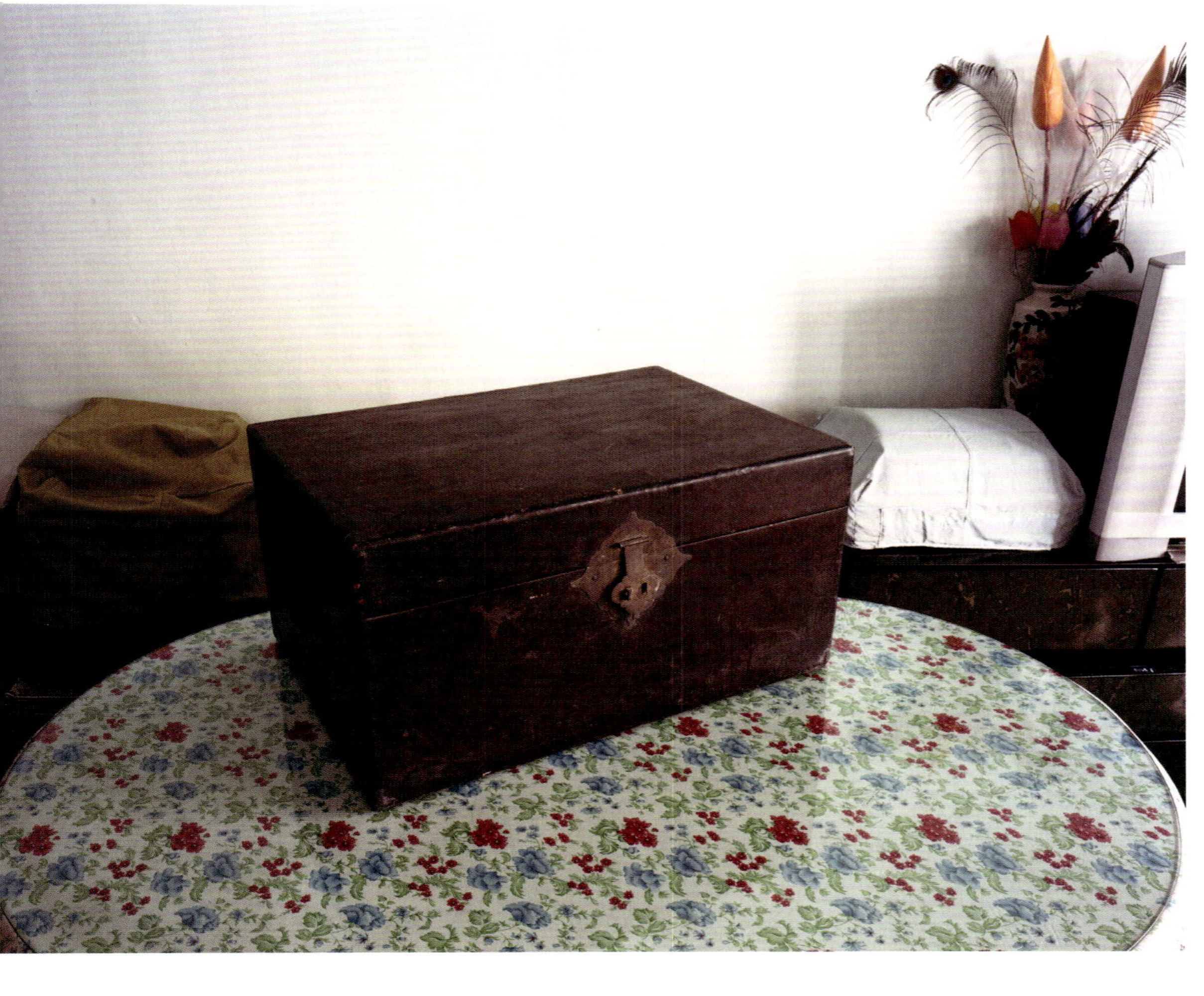

After arriving in Hong Kong, Chung Zak sent his family, except for his eldest son Woon Yin, to live in the Portuguese colony of Macau, where it was cheaper as it had a lower standard of living. Yip Hang can be seen here with her Portuguese friend (fifth from the left) and her sister Una (third from the left).

抵達香港後。仲錫讓除了大兒子煥延以外的家人搬到澳門居住，因為澳門的生活水平較低，比較便宜。照片中可以看到業恆（左五）和她的葡萄牙朋友以及姐姐業彤（左三）。

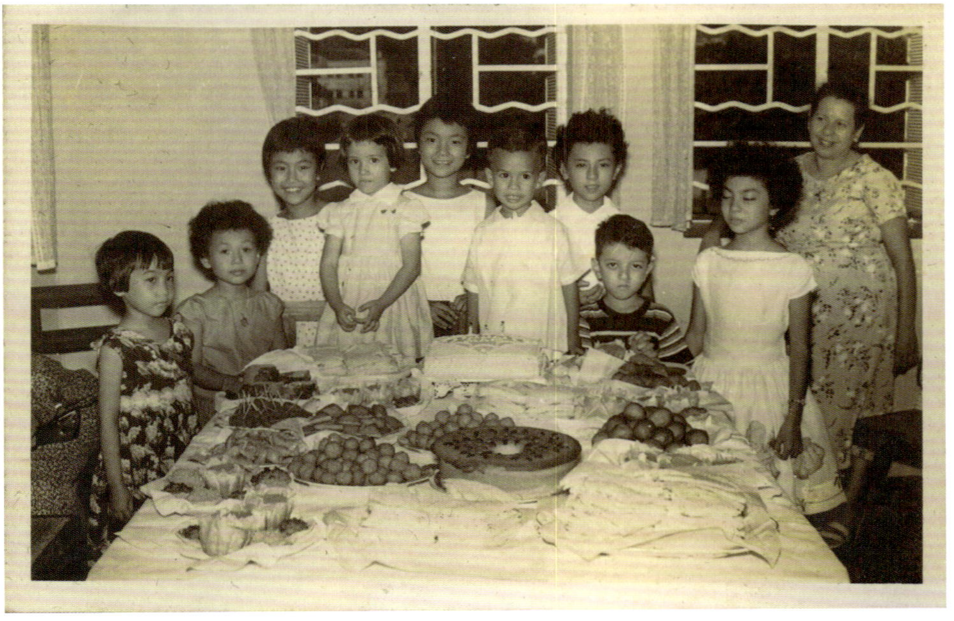

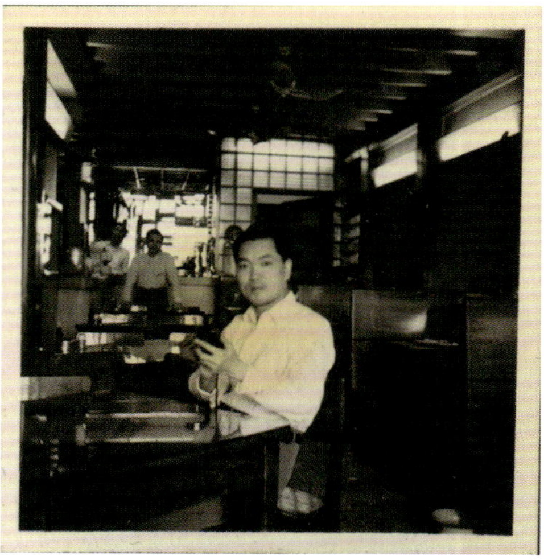

Meanwhile Chung Zak used the money that he had to open a hotel on the sea front in Hong Kong, near the docks of Sheung Wan. It was called Tai Ton Hotel, after the street in which the Wong Mansion was located in Guangzhou. Woon Yin, who attended school in Hong Kong recalls the hotel was frequented by sailors and that he had to walk past crowds of prostitutes on his way to school every morning.

與此同時，仲錫用剩餘的錢在香港上環碼頭附近的海邊開了一家酒店。酒店的名字叫大同，以廣州黃家所在的街道命名。在香港上學的煥延回憶說，這家酒店是很多水手經常光顧的地方，每天早上上學的路上都會經過成群的妓女。

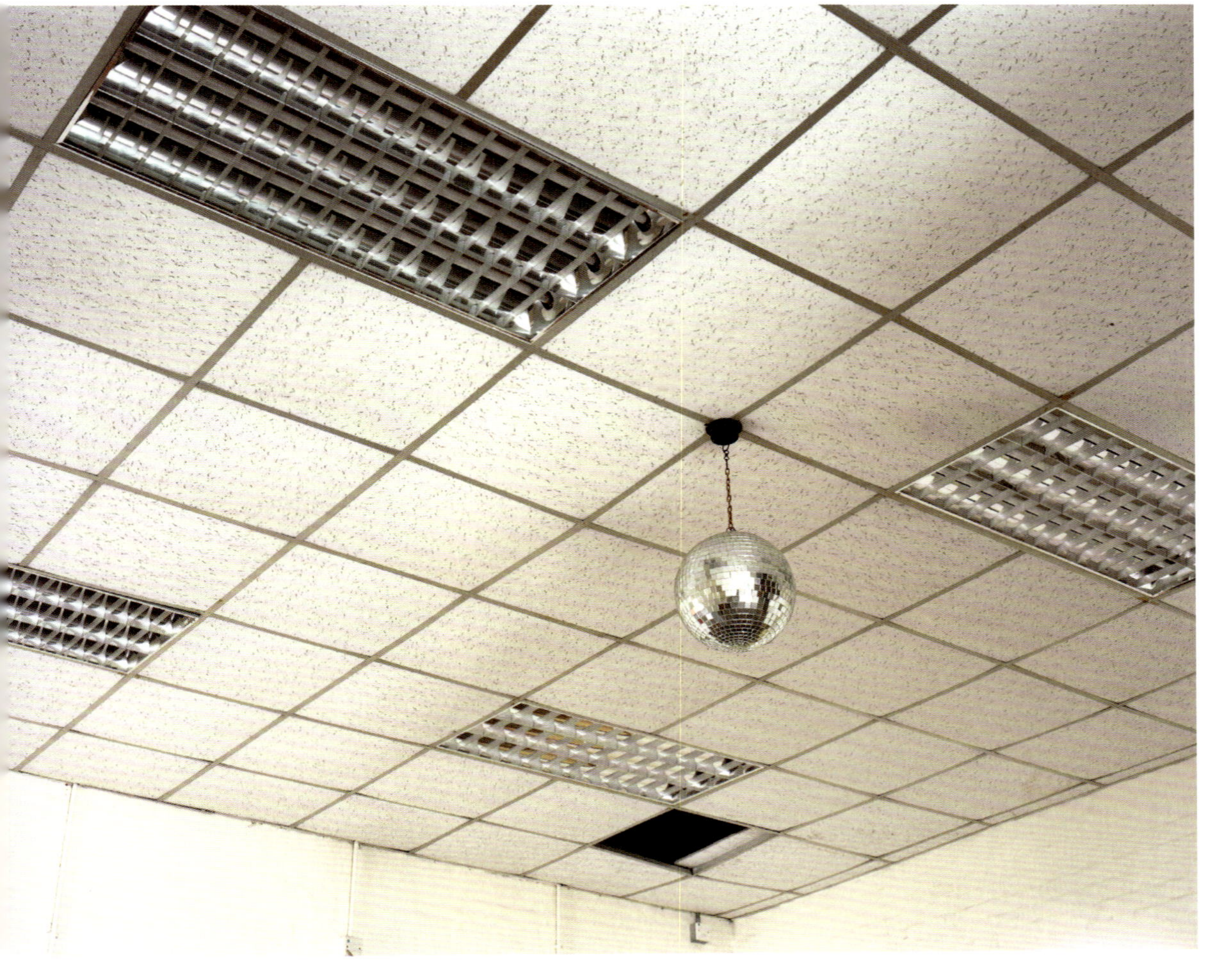

A luggage tag from Tai Ton Hotel. When relatives started arriving in Hong Kong from Guangzhou as refugees, many stored their belongings in the hotel.

大同酒店的行李標牌。親屬們從廣州離開至香港後，許多人會先將財物寄放在該酒店。

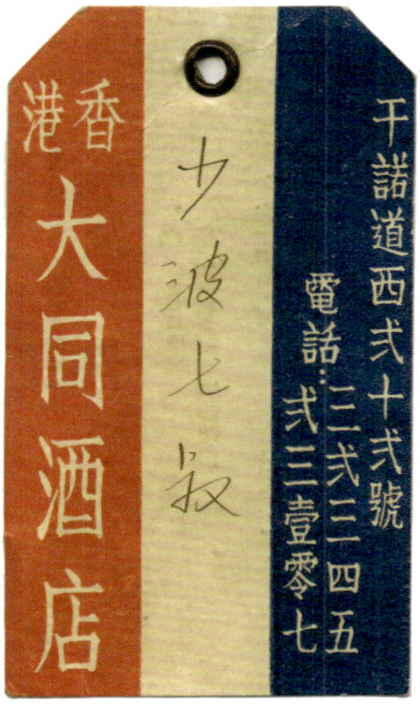
香港
大同酒店
少波七叔
干諾道西弍十弍號
電話：三弍二二四五
弍三壹零七

Having grown up with almost limitless money, Chung Zak did not run a successful business. Within a few years, most of the money he'd brought with him had run out. Yun Nan, still living in Macau with five children, relied on the little money he sent back each month to make ends meet.

As a child, Yip Hang remembers that at the end of the month the messenger would arrive on his bike to deliver the month's money. She would listen out for the clinking of the jars containing the treats her father had sent and would run up the road to greet the messenger. Another memory she vividly recalls is of the nuns, who ran the missionary school she and her sisters attended, using the universal sign of money by rubbing their fingers together and asking for their school fees, which were always late.

從小在無需為生計擔憂的環境下成長，仲錫的生意並不成功。幾年後，他帶來的大部分錢都用完了。而苑蘭和五個孩子還住在澳門，靠仲錫每月寄回的一點錢維持生計。

業恆還記得小的時候，每個月的月底郵差都會騎著自行車將生活費送來，自行車上父親送來的零食罐叮噹作響，她一聽到聲音遠遠傳來就會跑出去迎接郵差。她也忘不了教會學校的修女們總會用大拇指和食指指頭來回揉搓作出索要金錢的手勢，因母親總是遲交學費。

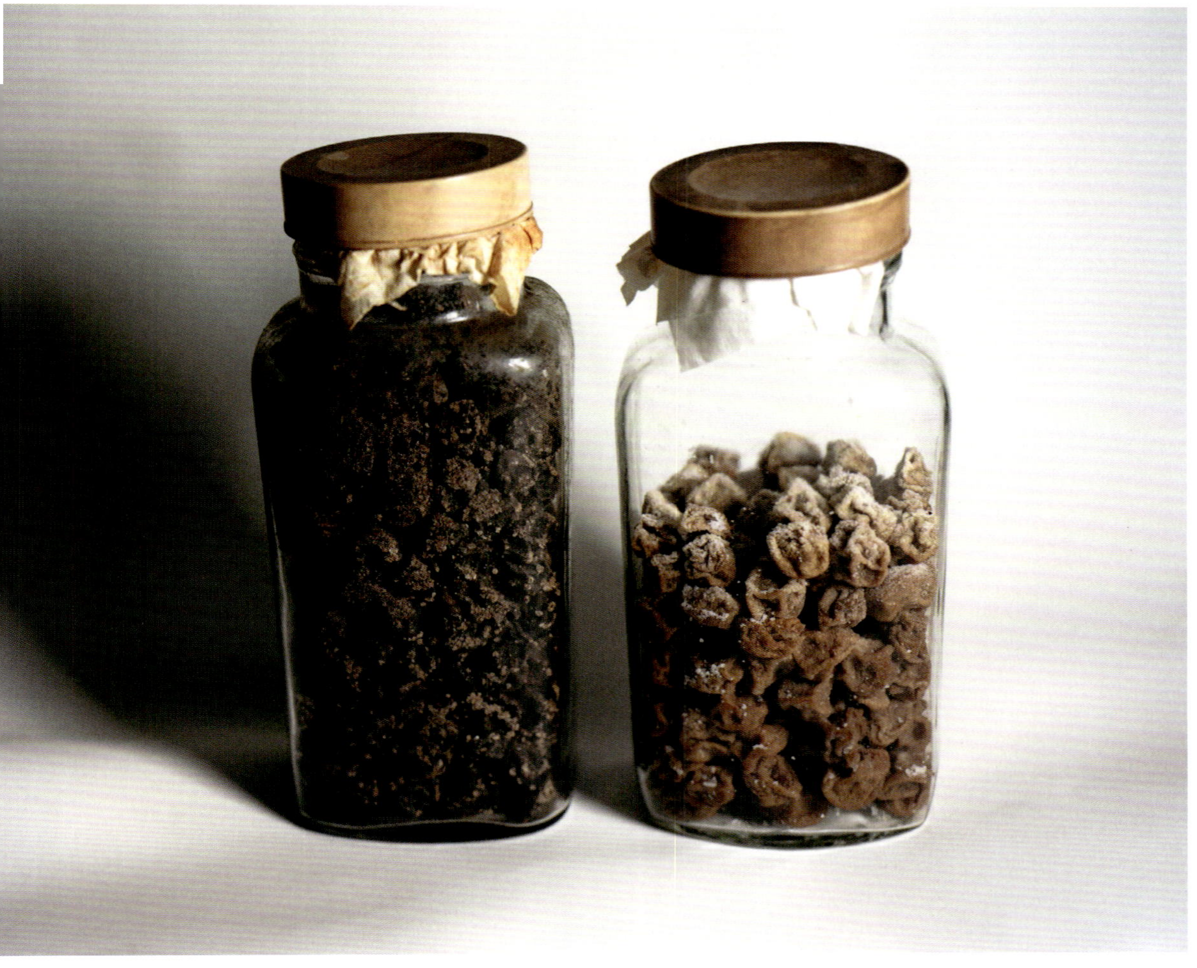

IX 打工仔
Working class

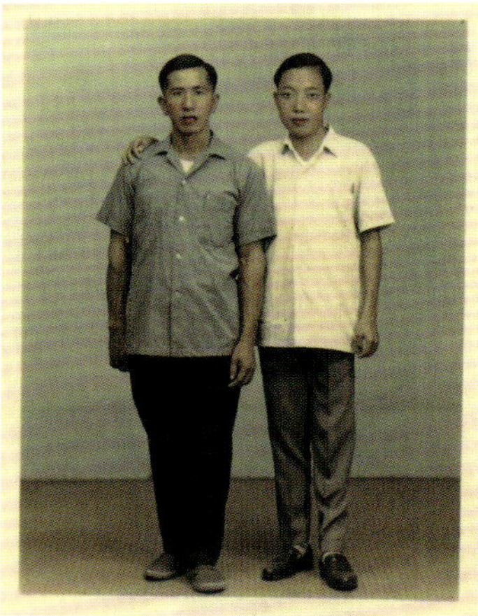

When the People's Republic of China was proclaimed in 1949, as many as 100,000 people fled to Hong Kong each month. An officially controlled border was established in June 1951 to halt this flow of people but thousands still continued to cross illegally for the next 50 years. Many chose to swim the Shenzhen Bay, including Bunnan's caretaker in the late 1950s and his son, some 30 years later. Thousands drowned during this swim. The three-mile crossing is now connected by a six-lane highway.

1949年中華人民共和國初成立時，每月約有十萬人前往香港。1951年6月，政府正式設立了邊境，但在接下來的五十年中，很多人依然嘗試非法越境。大部分人選擇從深圳灣水路偷渡，包括二十世紀五十年代末賓南的管家和三十多年後他自己的兒子。數以萬計的人在游泳過程中溺水身亡。這條三英里長的水路現在已經由擁有六車道的高速公路連接 。

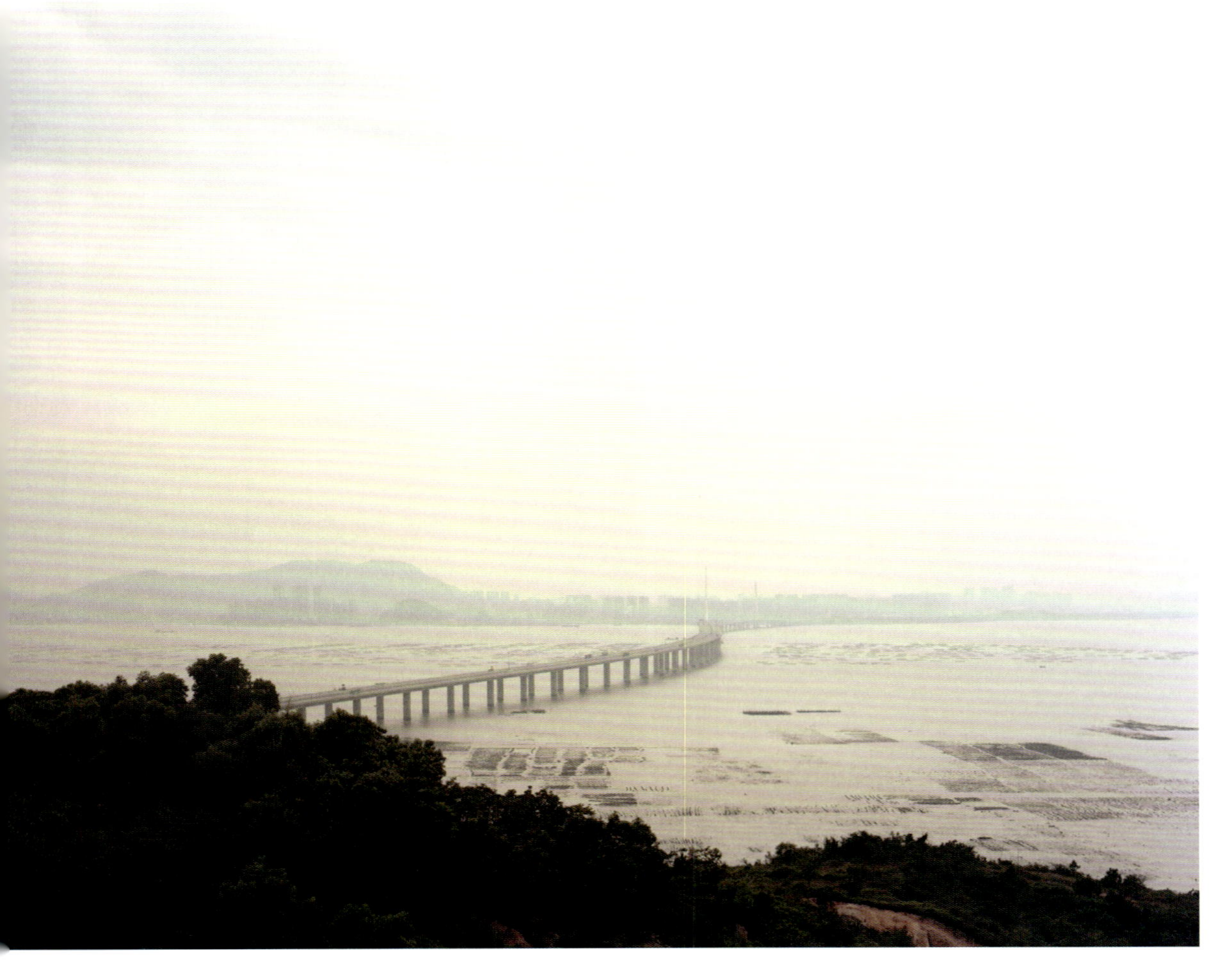

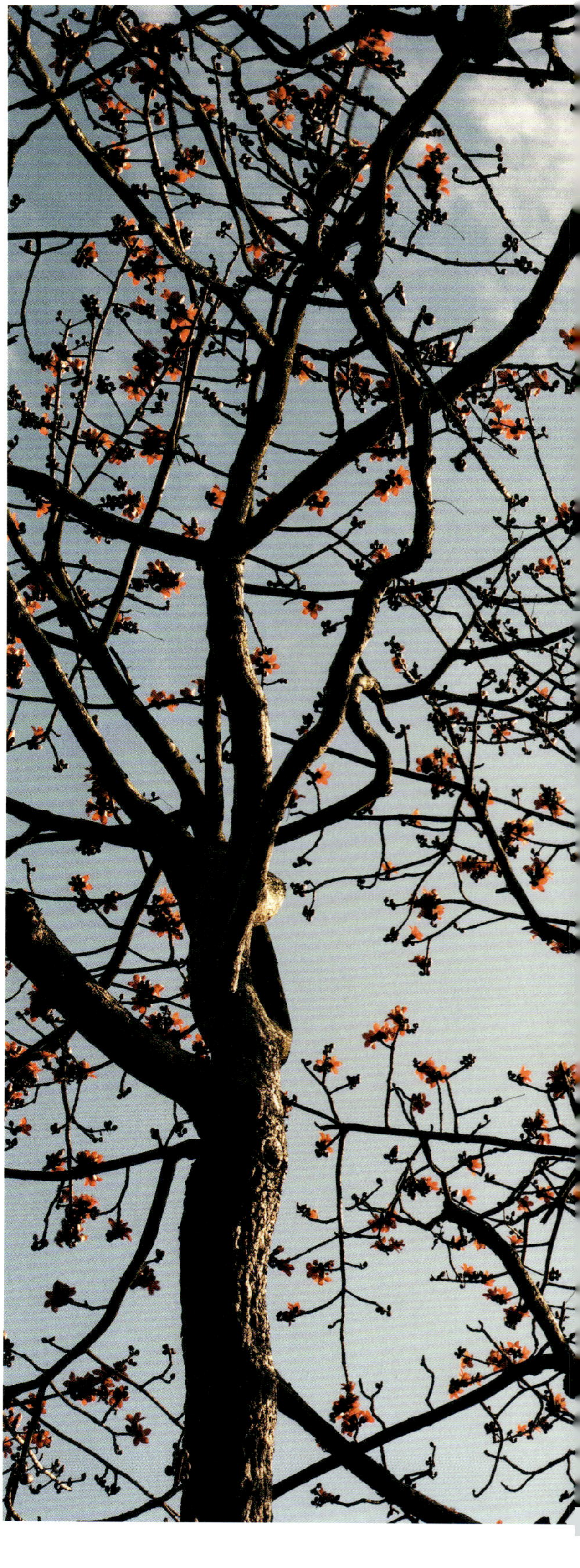

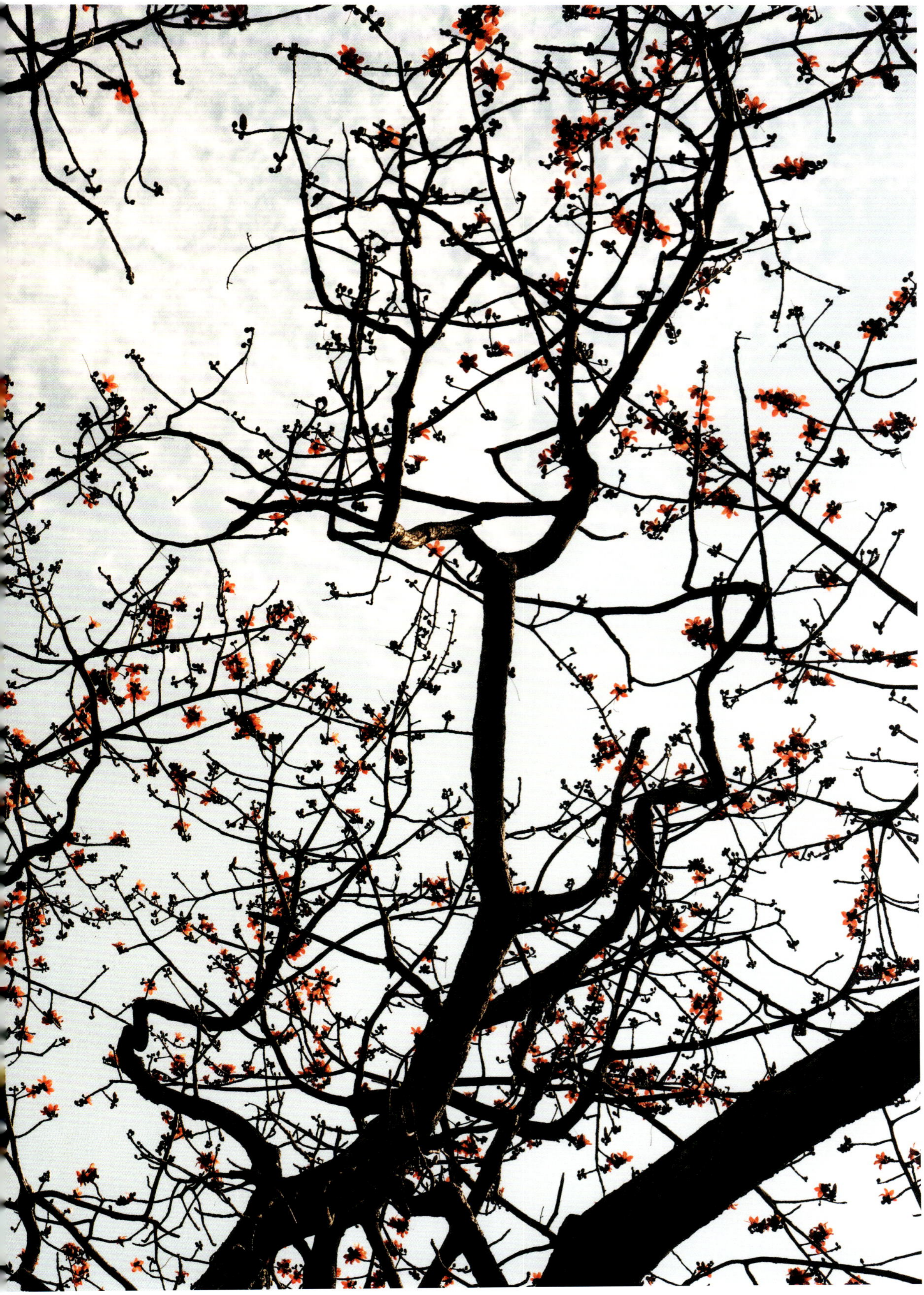

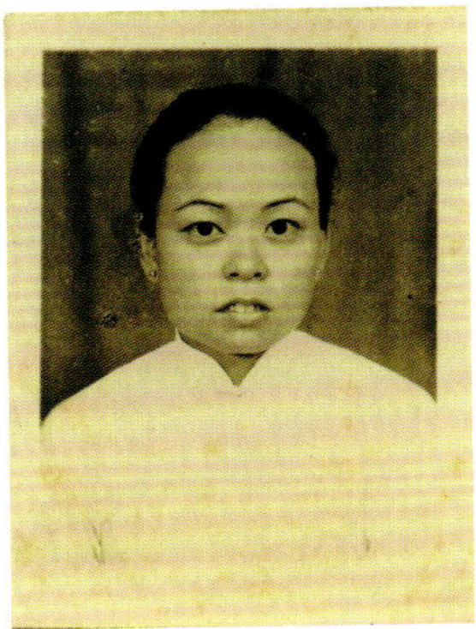

This traditional tunic belongs to Mak Ngan Yuk who worked as an Ah Mar (nanny) for 60 years until she retired a few years ago. She spent 40 years working for Tai Ching and was also the nanny for his youngest son, Ah Fung.

At the age of 82, she is one of the few remaining women who performed the combed up ceremony. Once a woman has been combed, she vows never to marry, dresses in the traditional tunic and wears her hair in a long plait. She is no longer obliged to her parents and any money she makes is hers to keep. In the first half of the twentieth century, many women performed the ceremony, particularly those who worked as domestic serevants. They could be found all over Southeast Asia.

這件傳統的束腰外衣是媽姐麥顏玉的，她在香港工作了六十年，直到幾年前才退休。她在大楨身邊服務了四十年，是大楨的小兒子阿鋒的保姆。

八十二歲的她是僅存為數不多的自梳女之一。一旦進行了自梳儀式，女性便發誓永遠不結婚，穿起傳統的束腰外衣，把頭髮梳成辮子。她不再對父母有贍養義務，掙的錢都是自己的。二十世紀上半葉，許多女性都進行了自梳儀式，她們大多是家庭傭工，在東南亞隨處可見。

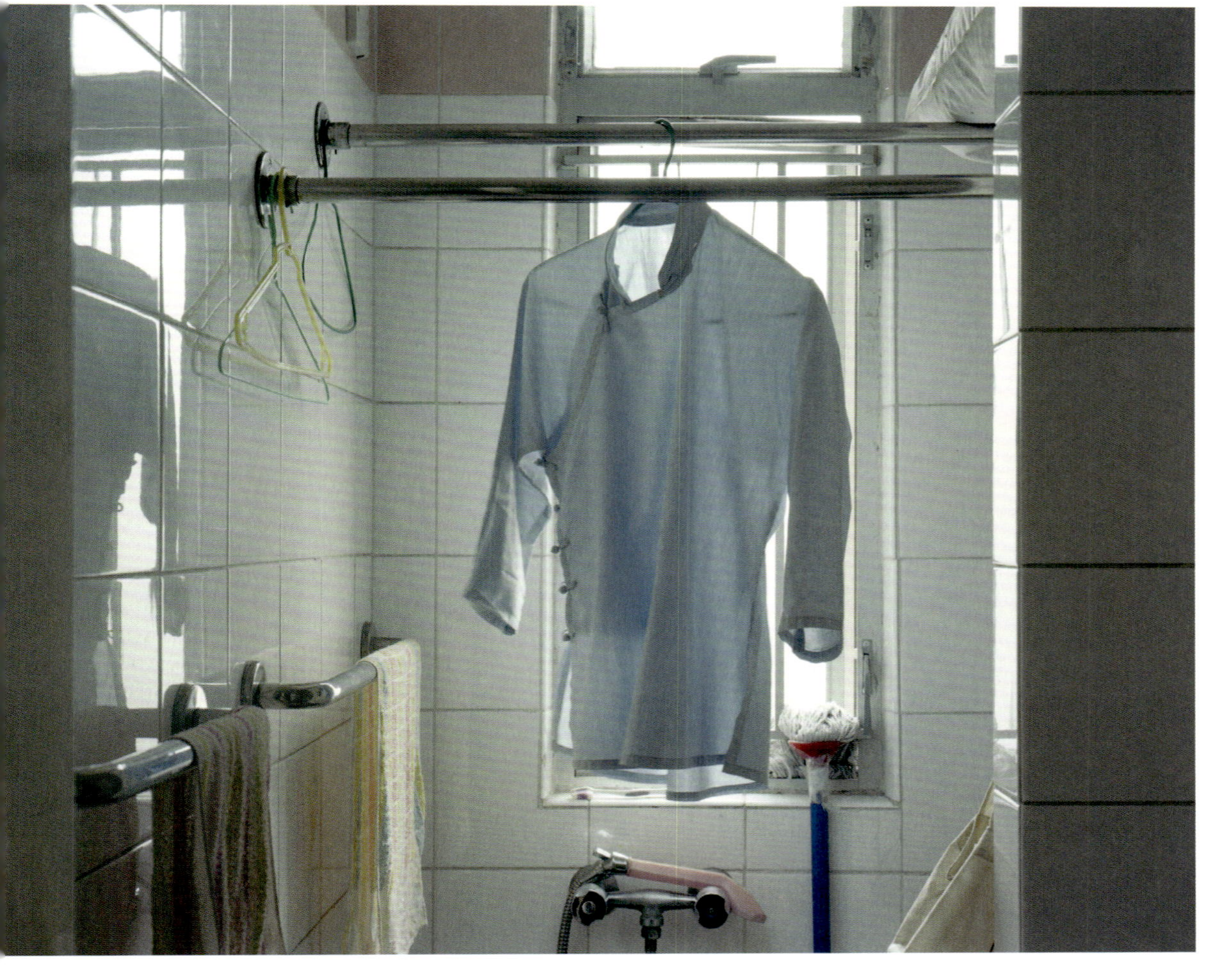

X 大英帝國勳章
Member of the Order of the British Empire

By the mid 1950s, Bunnan's two families were living separately. Zook Yin and her children remained at 84 Robinson Road while his second wife and her children were given a house at Yau Yat Chuen, a new district designed for the wealthy Chinese.

二十世紀五十年代中期，賓南的兩個妻子正式分開居住，淑英和她的孩子們仍舊住在羅便臣道84號，而他的第二任妻子和她的孩子們則搬到當時為有錢人設計的新區又一村居住。

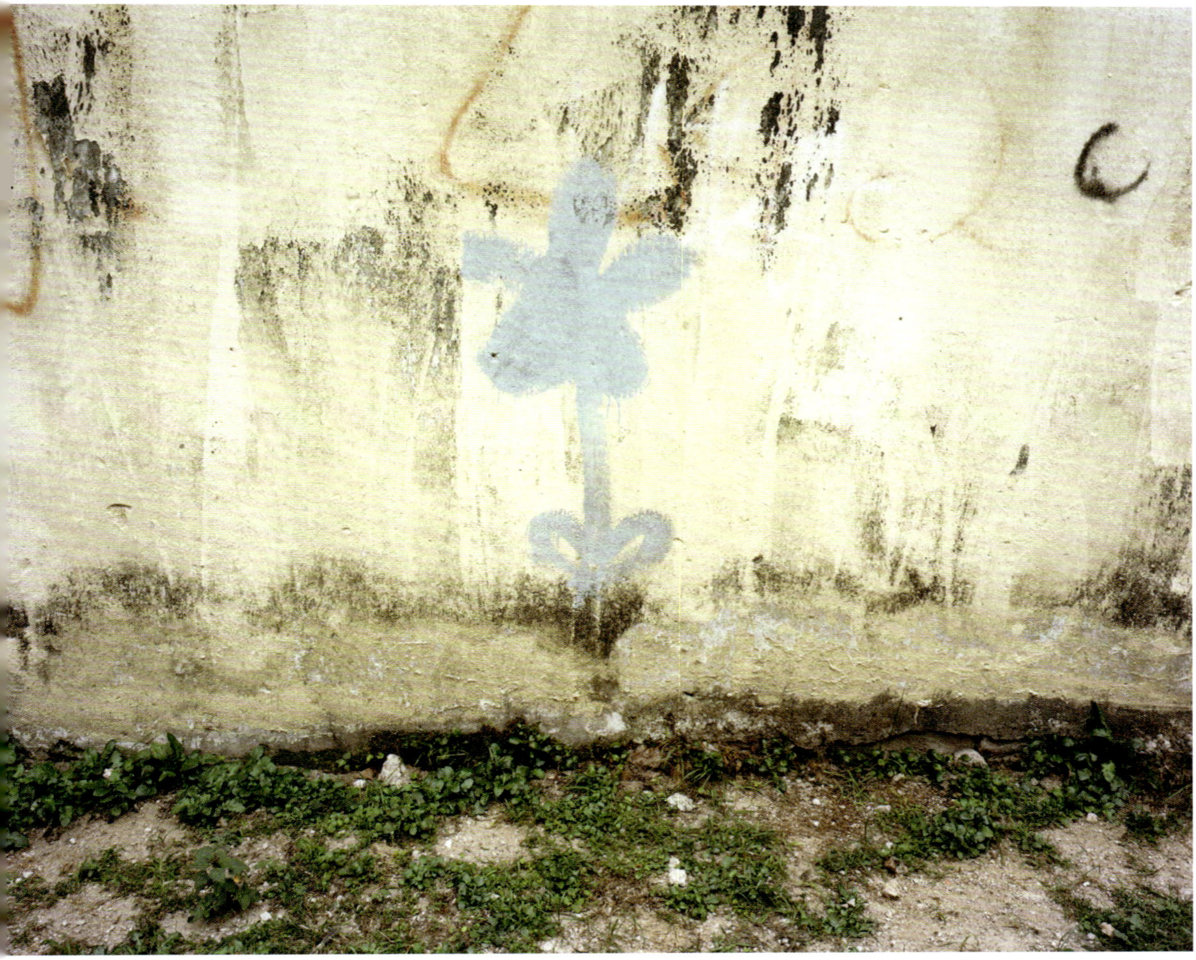

Bunnan preferred to pose almost every family photo in front of the bamboo bushes at 84 Robinson Road, the Tong's family backdrop.

賓南總喜歡在羅便臣道84號後院的竹叢前拍攝全家福照片。

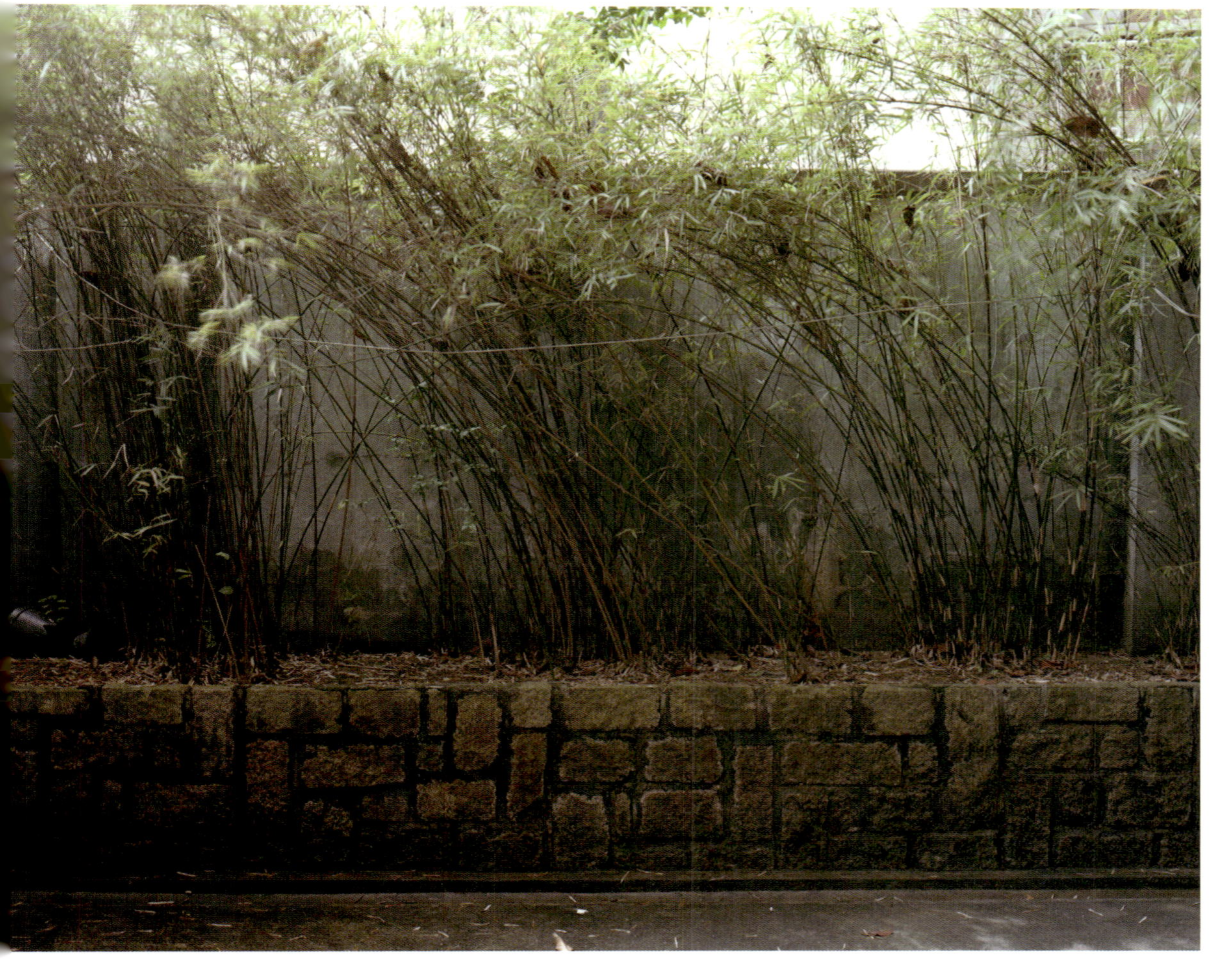

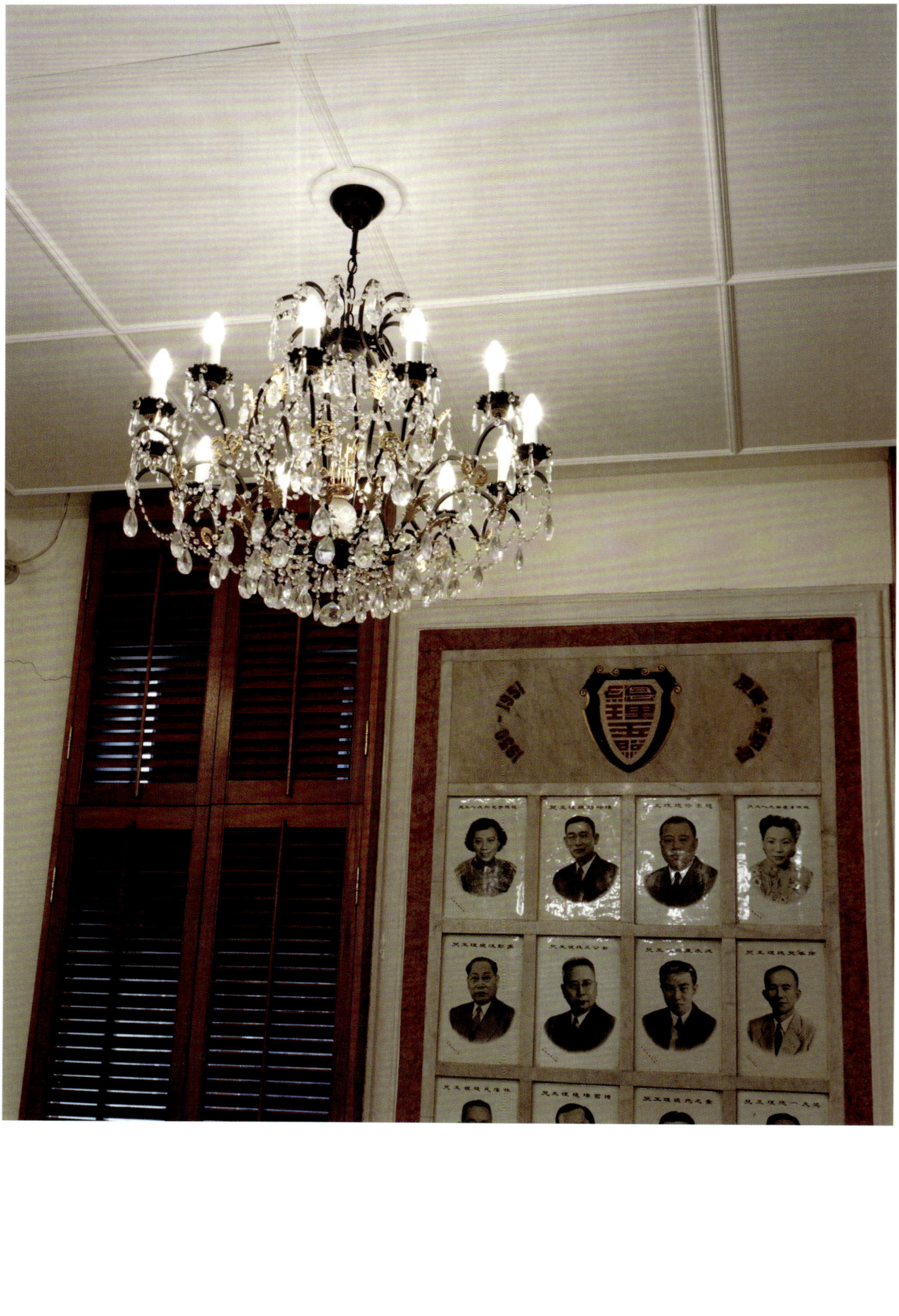

Bunnan began to get involved with a number of charities after WW2. In 1950, he was asked to be on the Governors' Board at Po Leung Kuk, one of the biggest charities in Hong Kong and which ran orphanages, women's shelters and schools. However, he was only interested if he could be chairman, and so Shook Ying took his place on the board that year. A year later, Bunnan got his wish and became chairman of Po Leung Kuk. During his term of office, he pushed through the construction of several new schools for disadvantaged children.

第二次世界大戰結束後，賓南開始參與一些慈善事業。1950年，他被邀請加入保良局董事會，保良局是香港最大的慈善機構之一，負責管理孤兒院、婦女庇護所和學校等。可是賓南只對當保良局的主席感興趣，因此當年淑英代替他擔任董事會董事一職。一年後，賓南如願以償，成為了保良局主席。在他的任期內，他推動了幾所新的弱勢兒童學校的建設。

In 1955, Bunnan ran for the presidency of the Traders Association. Several articles featured in trades paper about his achievements. He lost the election, failing to break into what was a very exclusive circle. Without the right friends in high places, no one close to him had thought that he had a chance.

賓南還在1955年競選商會主席。當時的商界報章刊登了一些有關他成就和貢獻的文章。可惜最後他在選舉中落選，未能進入這個非常排外的圈子。由於沒有和商界的上流人士建立關係，他的所有親戚朋友都認為從一開始他就沒有機會獲勝。

九龍深水埗區地價創高紀錄

中國綫轆廠址高價成交

（本報專訊）九龍方面深水埗工埔廠區地帶的地價近來瘋狂上漲，其地價之高已創空前記錄，就大埔道北河街口的「中國綫轆廠」而言，全廠五千英尺，爲置業中人以五十五萬高價成交，即每方英尺地價值一百十元之鉅。而該區較爲偏僻街道的地價亦漲至每方英尺六七十元之高，仍受「炒家」的注意，看來此一漲勢，會越來越熾。

港製傢俬優美　美歐訂購日多

（本報專訊）香港製的傢具，自去年冬天開始，已大受歐美貿易商的垂青，紛紛來單訂購，數量相當可觀。今年以來，傢具的輸出情況較去年更佳，因爲港製傢具的質地、款式與色澤可與歐美第一流傢具並駕齊驅，同時價錢較歐美貨便宜甚多，便構成港製傢具輸出數量與時俱增，在銷行地區有喧賓奪主之勢。

目前港製傢具，包括一般床椅、衣櫃及家庭裝飾用品等。聞近來有一部份外來游資，已投入此一行業中，設立一規模宏大的造木廠，所有出品均作輸出云。

百葉簾生意興盛　經營者多競爭烈

（本報專訊）港九兩地繁盛的市區裏，近兩年增加不少製造「百葉簾」的店舖，尤其是今年更見此一行業蓬勃異常，大有方興未艾之勢。

「百葉簾」業的興起，完全是環境使然。因爲「百葉簾」較前時流行的「布帳」「竹簾」或「百葉窗」更覺便利而且美觀，所以採用者日漸增加，不僅新建樓宇幾全部裝置「百葉簾」，同時很多舊樓宇也改裝了「百葉簾」，因此促成「百葉簾」業的繁盛景象。

製造「百葉簾」的主要原料是鋁片，大部來自美國。現在「百葉簾」的價錢比去年便宜許多，每方英尺自一元五毛至一元八毛，去年最貴的時候每方英尺會高至兩元八毛至三元左右，降價的原因是同行競爭所致，所以經營此業的利潤逐漸在落低中，不若從前的厚利了。

據調查：目前港九兩地的「百葉簾」店舖約有七十多家，正在籌設中的倘屬不少，看來「百葉簾」業同行的競爭越來越劇烈。

唐賓南跌傷手

（本報專訊）本港商界巨子，高技洋行總經理唐賓南氏，日前赴豪華戲院觀劇，不愼摔在地上，致左手臂拗骨節脫離，傷勢非輕，當即延跌打名醫廖係診療，傷勢已有進步，預算半個月始可復原。

鱷魚牌恤衫廠建議選舉工展小姐

鱷魚牌恤衫廠經理陳賢進氏，爲本港青年工業家，富進取，重公益，上屆工展會期間，爲振奮工展會塲，會舉辦選舉鱷魚小姐，但碍於大會當日之規限，未獲通過。陳氏認爲至深可惜，據陳氏表示：選舉工展小姐，可以提高遊客興趣，增加宣傳資料，並藉以籌募工業學校基金，一舉三得……。並已擬具專函及其具體辦法致香港中華廠商聯合會，以資策動，其原函如左：

逕啓者，近閱報載，關於第十三屆工展，已在急鑼緊鼓，加緊籌備中，規模較去年偉大，足見當局諸公過去努力之成，有以致之，本人頓憶去屆工展時曾舉辦選舉鱷魚小姐，嗣大會格於某種理由，致選舉中止，迨乎本年度廠商會舉辦之星洲展覽會，由於舉辦選舉工展小姐關係，增加熱鬧不少，盛況空前，證之七月廿一日甄文亮團長在大華飯店歡宴時所發表之談話，已無可否認，故本人認爲第十三屆工展，實有舉辦選舉工展小姐之必要，茲列出下列三點：

（一）提高遊客興趣，增加會塲熱鬧。

（二）增加宣傳資料，俾對工業出品予以深刻之印象。

（三）選票收入撥充籌建工業學校基金。

至於具體辦法，請參閱敝廠去年舉辦鱷魚小姐辦法，以觀衆評判爲標準，旣公允，又民主，利多於弊，定必大收宣傳之效，想袞袞諸公，當有同感本人謹淺言微，如不以有瀆清聽，見棄，請三思之，本人忝屬會員一份子，爲發揚本港工業前途計，謹獻芻議，幸垂察焉，並希賜教爲荷！此致

中華廠商聯合會

一九五五年九月八日

韓國商業考察散記　圖文並茂業已出版

中華廠商聯合會

副監事長張軍光於去年九月率領廠商會組織的考察團前往韓國考察商業，曾將其觀察流露於紙上，全部文字已由本報印行單行本，內容將今日韓國工商業、貿易、外滙等問題均有透徹論述，此外有關韓國歷史、地理與及人情風土項均以淸新筆調論述，有聲有色。全書有圖片四十幀，文字六萬言，彩色封面，誠是圖文並茂，該書全部已印就，除寄發海外各地外，港九各報攤及書局均有出售，每册售港幣一元二毫。

彩色瓷相

·特級採訪·

「瓷相」在香港已有相當歷史，可是「彩色瓷相」還是去年創見的事。因爲瓷相着上天然彩色，自然是有別於我們所習見的古老黑白瓷相。

「彩色瓷相」（Colour Photo China）是香港「琴氏藝術舘」所創製，這不啻創瓷相製品的又新一頁。「彩色瓷相」是具有高度藝術氣氛的裝飾品，除了充作家庭的擺設外，並且用以作彌月、喬遷等都是很美妙的紀念品。永久紀念物如：結婚、壽誕、饋贈親友，該屬最實惠的禮物之一。

目前「彩色瓷相」祇有「琴氏藝術舘」獨家出品。「彩色瓷相」的形式有圓形、鷄蛋形、長方形等三種，而色澤是自然彩色，也就是我們所稱的「特藝彩色」，這美麗的色彩的特點是歷久不變。因爲「彩色瓷相」是多采多姿的藝術品，自今年問世以來大受中外人士所歡迎，短短半年，已在海外展開前途，而在本港方面，不少中上的家庭中已擺設了這種新興的藝術紀念品，看來將會普遍到每個家庭去。

廣泛地說：「彩色瓷相」不僅流行於家庭，因爲它富有吸引力，一部份已作爲廣告的宣傳品了。同時，它爲香港的藝術工業製品發射出新的光芒，今後輸出產量的逐漸增加是可期望的。（六）

◇◇◇◇◇◇ 香港貨圖說 ◇◇◇◇◇◇

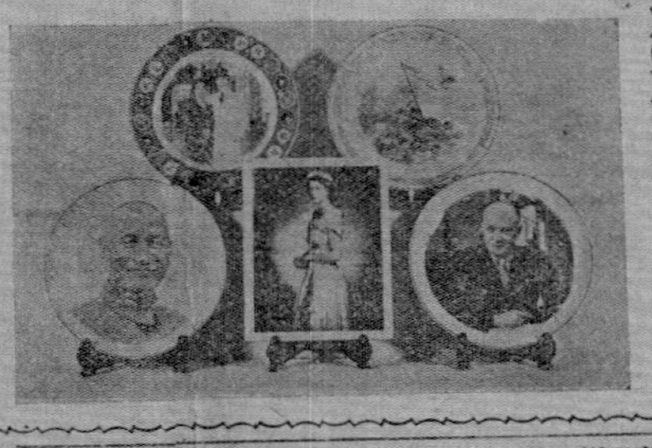

唐賓南擎天一柱

·中歌·

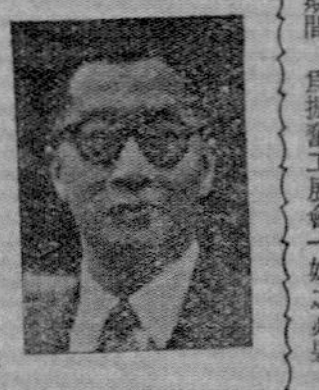

想每一個香港人都可鮮明憶起去年「中華總商會」競選浪潮的奮事罷：香港商界的權威人物——唐賓南——受到廣大人羣的擁戴，挺身而出向「中總」進軍，向高卓雄挑戰，唐氏爲自由奮鬥的果敢精神，倍令到香港朝野人士和對手們的關心與矚目，可見唐氏今日在香港商界的聲隆名噪，實具有其舉足輕重的分量殆無異義。

唐賓南係廣東中山唐家灣人氏，現年五十三歲，遜清光緒廿九年間誕生於唐家灣故鄉。唐氏在童年時期的家庭情況並不好，其先翁曾畢公側身於航業，辛勞所獲酬報實不足以應付家庭生活之需，所以唐氏在十歲以前的學齡期間已蒙受失學的苦痛。直至彼十歲那年，乃父鐸聊公的事業有了轉機，在香港一家航務公司任買辦之職，此一轉變對於他整個家庭（甚至可說唐氏畢生關鍵）發生極大影響，而唐氏也就此舉家遷港居住。

賓南先生在十歲時因家境好轉才獲得求學的機會，起初在私塾習讀國學，爲期僅三載，十三歲轉入「育才書院」與「皇仁書院」，直至十八歲卒業。這裏值得一提是唐氏當求學時的勤學苦讀精神，因爲早年失學苦痛所譬傷，深悉有機緣進學的寶貴，所以他手不釋卷埋頭於學業，再加上天賦聰穎，及後已在校中被師長目爲優秀學生，完全是個人苦學勤奮的結果。總而言之，賓南先生是一個聰明的勤學後者，他來獻身社會從容發揮超人的才幹，所獲致的成果可說大半得力早年的勤學。

唐氏十九歲以「皇仁書院」高材生的資格爲政府所錄聘，先後曾任職於布政司署、財政司署、工商署及海事處等政府機構，服務政府職守年餘，留下一個良好紀錄，深得政府上下同寅讚許。唐氏脫離政府職務後轉進英商渣甸洋行任職，此爲他獻身商界的最初階段，在「渣甸」服務七年，他對工作表現處處顯示出人頭地的風範，不僅爲上級讚爲難得，即同級或下屬對唐氏的爲人與服務精神亦致以敬佩。而唐氏在「渣甸」的七年間，不少軼事於今仍爲識者所傳誦，可見唐氏當年的種種不凡處事待人事蹟，深深爲人懷念，此細節已崇唐記者再事細表矣。

一九三五年間，本港德人經營的「高技洋行」因業務不前，漸陷困境，邀唐氏投資合作，改組爲中德合營的「高技洋行」。「高技」在唐氏的一番刷新與銳意經營下，呈現一片新景象，業務飛黃騰達，短短三年完全改觀了「高技」的舊有面貌。迨至一九三九年間，國際環境轉變，與唐氏拍檔的德人返回祖國，「高技」遂由唐氏獨資經營，成爲純華資的貿易商行。

戰後以還，「高技」在唐氏積極擘劃發展下，今日被目爲香港華資貿易商的權威，每歲貿易數字達港幣二千萬元以上，尤其年來「高技」以其雄厚經濟來扶植協助香港工業的發展，當年許多小規模的廠家在唐氏的培養下，今日已成爲具有規模的大廠，證之種種，可窺知唐氏以其權威貿易商來推動香港工業的成就，直接間接所予港人的恩澤，誠有罄竹難盡之感。

綜觀唐氏過去半生，他善自珍重過人才華加以發揮，並運用機警智慧才造成他今日在社會上的崇巢地位，而其處事認眞態度與俠義的心腸去對待所認識的朋友們，尤爲令人折服。他有傲骨的風格，却沒有傲氣的陋習，對仍健在的慈母盡其孝親之能，對胞弟賽南先生彼此保持「兄友弟恭」的手足情誼，這便是唐氏爲人處世的縱橫面，雖然他忠耿剛直的不免流露容色，但這小疵是無損他受人崇拜的人格。

這位擁有兒女十五人的香港商界巨子唐賓南，他仍一貫雄才大略精神來致力香港工商業的錦繡前程。今日「高技」雖蜚聲國際貿易圈，可是唐賓南却不以此爲滿，繼續努力於未來，眞是「百尺竿頭，更進一步」矣。

本文所記唐氏過去僅係粗枝大葉的片片斷斷，紙短意長，未能把唐氏卅年餘年來的事蹟盡情描摹，引以爲憾。但，賓南先生的「擎天一柱」於今日香港商界，受到各界人士的擁戴，記者實無再事述的贅必要。

唐賓南先生除事業上鉅大的成就外，對香港社會福利事業倍具熱忱，大受各界所器重，先後歷任高等法院承審委員、香港大學校董、保良局永遠總理、華人銀行永遠董事、又一邨建設有限公司創辦人兼副主席、惠康有限公司董事、唐氏宗親會理事長、華僑子弟學校董事、鐘聲慈善社名譽社長、兒童安置所委員、其他社團任職不勝枚舉，唐氏的爲香港朝野上下人士器重。

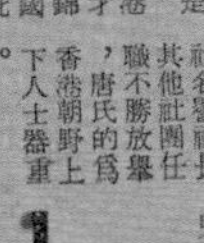

In 1963, Bunnan was awarded the MBE by the Duke of Edinburgh during his visit to Hong Kong. This was given for his public service, though some within his family felt his involvement in charity work was to get recognition in Hong Kong's high society rather than any desire to help.

賓南在1963年因其在香港公共服務領域作出的貢獻而獲得當時訪港的愛丁堡公爵所授予的大英帝國員佐勳章。但他的家人覺得他參與慈善工作只是為了在上流社會中獲得名氣，而不是為了幫助社會。

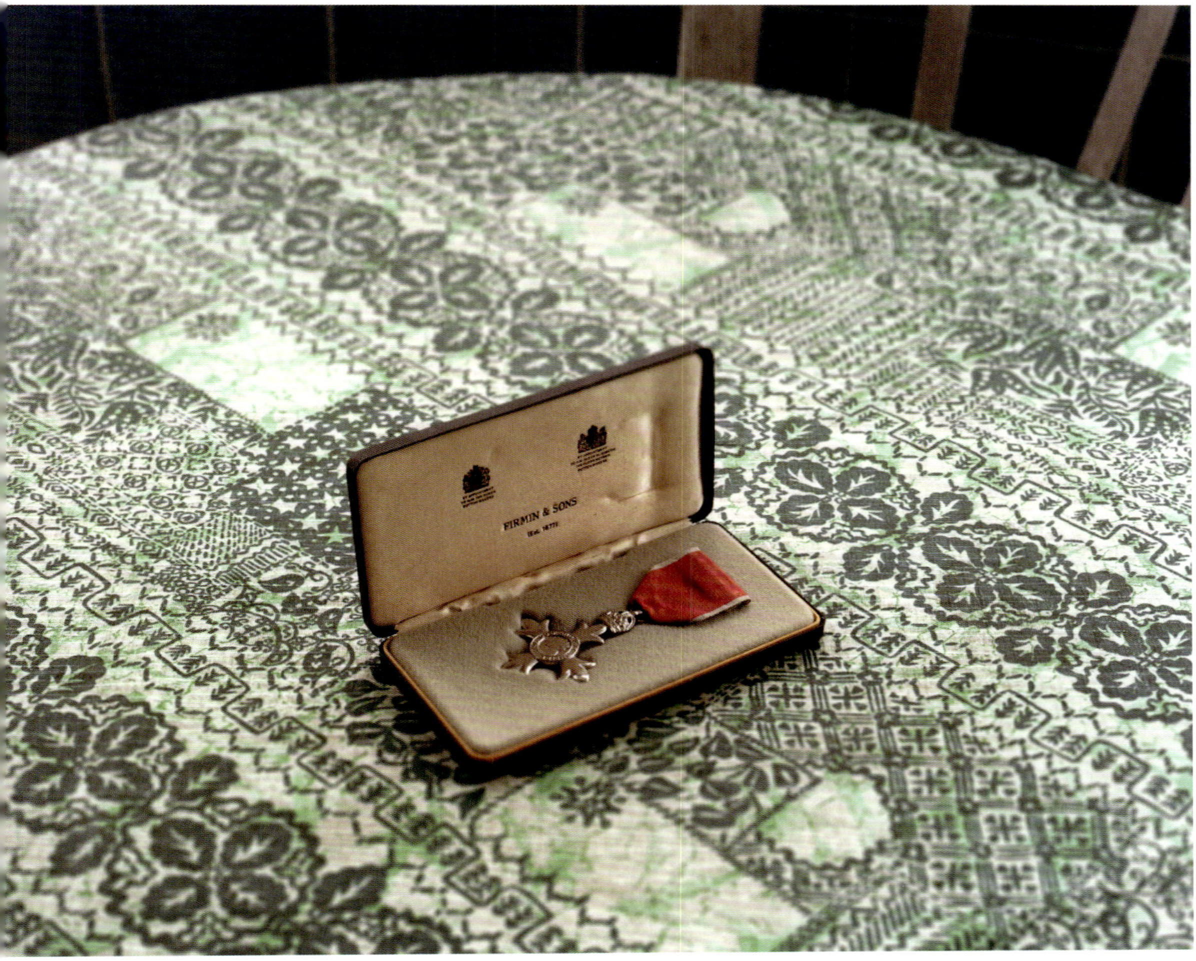
FIRMIN & SONS

XI 大英帝國勳章ii

Member of the Order of the British Empire II

從小到老

黃鍾麒

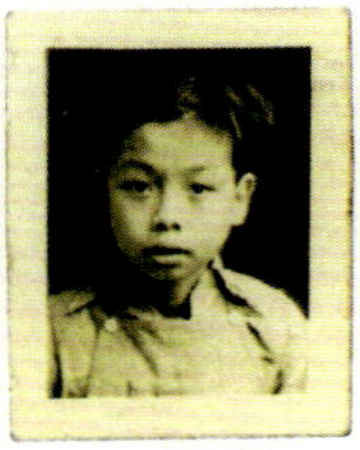
1945

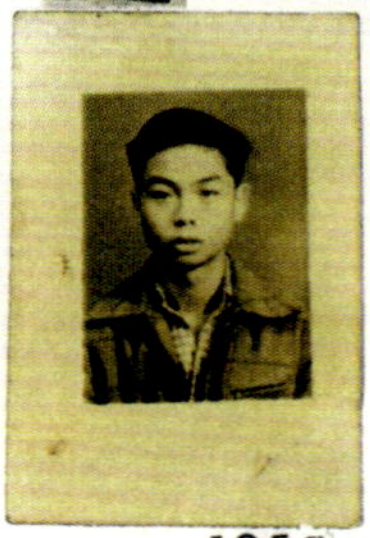
1952

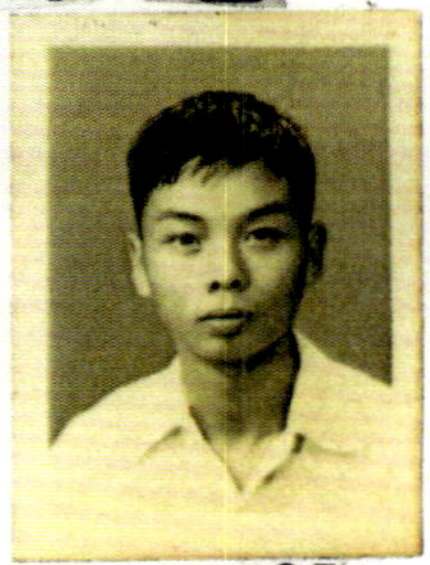
1954

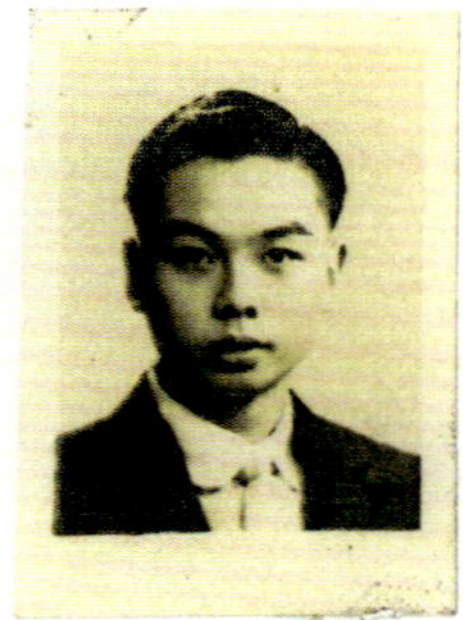
1955

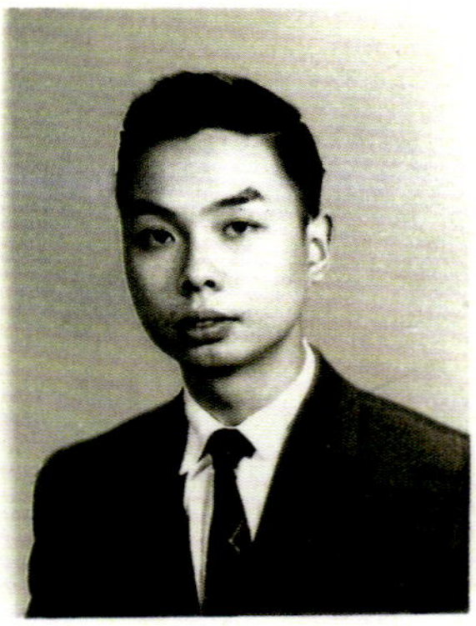
1958

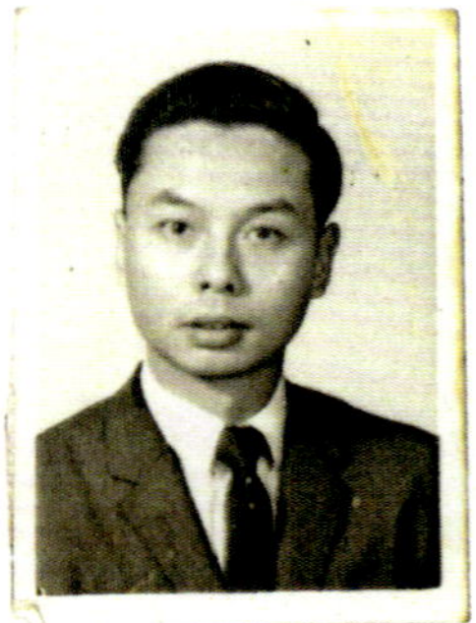
1967

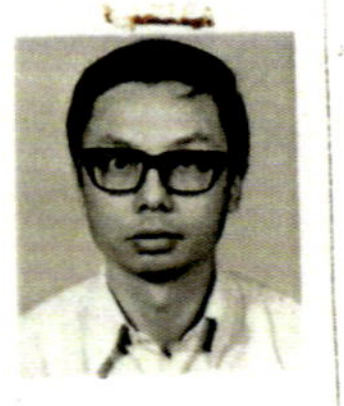
1976

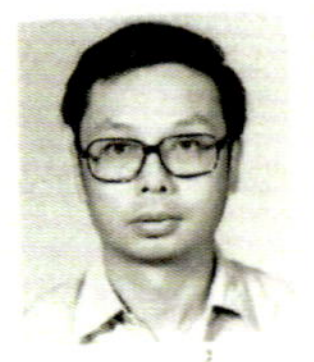
1980

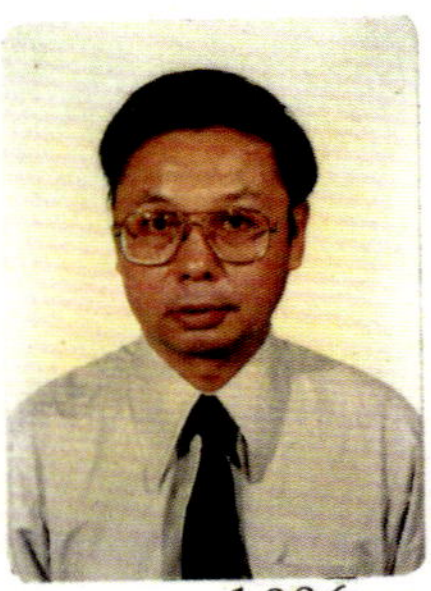
1986

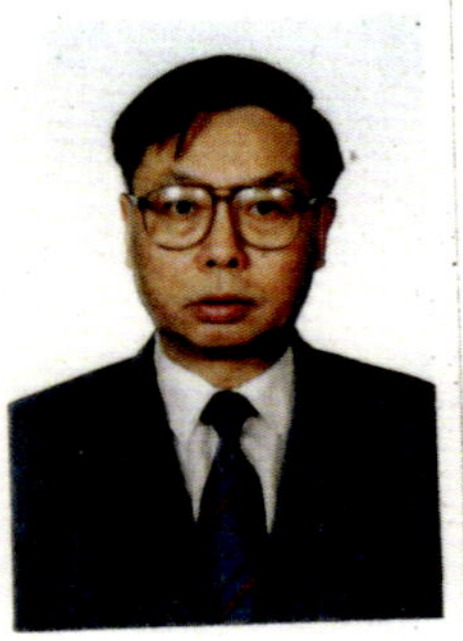
1992

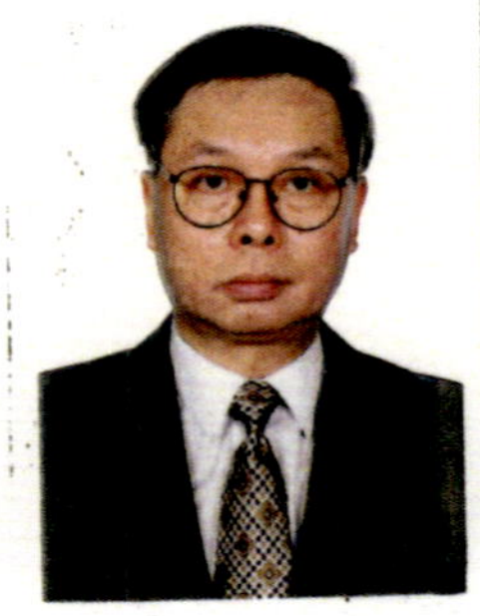
1996

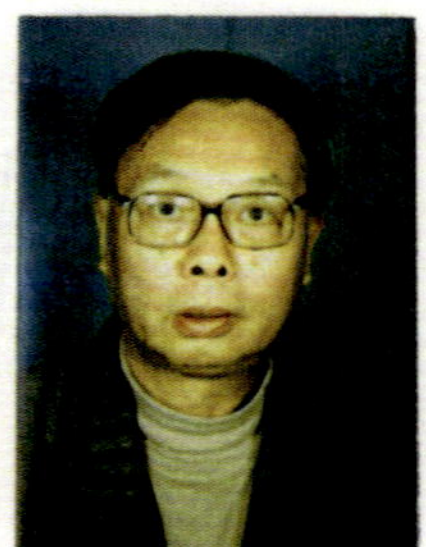
1998

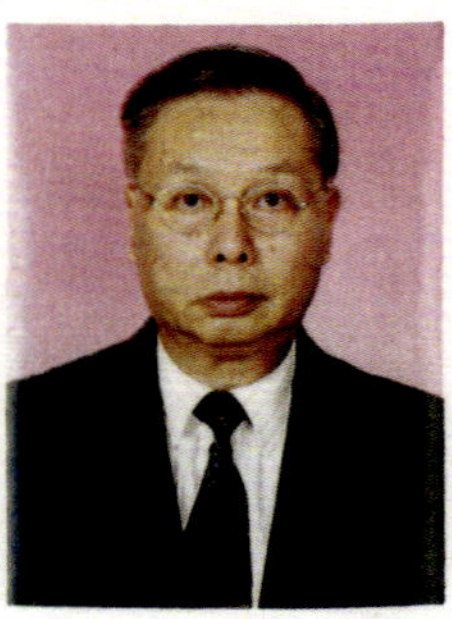
2001

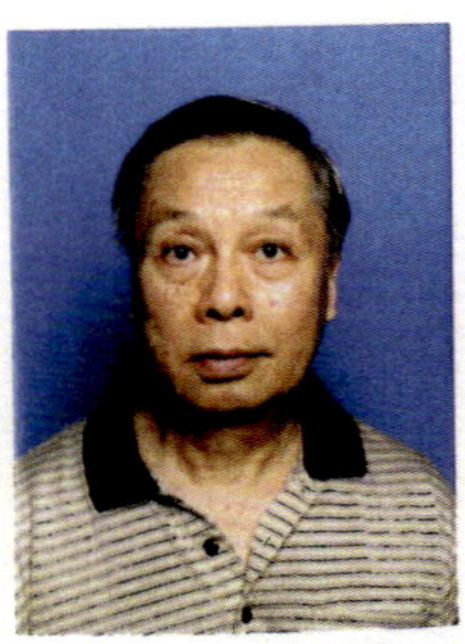
2005

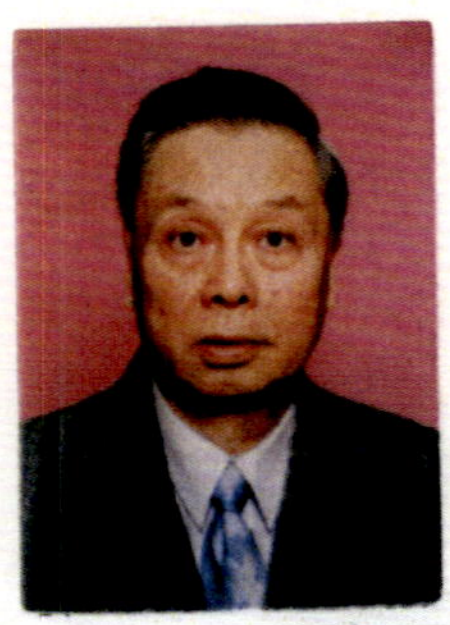
2005

Born in 1936, Chung Kai shared the same great grandfather as Chung Zak. Being the same age as Chung Zak's eldest son Woon Yin, they grew up together in the Wong's mansion in Guangzhou until they both sought refuge in Hong Kong in 1949. On 30 June 1997, he was awarded the MBE by Prince Charles, who was in Hong Kong for the Handover the following day.

Kai was awarded the MBE for his dedication to the Royal Hong Kong Post Office where he worked for 40 years.

仲麒出生於1936年，與仲錫擁有同一個曾祖父。他與仲錫的大兒子煥延年紀相同，在廣州的黃家一起長大，直到1949年前往香港。1997年6月30日，在香港參加交接儀式的查爾斯王子為他頒授大英帝國員佐勳章。

仲麒在香港郵局工作了四十年，貢獻良多，因此獲頒此榮譽。

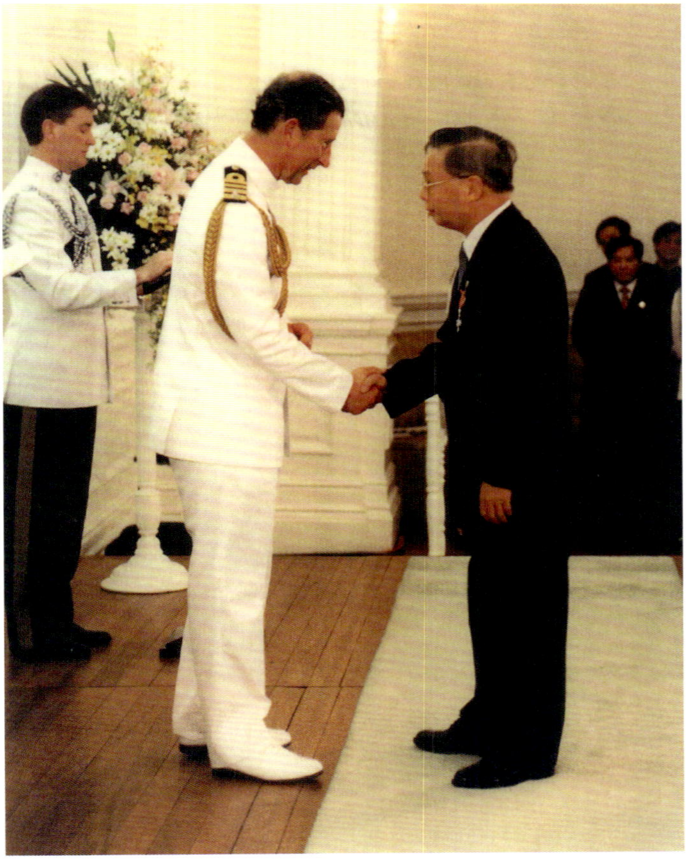

XII 雞是最便宜的
Chicken is the cheapest

By the late 1950s Chung Zak had lost his hotel business, and the whole family came to Hong Kong after having lived in Macau for ten years. They rented half of a two bedroom flat on Bonham Road. Two parents, with six grown up children, shared with the landlord's family: fourteen of them altogether. It was hardest for Chung Zak who had been used to a life of luxury.

二十世紀五十年代末，仲錫關掉了酒店的生意，在澳門生活了十年的家人也終於搬到香港。他們在般咸道租了一個兩居室公寓的其中一間房，夫妻倆帶著六個成年子女與房東一家人合住，合共十四人。對於早已習慣奢華生活的仲錫來說，這是他人生中最艱難的日子。

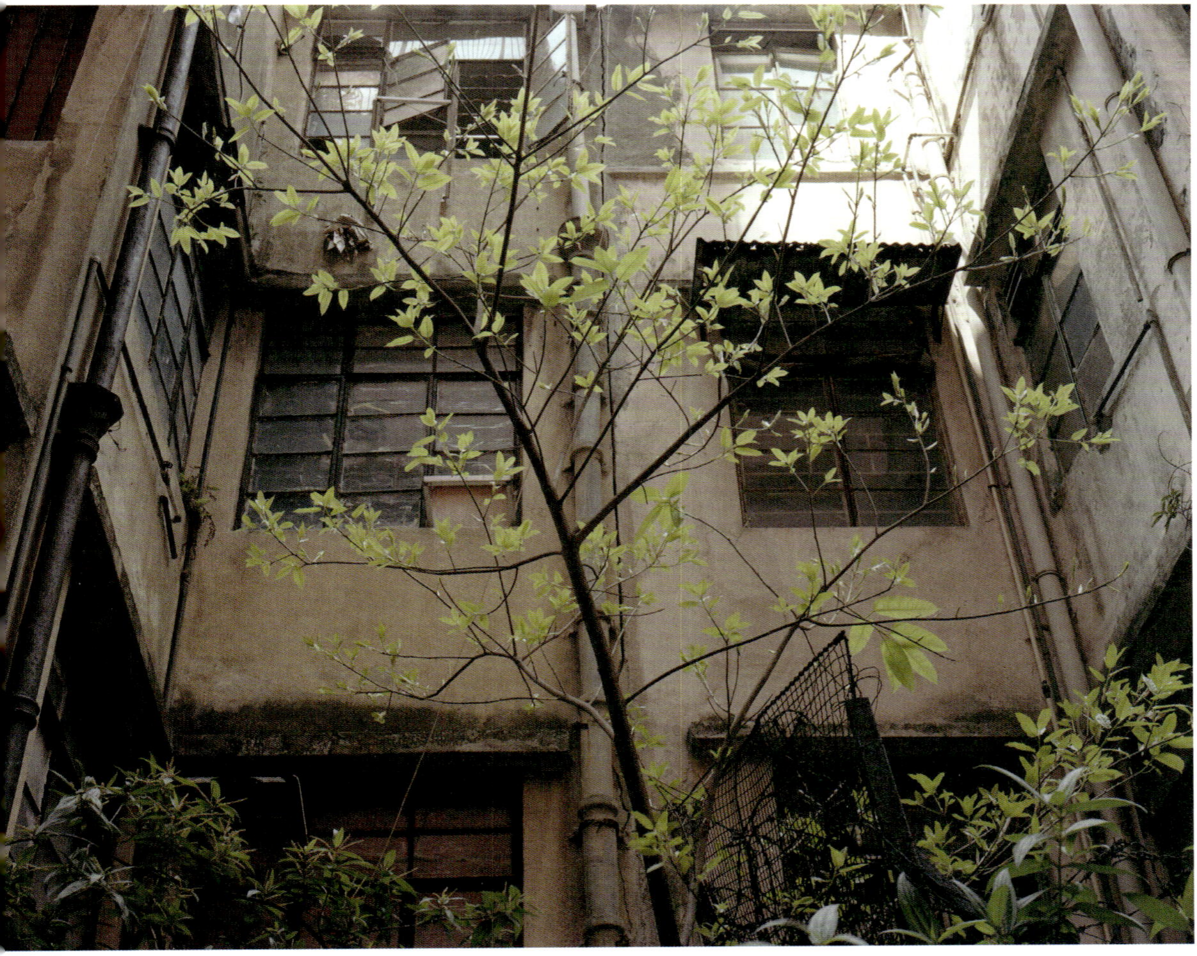

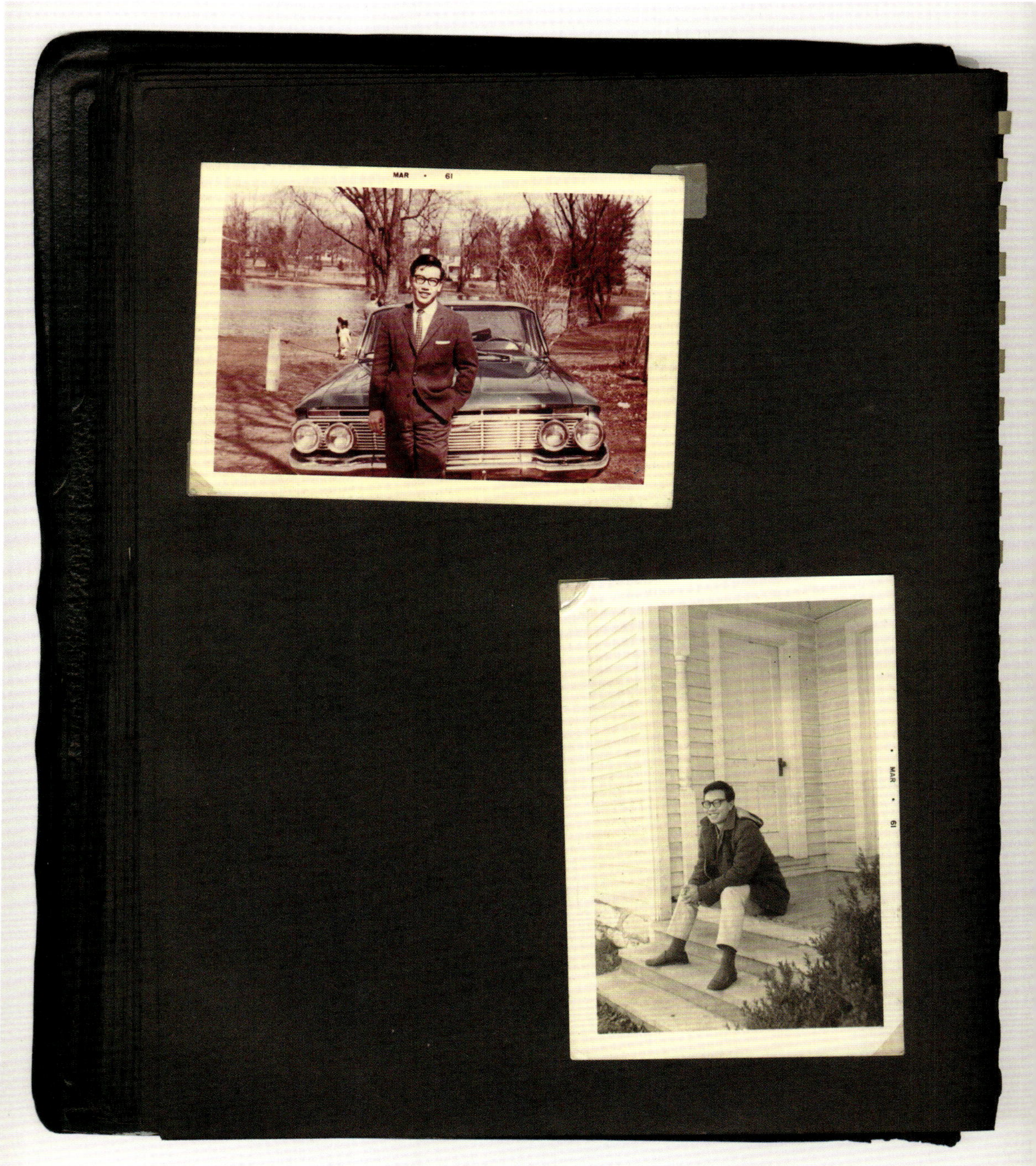
MAR • 61
MAR • 61

After getting his first degree in Taiwan, and working for several years in Hong Kong, Woon Yin, with the help of a friend, had saved enough money to go to America for further studies.

The week before he left, his mother would prepare chicken for him each night even though the family had little money. In Chinese ceremonies and celebrations chicken is significant, and it is expensive. After arriving in the USA, Woon Yin went to a local diner. Budget conscious, he asked for the cheapest meal available. It was the chicken.

在台灣獲得大學學位並在香港工作了幾年後，煥延在朋友的幫助下攢下足夠資金前往美國深造。

在他離開的前一周，他的母親每天晚餐都會為他做雞肉，儘管那時家裡已經沒有多少錢了。雞在中國的儀式和慶祝活動中佔有非常重要的地位，而且在當時價格昂貴。到了美國後，煥延在當地的餐廳吃飯時，為了省錢，他總點最便宜的食物，也就是雞肉。

Having fled Guangzhou, perhaps Hong Kong never felt like home for Chung Zak's children. Four of his six children emigrated during the 1960s and 1970s.

Woon Yin married Brigetta, a German au pair whom he met in Charlottesville; they settled in America. His brother Woon Ping fell in love with a Danish girl, Lillian, whom he'd met in New York; they now live in Denmark. Woon Kwong married a Korean-Chinese girl he'd met in Taiwan and they emigrated to America, whilst his sister Yip Yung married a Jamaican-Chinese and moved to Canada.

Esben, Brigetta, Woon Ping and Lillian, Denmark, 1970.

離開廣州後，仲錫的孩子們一直都不認為香港是自己的家。他的六個孩子中有四個都在二十世紀六十、七十年代選擇移民國外。

煥延娶了一名叫布里格塔的德國交換工，他們在夏洛特斯維爾認識後定居美國。他的弟弟煥平愛上了一個在紐約市認識的丹麥女孩莉蓮，現居丹麥。弟弟煥剛娶了一個在台灣認識的韓國華裔女孩，並隨後移居美國。他的妹妹業楊嫁給了一名牙買加籍華人並移民加拿大。

埃斯本、布里格塔、煥平和莉蓮，1970年拍攝於丹麥。

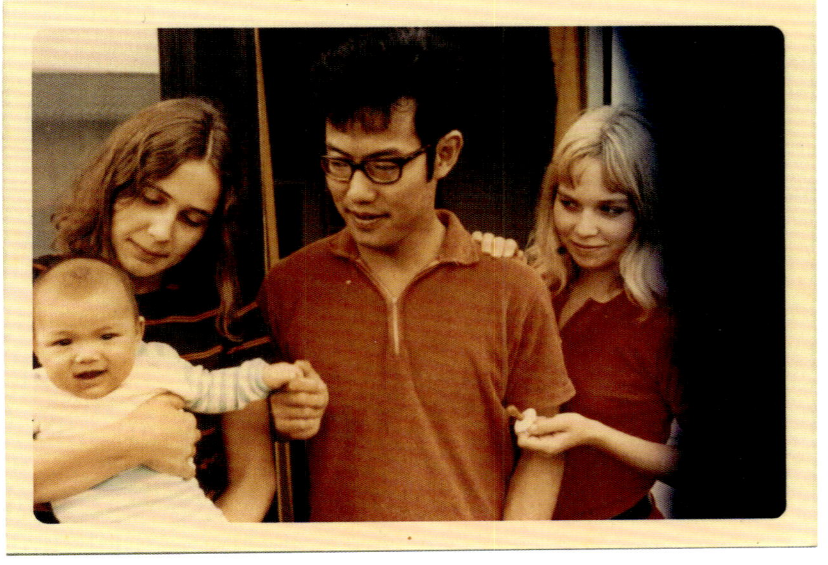

Oct. 1, 1972

Dear Etta

Woon Gin just called to advise that Woon Kwong is getting married on Oct. 22 (just 3 wks away). We don't know what our parents would be giving Yuen Lan. I don't care but please explain to ~~her~~ Mom that she should give her an identical set of pearls ~~so~~ especially when both Woon Gin & Woon Ping's wife had pearls & both of them ~~bea~~ being Europeans. If Mom gives diamond to Yuen Lan they might think that Mom gives her diamond because she likes Yuen Lan better, her being CHINESE & they just get pearls, being Europeans. ~~I don~~ Diamonds or pearls might be

P.T.O.

(2)

the same price but in their
eyes (or anybody's) diamonds
are diamonds!! I'm not saying
that they (Lillian & Gitte) would feel envious
but it is highly probable
(you know women!) I'm writing
this because I'm afraid that
mom might have overlooked
this point & I want to
prevent any misunderstandings
which might arise between
these three in-laws
(Lillian, Gitte & Yuen Lam). But
if Mom realizes this & still
thinks that it doesn't matter,
she would be the one to bear
the consequences & I'm sure
if misunderstandings does
arise I'm afraid it wouldn't be
very pleasant for her &
prevention is better than cure & the
explanation of it being the same price wouldn't do.

XIII 保羅利文
Paul Newman

In 1958, Bunnan's second wife persuaded him to send her son to study in America. In response, Shook Yin sent three of her daughters to study in America and Tai Ching to study in London. Since Hong Kong was a British colony, a degree from the United Kingdom was seen as far more prestigious.

1958年，賓南的第二任妻子說服他送兒子去美國留學。因此第一任妻子淑英也決定派三個女兒和大楨分別去美國和英國留學。由於香港是英國殖民地，英國的學位在當地然看來更為優越。

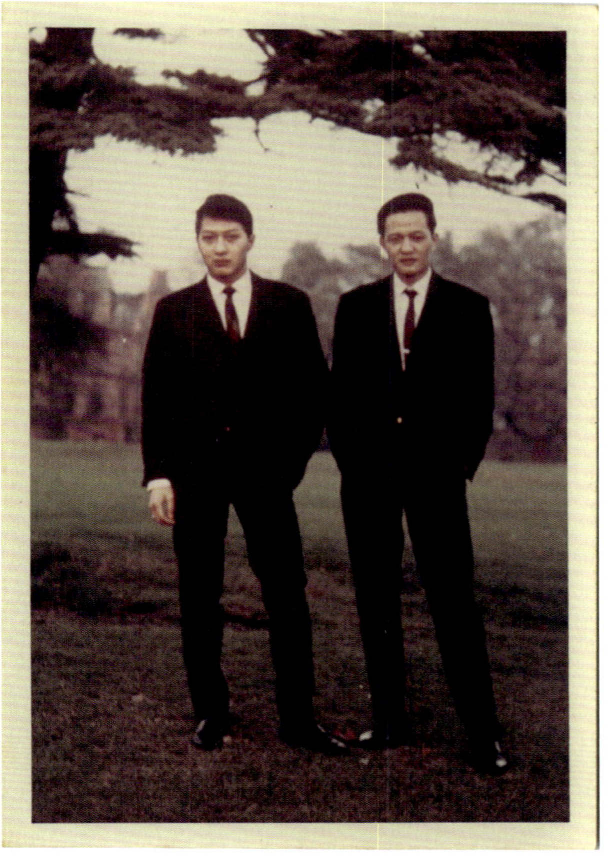

BUNNAN TONG & COMPANY LTD.

MARINA HOUSE

P. O. BOX 887 HONG KONG

CABLE ADDRESS
"BUNNANCO"

IN REPLY PLEASE QUOTE
REFERENCE

5th March, 1965.

PERSONAL

Mr. Tai Ching Tong,
c/o Henry Yim Esq.,
9A, Congress Road,
London. S. E. 2.
England.

My dearest Tai Ching,

Your letter of the 2nd inst. has been received. Evidently you did not know then that Tai Sing wanted to come back to Hong Kong or else you would have mentioned in your letter. Anyway, as he wishes, so it be. It may not be a bad idea for him to come home for a change and have some rest before making further plans for his future.

By the time you get this letter I hope you have already got in touch with Mr. Esmail and have settled the account with him. Also I wonder whether you have approached Dr. Low-Beer for a letter certifying that Tai Sing is healthy and normal.

As Tai Sing is coming back he does not need a guardian anymore. You don't have to pay any money to Mr. S. K. Lam as we formerly arranged.

Yesterday the 4th Mr. Leung Kei Ho invited me and your mother to lunch. Margaret and her parents were also his guests. Whether it was my over-sensitive imagination or not, your girl friend looked a bit depressed. She seemed to have something on her mind. You, probably.

Meantime, please take good care of yourself. Mother joins me in sending our love and best wishes.

Your loving father,

BUNNAN TONG

Margaret has booked the Quantas to fly to Australia by 10pm tonight. Your sisters Nancy & Peggie will be seeing her off as your representatives.

SL/BT.

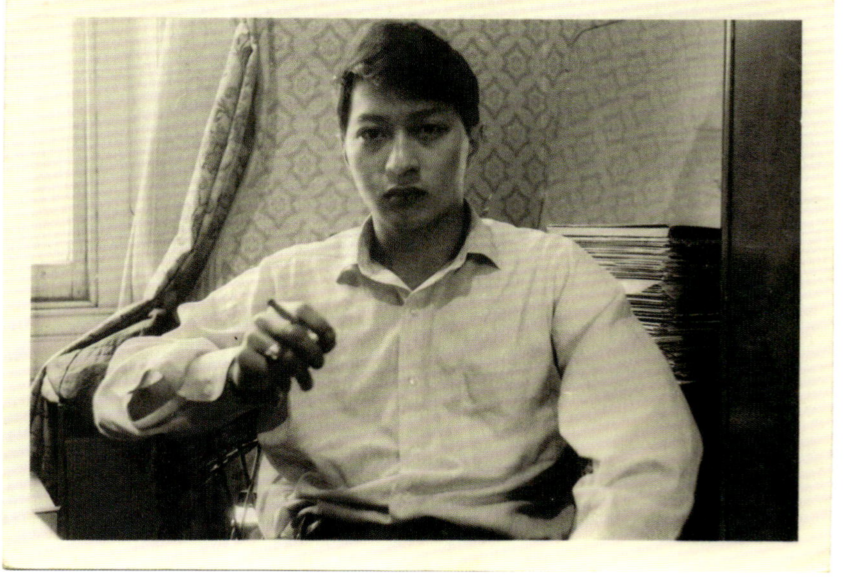

Tai Ching was an active member of the Chinese Students' Union and was elected Vice President. The USA government blacklisted him as a communist and were later to make his life difficult when he was trying to do business in America. Tai Ching also idolised Paul Newman and thought he looked a bit like him in this photograph.

大楨是中國留學生協會的活躍分子，並成功當選為副主席。可惜美國政府將他列入共產主義者黑名單中，這讓他日後在美的生意發展並不順利。他非常崇拜好萊塢老牌男影星保羅利文，認為自己在這張照片中有點像他。

Tai Ching often boasts about the number of German girlfriends he had during his time at University. He kept many pictures of them in a beef jerky tin. Not long after he got married, his wife caught him looking through the box of photographs in secret. She ripped them all up.

大楨經常吹噓自己在大學期間有多名德國女友。他把這些女友的照片保存在一個裝牛肉乾的鐵罐裡。結婚後不久，他的妻子有一天發現他在偷看盒子裡的照片。她一怒之下將所有照片都撕碎了。

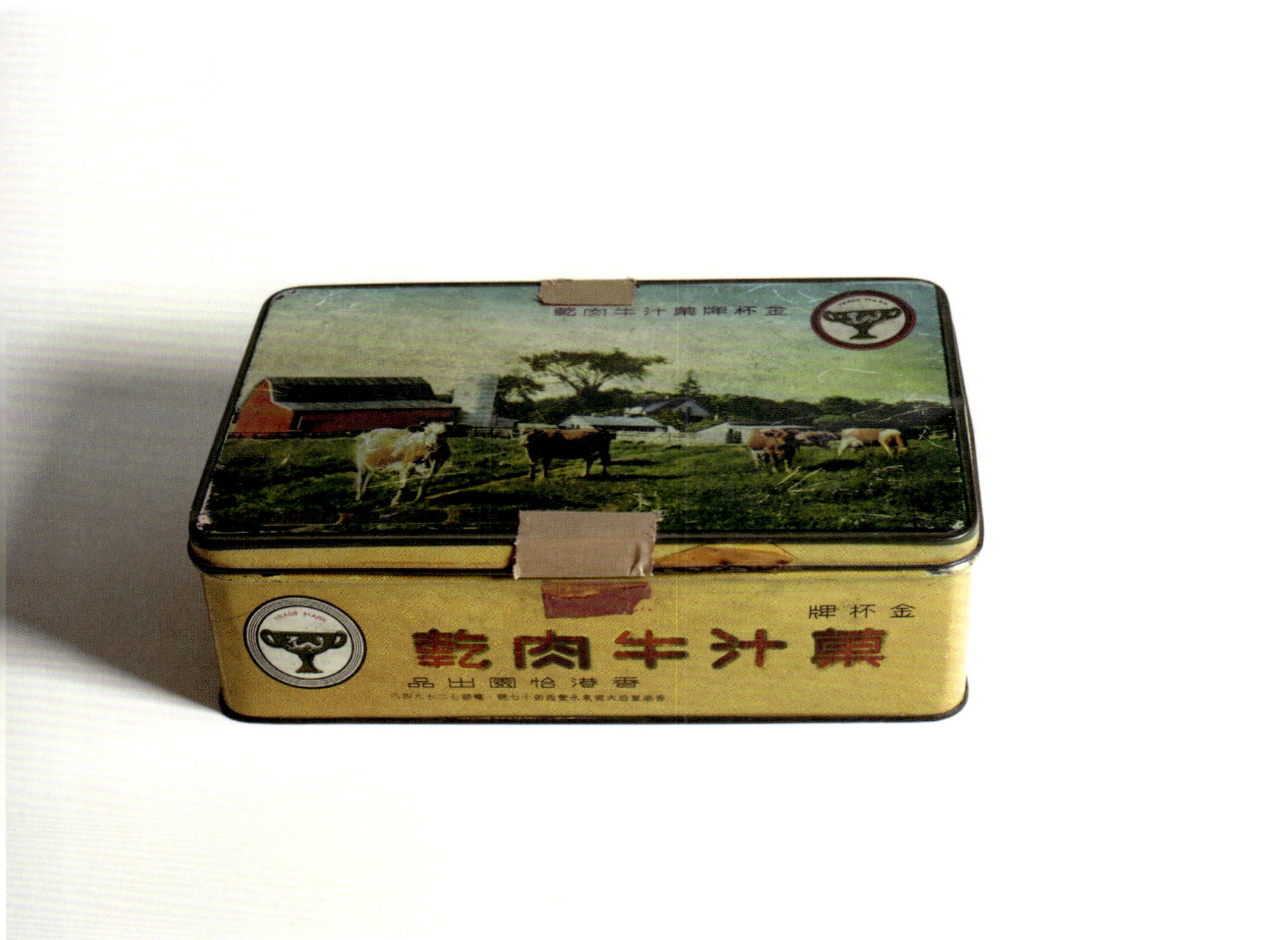
金杯牌薑汁牛肉乾
TRADE MARK
金杯牌
薑汁牛肉乾
香港怡園出品

XIV 半供讀

Half work half study

Yip Hang moved to Hong Kong a year after Tai Chin left for London.

業恆在大楨留學倫敦一年後搬到香港。

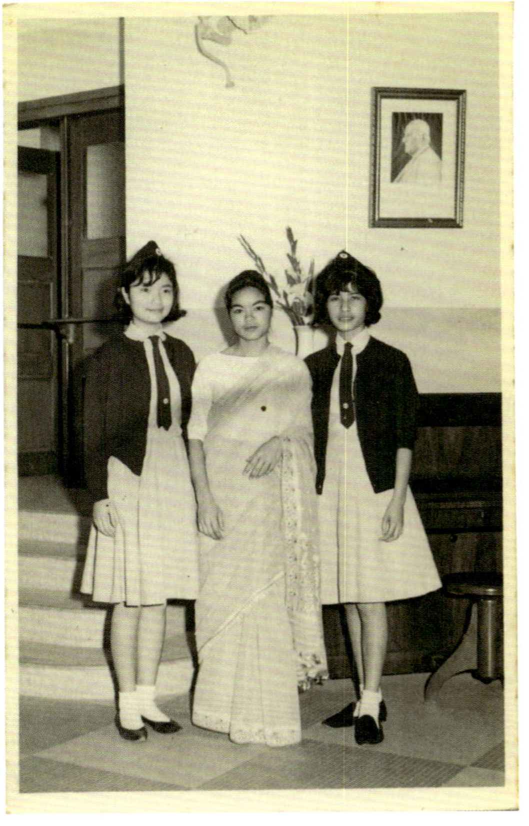

She had planned to follow her brothers' footsteps and study in America. She was accepted by a college in New York but was denied a student visa. She was told by the immigration officer that both her brothers were having to work in order to support themselves through their studies, "How are you going to support yourself?"

她原計劃跟隨哥哥們的腳步去美國學習。她被紐約的一所大學錄取了，卻被簽證處拒發學生簽證。移民局官員問她，她的兩個哥哥都要靠邊學習邊打工來養活自己，「你要怎樣養活自己？」

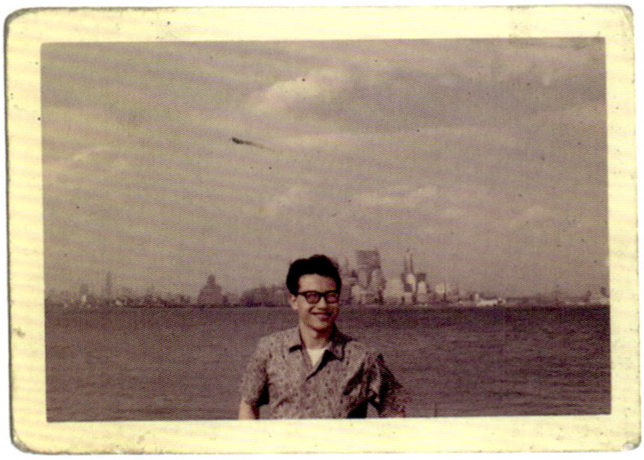

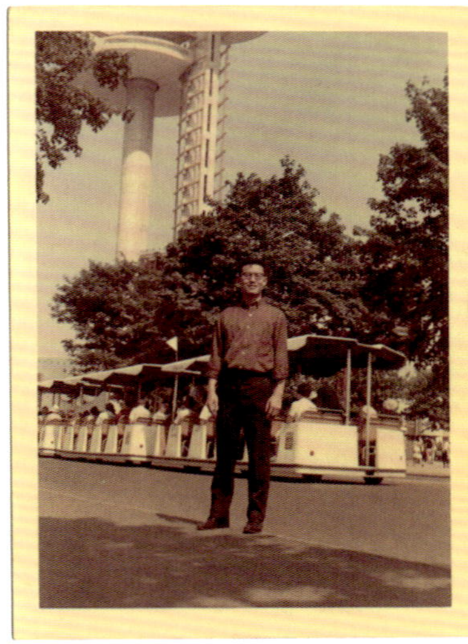

In 1964, Bunnan & Co. expanded their business and moved out of their original office into a bigger space. Parker Pens moved into the vacated space. After completing her secretarial course, Yip Hang's first job was at Parker Pens.

賓南於1964年搬進更大的辦公室打算進一步擴充業務。而因此空出的舊辦公室後被生產鋼筆的派克公司租下。業恆在修讀完秘書課程後，在派克公司找到了第一份工作。

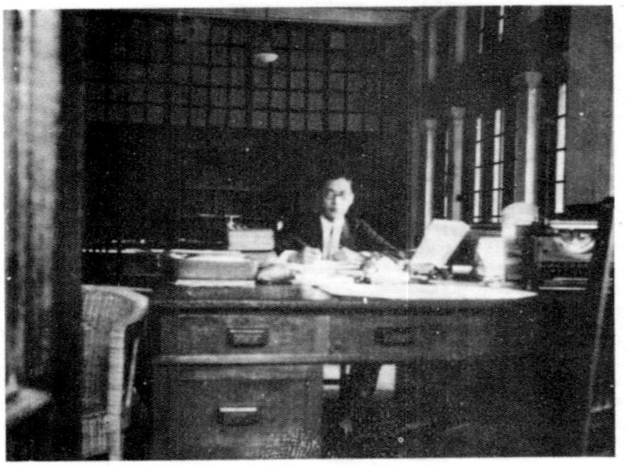

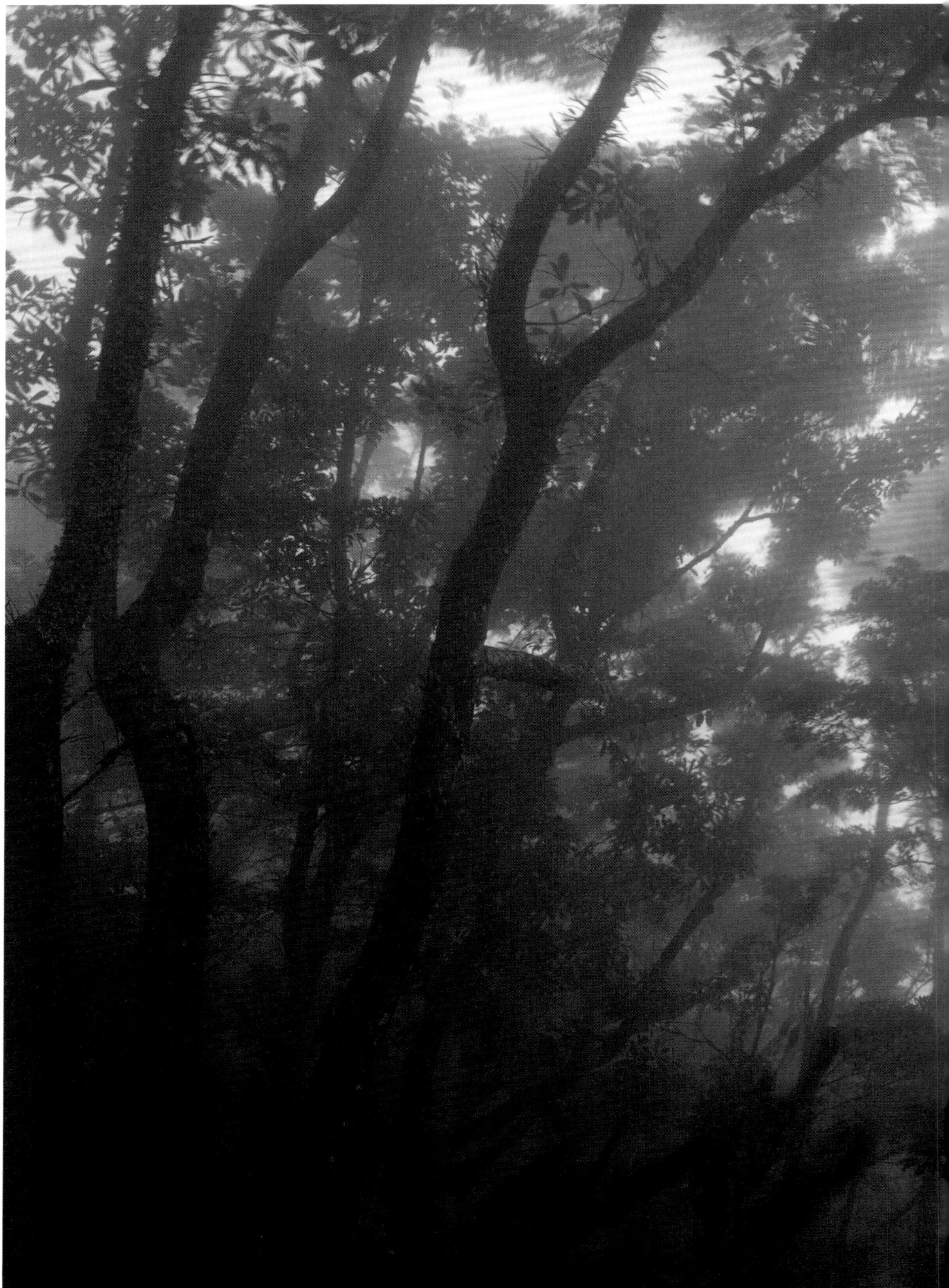

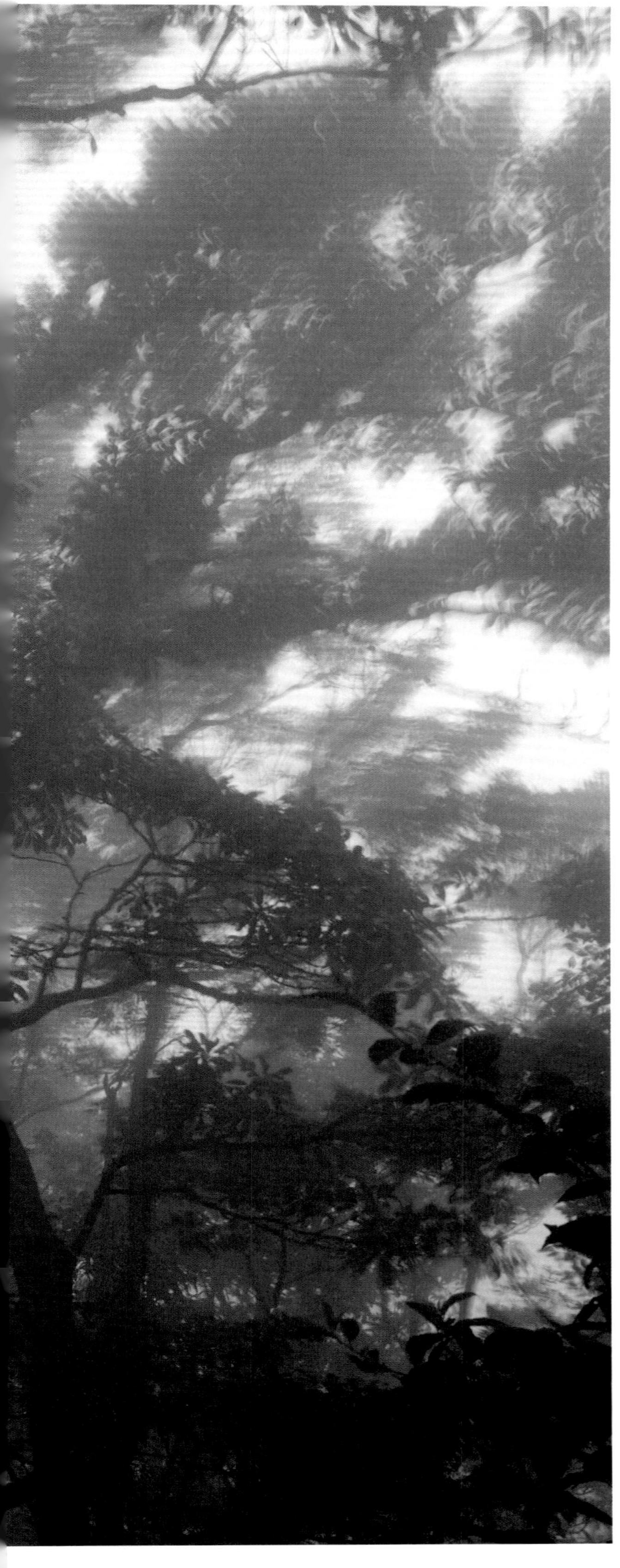

XV 你要多一個印章
You need another stamp sir

Tai Ching had wanted to do a PhD in London and had already been accepted when Bunnan demanded that he return to Hong Kong to work in his company. After years of spending all his time on his social ventures, the company was being taken over by his eldest son Tai Kung who, in a bid for control, had systematically fired anyone from the family.

Bunnan wanted someone on his side to work in the power struggle. Tai Ching was made to start at the bottom, as a stock checker, the lowest job available. Tai Kung then hired his sister-in-law as supervisor to keep an eye on his younger brother.

大楨原本想在倫敦繼續攻讀博士學位，當賓南要求他回香港在自家公司工作時，他已經拿到了錄取通知書。由於賓南多年來一直把時間放在社會事務上，他的公司實際上已經被長子大鈞接管，大鈞有計劃地把公司裡面的家族成員一一解僱，企圖自己獨自掌管公司。

賓南希望有人能夠在公司的權力鬥爭中站在他這一邊。大楨是從底層工作開始做起的，一開始被分配為最低級別的貨倉管理員。大鈞雇用他妻子的姐妹做大楨的主管，以方便監視他的一舉一動。

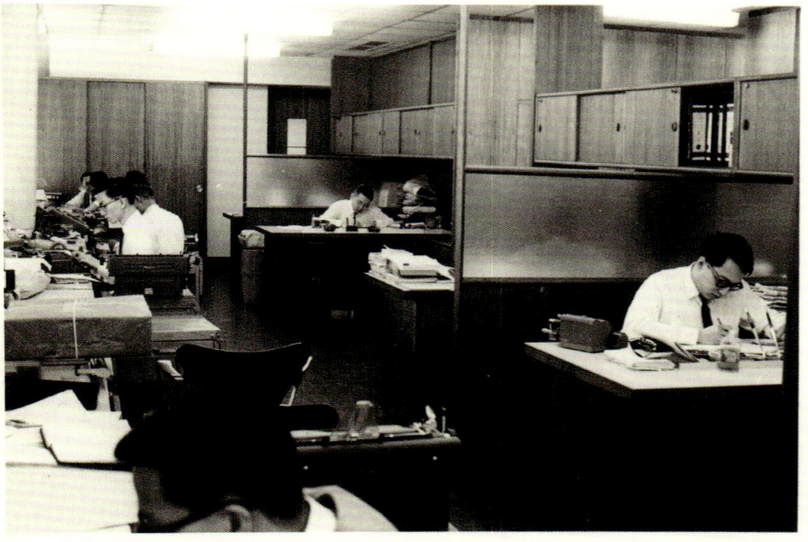

In May 1967, a labour dispute turned into large scale demonstrations against British Colonial rule across Hong Kong. Pro China leftists carried *The Little Red Book* and chanted communist slogans, calling for Hong Kong to be returned to China. Outbreaks of violence followed which resulted in numerous deaths. Although order was eventually restored, confidence in the colony's future declined with many Hong Kong residents selling their businesses and property and relocating overseas.

1967年5月，一次勞資糾紛升級成為反對英國殖民統治的大規模示威活動。親中左派高舉紅色小冊子，高呼共產主義口號，呼籲香港回歸中國。隨後爆發暴力事件。雖然秩序最終得以恢復，但很多人對香港前途的信心下降，不少市民變賣資產與物業，紛紛移居海外。

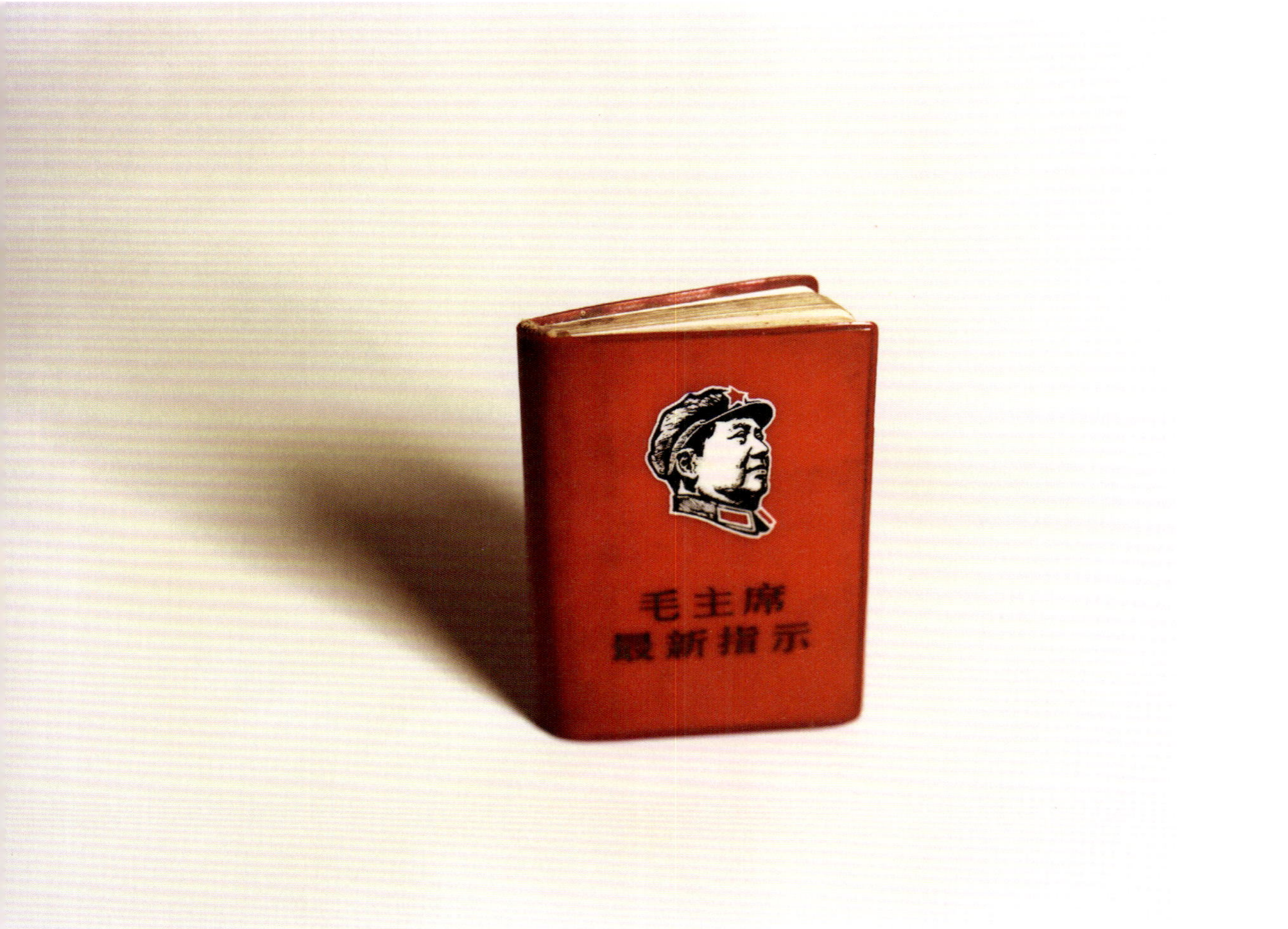
毛主席
最新指示

Following the riots, many residents wanted to sell off their businesses to move abroad, often at a low price to secure a quick sale.

Feeling the tide was turning away from imports and exports and into manufacturing, Tai Ching decided to risk his entire life savings to open his own factory. He had initially asked his brother Tai Kung to go 50:50 with him. Eventually his brother agreed to do so, but only if it was 70:30 in his favour. After Tai Ching had put down payment on the factory and machinery, his brother pulled out, giving no explanation. With no help from his father, Tai Ching was facing financial ruin until one of his university friends stepped in as a partner at the last minute. He would go on to make a 20,000% return on his investment within five years.

暴亂發生後，許多香港居民想變賣資產移居海外，往往以較便宜的價格爭取將物業迅速售出。

當時大楨認為經濟已經逐漸從進出口業轉向製造業，於是決定把畢生的積蓄投資開設工廠。他最初希望哥哥大鈞能夠和他每人投資百分之五十。他哥哥最終同意在佔七成股份前提下進行投資，但就在大楨付清了工廠和所有機器的款項後，大鈞沒有給出任何解釋就退出了合作。在沒有得到父親幫助的情況下，大楨面臨財務困境，直到最後一刻，他的一個大學朋友願意與他合作。在隨後的五年裡，他獲得了兩百倍的投資回報。

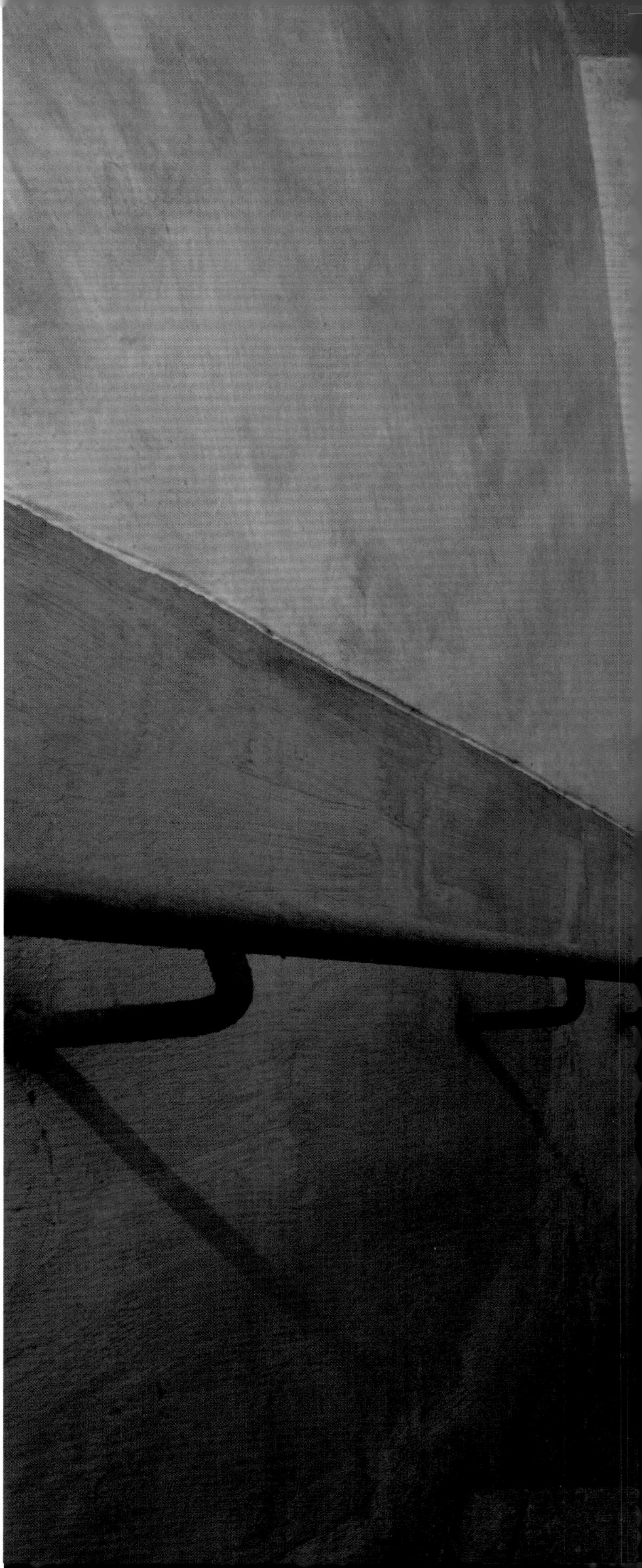

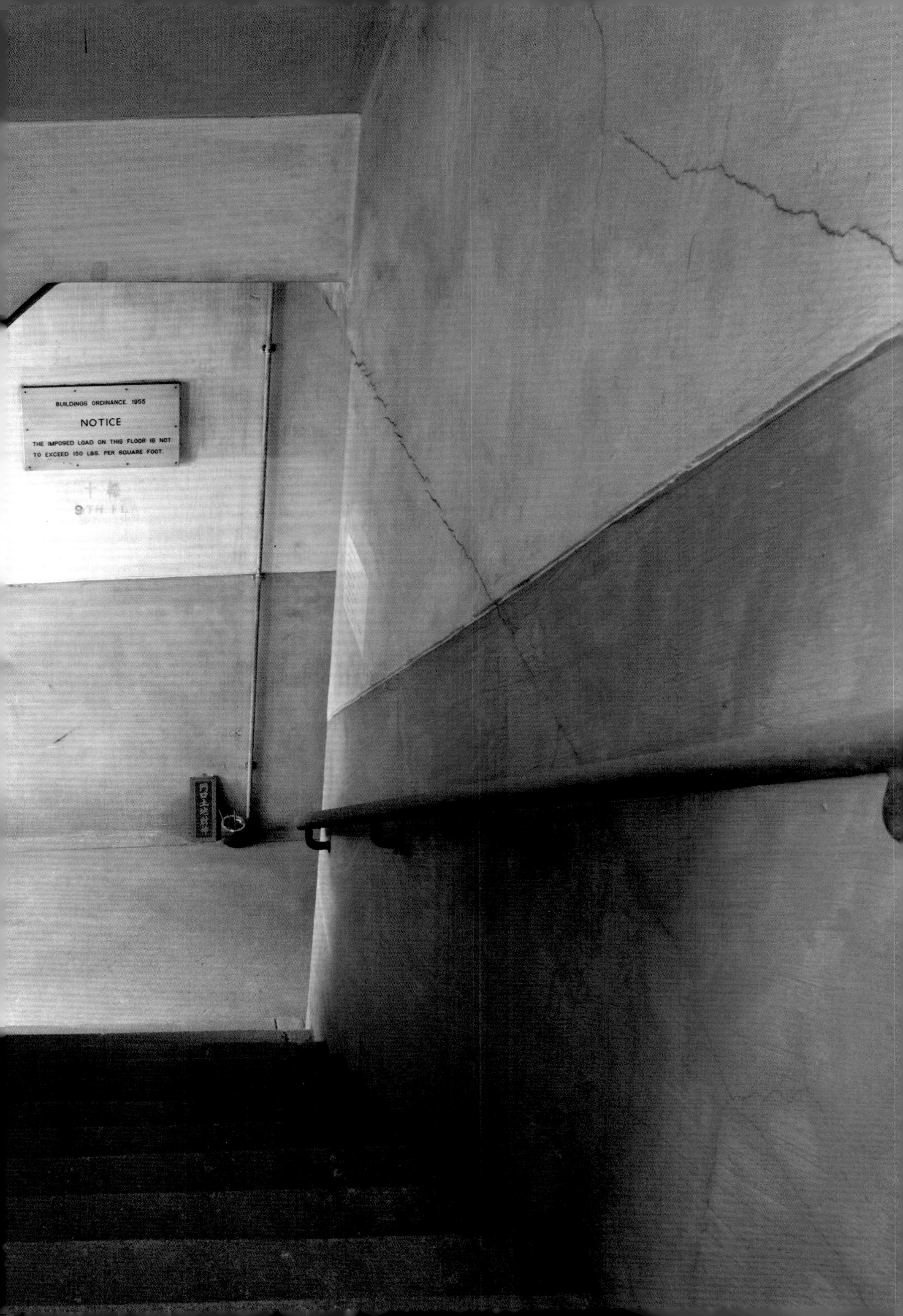
BUILDINGS ORDINANCE. 1955
NOTICE
THE IMPOSED LOAD ON THIS FLOOR IS NOT
TO EXCEED 150 LBS. PER SQUARE FOOT.

Shook Ying died in 1968, leaving behind lots of expensive jewellery, cash and stock certificates in her safety deposit box at the bank. According to her will, they were to be divided among her three sons, causing uproar from her eight daughters.

Just before she passed, she had reassured Tai Ching that his new business would be safe as he would soon be a millionaire.

Tai Ching and his brother-in-law were the two executors with authority to open the box after her death. After three months of bureaucracy, they eventually managed to open it. All they found were two bundles of one-dollar bills and a simple jade bracelet. Her husband, Bunnan, the only other person with authority to open it must have done so soon after her death, with his second wife taking everything else. Tai Ching is still bitter about the missing watch that was given to him by his mother.

Days following her death, Bunnan's second wife had their marriage officially registered, entitling her to his wealth.

淑英1968年去世，留下了許多貴重的珠寶、現金和股票放在銀行的保險櫃裡。按照遺囑，這些財產將由她的三個兒子平分，引起她八個女兒的極度不滿。

就在她過世前，她告訴大楨，他新工廠的生意將會非常順利，很快他就會成為百萬富翁。

大楨和他的姐夫是淑英過世後有權打開保險櫃的兩位遺囑執行者。經過三個月的漫長流程，他們終於打開了保險櫃，但在裡面只找到兩捆一元的鈔票和一隻普通的玉鐲。而賓南是以除他們倆外唯一能打開櫃子的人，他在淑英死後就打開了櫃子，與第二任妻子一起取走了所有其他東西。大楨對遺失了母親送給他的手錶仍耿耿於懷。

在淑英過世後不久，賓南和他的第二任妻子便正式登記結婚，好讓她有權繼承他的財產。

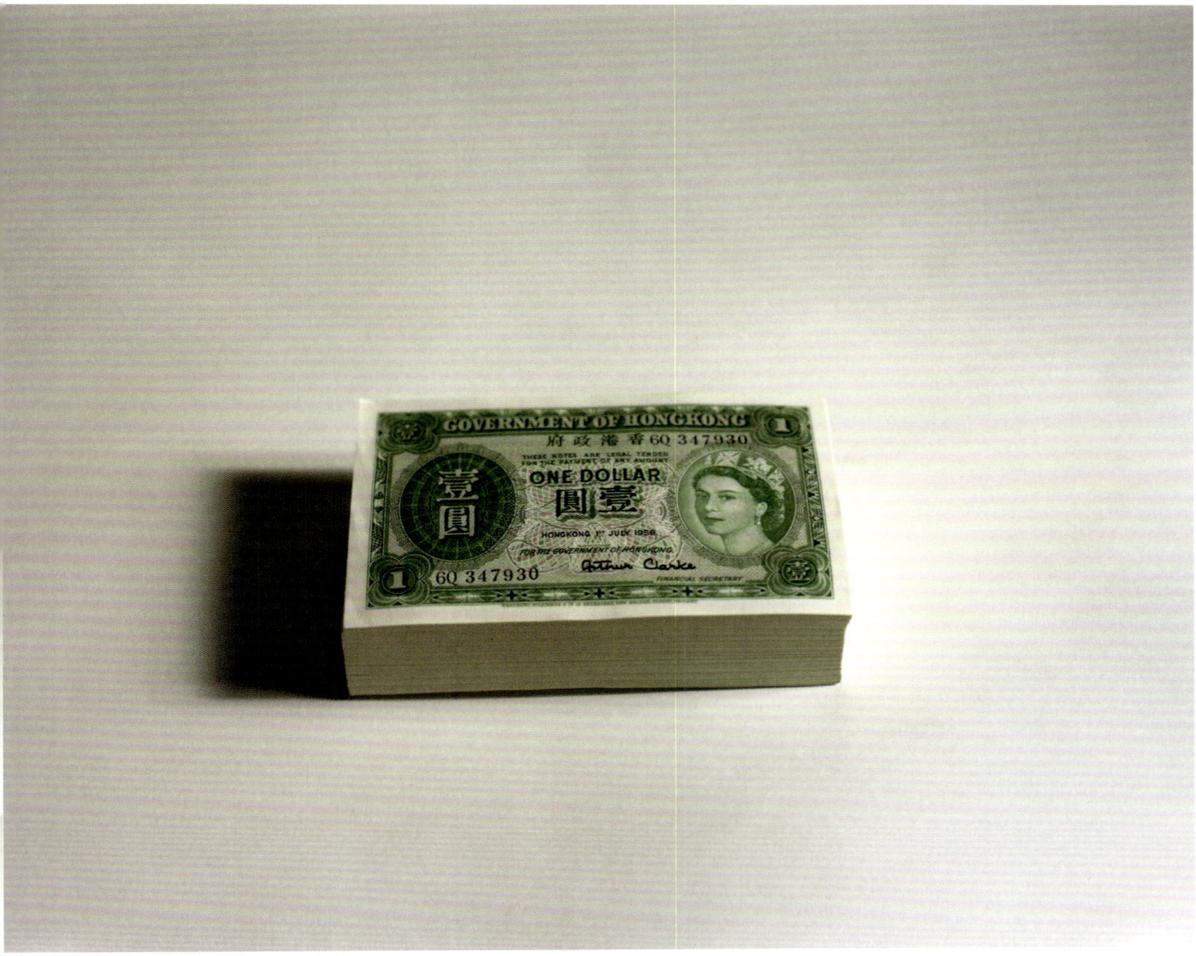
GOVERNMENT OF HONGKONG
香港政府 6Q 347930
THESE NOTES ARE LEGAL TENDER FOR THE PAYMENT OF ANY AMOUNT
ONE DOLLAR
壹圓
HONGKONG 1st JULY 1958
FOR THE GOVERNMENT OF HONGKONG
Arthur Clarke
FINANCIAL SECRETARY
6Q 347930

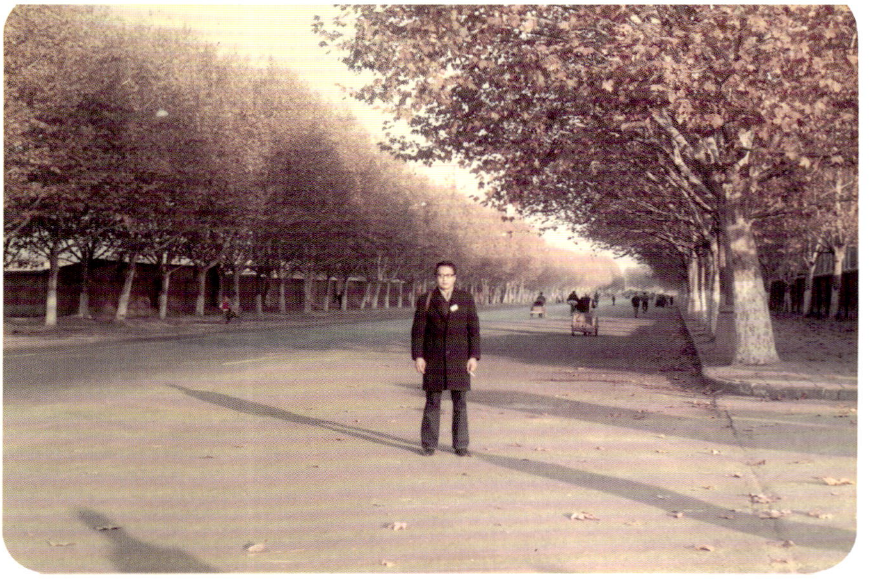

Tai Ching sold his factory in the mid 1970s. By then factories had started to move away from Hong Kong due to the increasing labour cost: Vietnam, Taiwan and Mainland China being the three main destinations that manufacturers moved to. He explored the possibilities of opening a new factory in these regions in 1977, going on specially designed trips for potential investors.

"In Hong Kong, anyone can open a factory and worry about the paperwork later. In these places, I was constantly being told that I will need another stamp; another department, another person to bribe. I just can't work like that."

Tai Ching in China in 1977.

大楨在二十世紀七十年代中期賣掉了工廠，當時勞工成本增加，製造業開始遷離香港。越南、台灣和中國大陸是工廠轉移的三個主要目的地。1977年，他參加了一個為投資者特別設計的旅程，去這些地區研究開設新工廠的可能性。「在香港，任何人都可以開一家工廠，然後再完成剩下的申請文件，但在這些地方，我經常被告知我需要蓋另一個章，找另一個部門或另一個人行賄。我實在不能適應這樣的工作方式。」

大楨在中國大陸，攝於1977年。

XVI 生咗個仔啊
It's a boy!

Tai Ching was introduced to Yip Hang, a friend of his younger sister. He used to bring her up here for dates, she thinks it was just an excuse for him to hold her hand.

大楨被介紹認識了業恆，他妹妹的朋友。他過去常帶她來這里約會，她認為這只是他想找機會牽她的手。

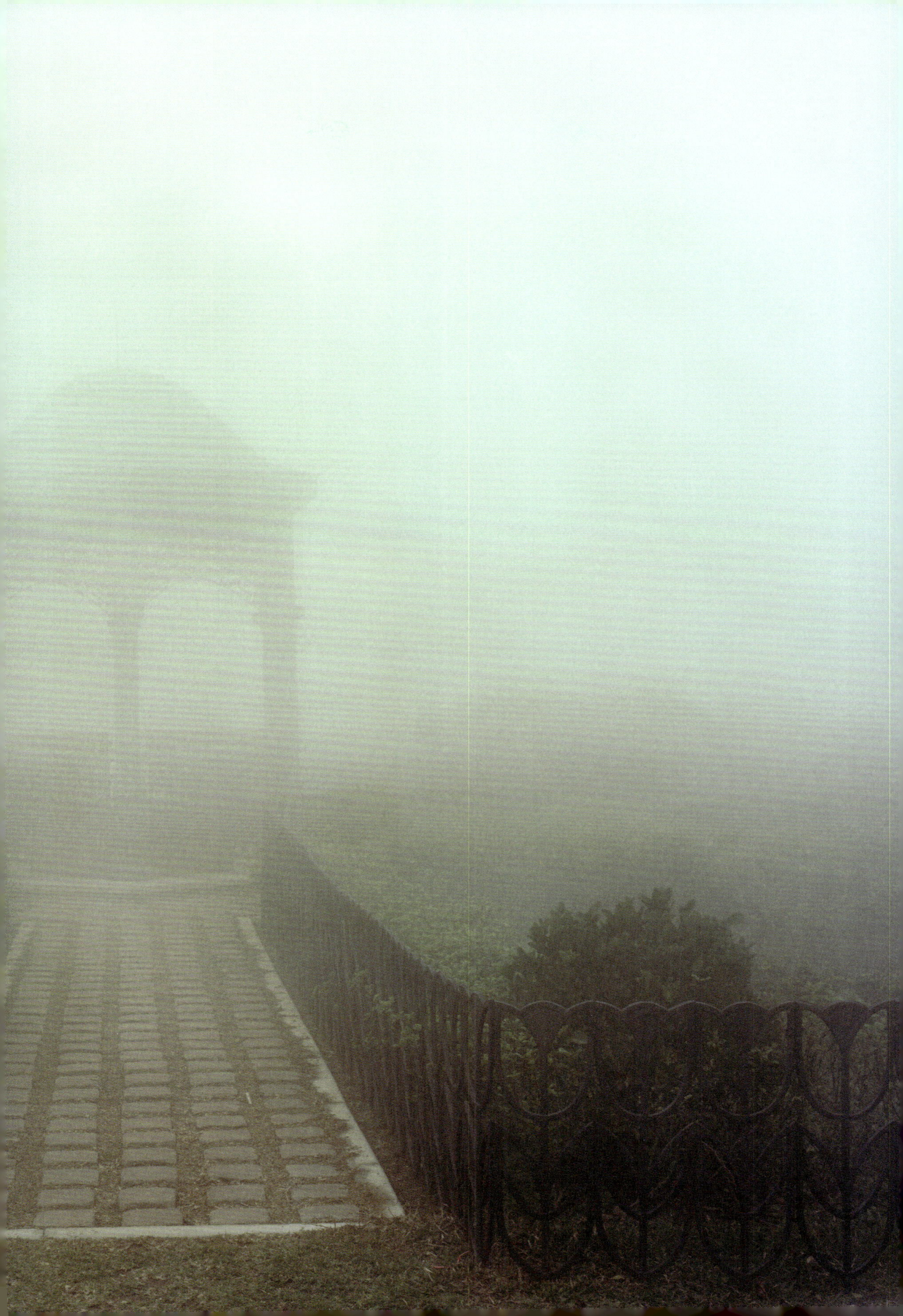

15/02/1968

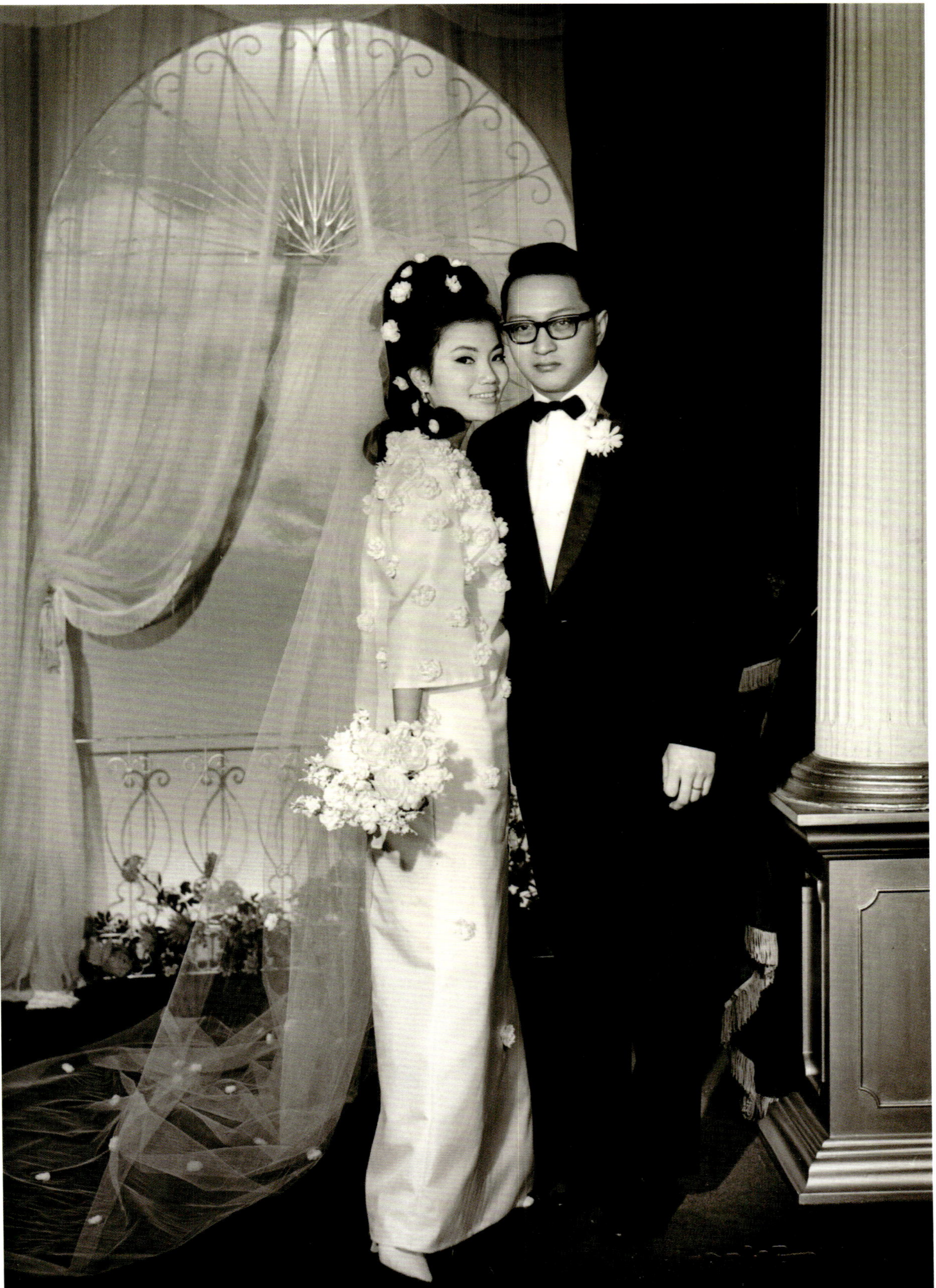

They welcomed their first child, a daughter call Ling Yee. She was joined by her sister, Ling Sze, a year later.

When Yip Hang was in labour with Ling Yee, Tai Ching's sisters, in full knowledge that Yip Hang had given birth to a girl, told Bunnan that it was a boy, so that he would be more disappointed when he found out the truth.

他們迎來了他們的第一個女兒令儀。一年後，妹妹令詩出生。

當業恆剛剛生下令儀時，大楨的姐姐們在明知業恆生了一個女孩的情況下，卻告訴賓南她生了一個男孩，這樣當他發現真相時將會加倍失望。

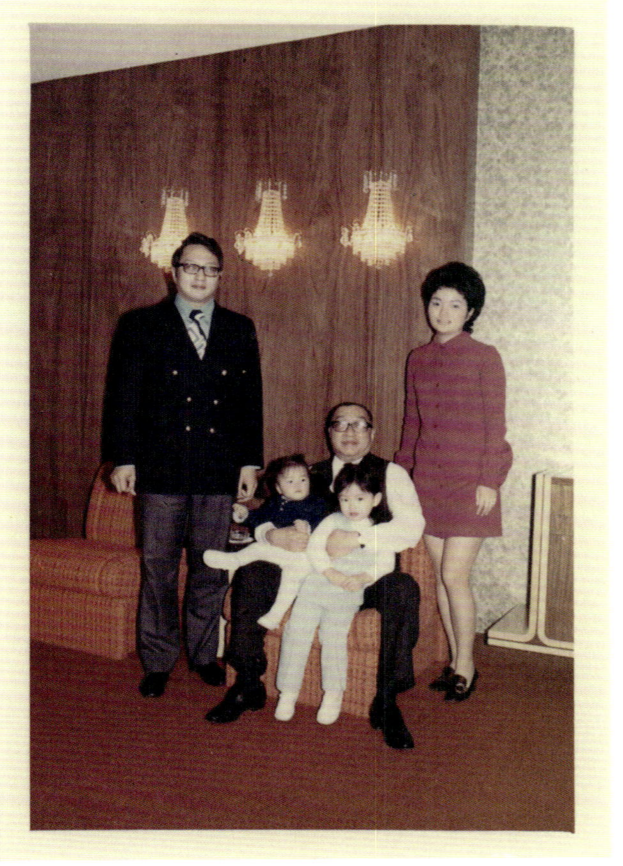

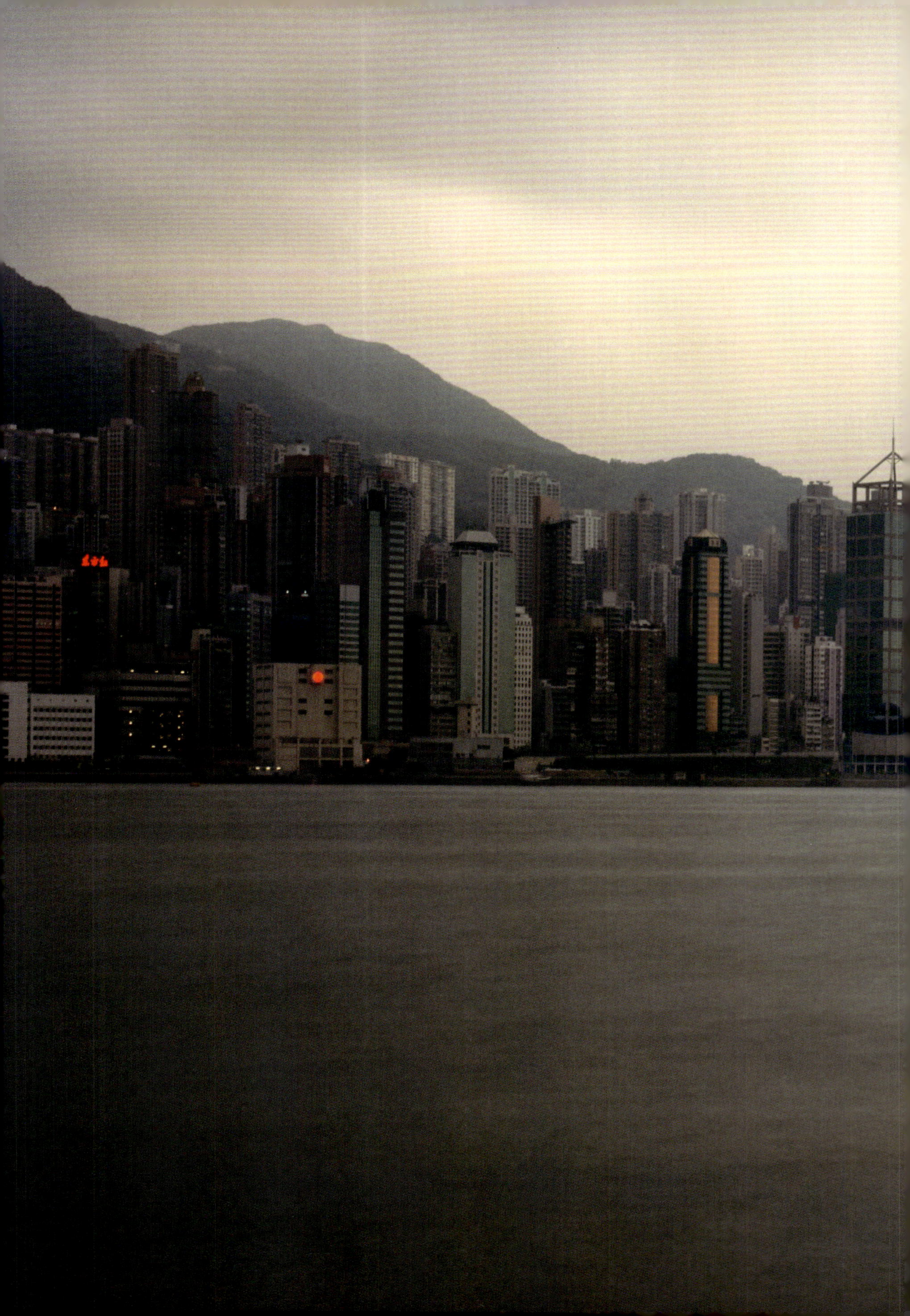

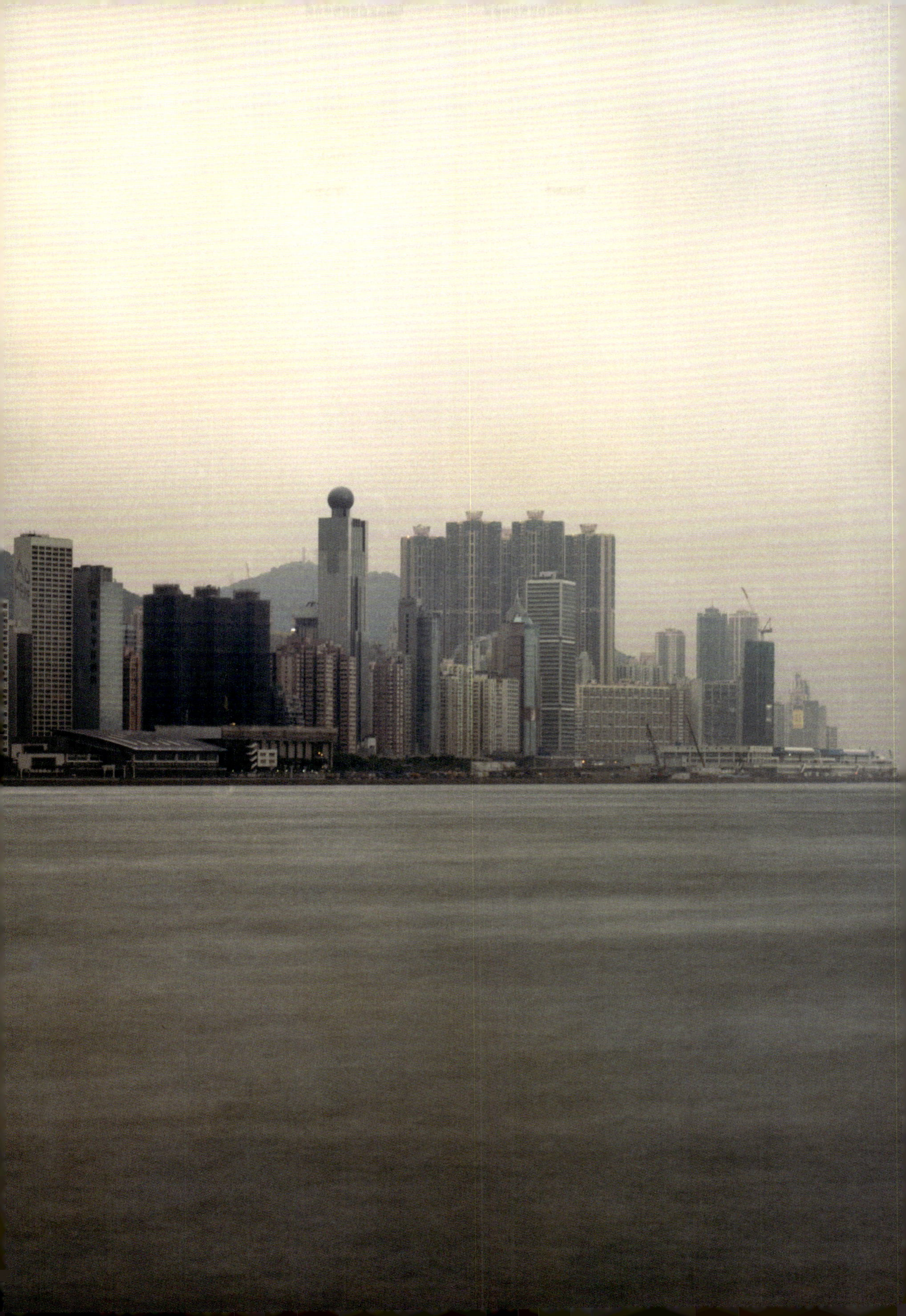

under-estimate their probable illogical move, as our parents & many others did so many years ago when they took control of China.

Belina also told me about Auntie No 6's misfortune & I really feel so sorry for her. But I don't see what we can do except offer her a willing & patient ear & offer whatever comfort we can. I don't think Mom nor Dad would be understanding or comforting in this respect & with ~~out~~ us all out here, I'm afraid, & I hope you will, bear it with her & comfort & do the best you know how. I hope, someday, to do something for her at least to show my appreciation & gratitude for all that she did for us.

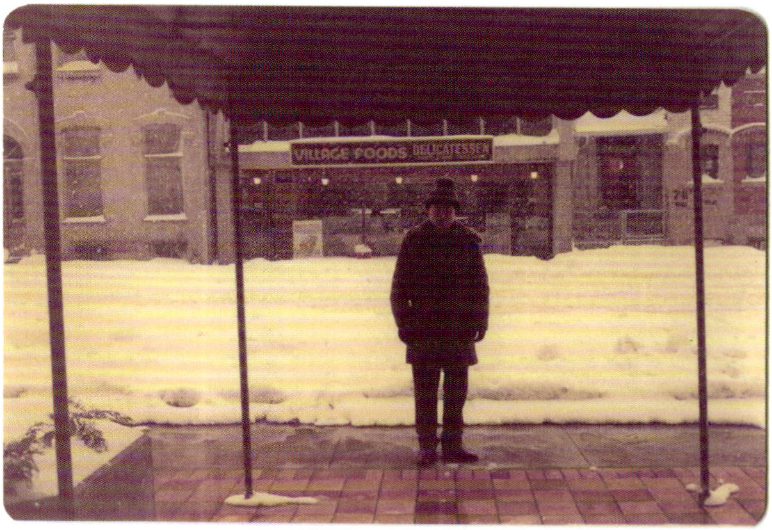
VILLAGE FOODS DELICATESSEN

Against many peoples' advice, Chung Zak and his wife emigrated to Canada in 1976. They rented an apartment in Chinatown that was beyond their means and worked for his daughter in her chain of bookshops. The arrangement never worked out and they returned to Hong Kong exactly a year after they arrived.

Having spent the first 40 years of his life with limitless money, he would never have thought that he would end up in a different country, especially one speaking a different language, and taking orders from his own daughter. Yun Nan became sick after returning to Hong Kong and was diagnosed with Parkinson's disease.

在眾人的反對下，仲錫和他的妻子於1976年移民加拿大。他們在唐人街租了一套超出他們經濟承受能力的公寓，並在女兒的連鎖書店打工。在那兒的生活一直不如人意，最終在他們抵達加拿大剛好一年時他們決定返回香港。

度過了無憂無慮的人生前四十年後，他從沒想過自己要去到一個不同的國家居住，尤其是一個說著不同語言的國家，並在工作上被自己的女兒差使。苑蘭在回到香港後被診斷患有柏金遜症。

XVII 又生多個仔
It's another boy!

Tai Ching and Yip Hang welcome their third child, a son called King Tun in 1974.

Ling Yee remembers that everytime they went to visit their granddad, he would give them a 'Lai See', a little red packet containing money. Her sister and her would get ten dollars. King Tun, a grandson, would get twenty.

大楨和業恆在1974年迎來了他們的第三個孩子，一個名叫景端的男孩。

令儀記得每次她們去看望爺爺，他都會給她們每人一封利是。她的姐姐和她每次都得到十元，而身為男孫的景端則會得到二十元。

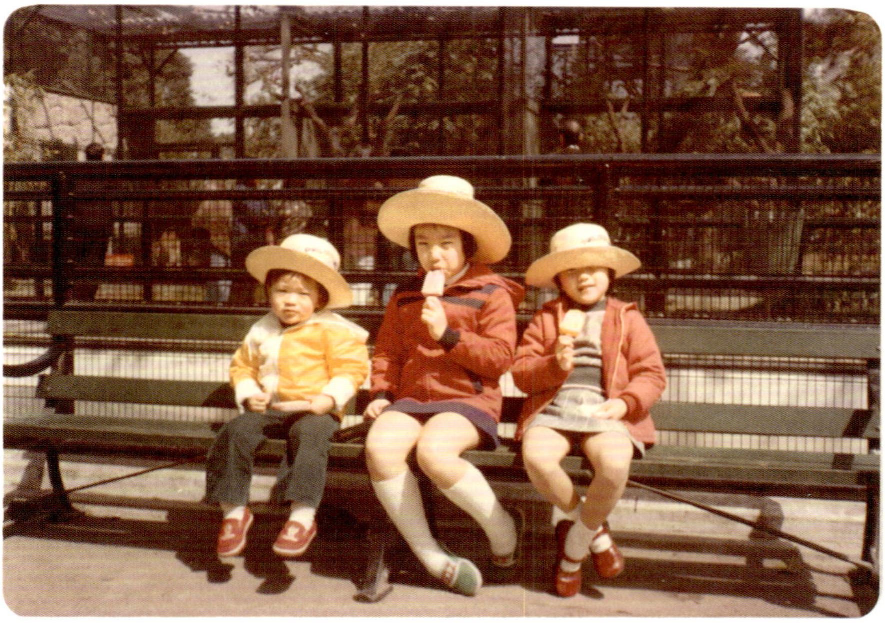

Bunnan passed away on 4th July 1976. A traditional Chinese obituary listing all his family members ran in the papers: two wives on the right, seven sons and their partners to their right, ten daughters after that, eleven grandchildren from his sons followed by 24 grandchildren from his daughters.

賓南於1976年7月4日過世，報紙刊登了印有他所有家庭成員名字的訃告，他兩個妻子的名字在最右邊，然後是七個兒子和他們的妻子，接著是十個女兒，最後是十一個內孫和二十四個外孫。

March 29. 1972

Dear Etta,

It's really nice of you to remember my birthday & thanks a million for the big fat cheque. I do appreciate it so much. Also, please convey my sincere thanks & appreciation to T.C. By the way, has T.C. left for the States yet? Hope we would have a chance to have a chat with him by phone when he's out this way.

I don't really have very much knowledge about Red China's policies nor am I following it closely now. If it is the majority's opinion & T.C.'s that there isn't any eminent danger of R.C. taking over H.K. soon, so much the better, but I do hope that you all would keep an open eye on them & not

先夫唐公賓南府君於公曆一九七六年七月四日下午七時四十五分在港寓壽終正寢積閏享壽七十有七歲奉移香港殯儀館治喪謹擇公曆七月八日(星期四)中午十弍時半大殮一時在該館大禮堂辭靈隨即出殯安葬香港仔華人永遠墳場哀此訃

聞

奠儀撥助
保良局
香港防癌會
香港公益金
華僑日報救童助學委員會
充作善舉

未亡人 唐陳淑英 伍玉美

孝男 大星 大楨 大鈞 大衛 大炫 大永 大京

媳 郭漢華 黃業恒 蘇曼婷 趙翠蘭 林穎莊 尹彩嫦

孝女 碧薇 碧齡 碧婉 碧珍 碧堅 碧馨 碧儀 碧環 碧鸞 碧錦

婿 馮蔭坤 潘仕良 馮元弼 許賢謙 林安紹 趙大偉 陳天樂 李耀庭 鍾明烈

孫男 景泰 景炘 景勳 景康 景端

孫女 海蓉 慧儀 倩明 令儀 令詩 可欣

胞弟 賡南　弟婦 潘麗珍

胞妹 金蓮　妹倩 甘華鉅

外孫男 林邦成 林邦怡 許佐之 趙善麟 趙善智 趙善仁 馮永和 馮基和 陳　聰 潘文豁 潘永鏗 李智仁 李智權 馮基敏 馮基偉

外孫女 趙巧兒 許心麗 馮靜嫻 馮靜思 潘慧敏 潘慧琪 李穎琪 鍾懸儀 鍾懸賢

司書侄 樹培 侄媳 蘇氏 親屬繁衍 恕未盡錄

泣告

治喪處：香港殯儀館 英皇道六七九號 電話：六一五弍二六一八

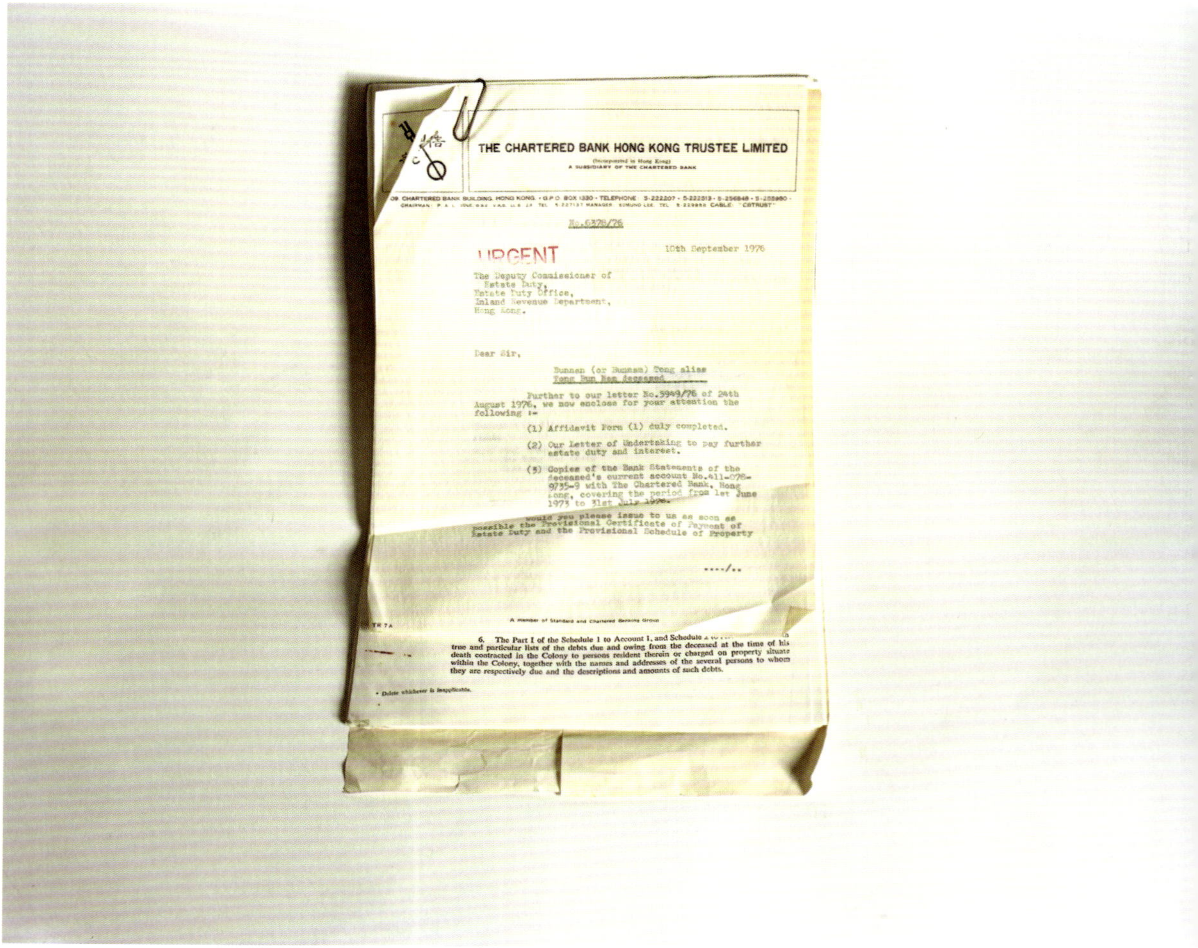
THE CHARTERED BANK HONG KONG TRUSTEE LIMITED
A SUBSIDIARY OF THE CHARTERED BANK
No.6378/76
URGENT
10th September 1976
The Deputy Commissioner of Estate Duty,
Estate Duty Office,
Inland Revenue Department,
Hong Kong.
Dear Sir,
Bunnan (or Bunsam) Tong alias Tong Bun Sam deceased
Further to our letter No.5949/76 of 24th August 1976, we now enclose for your attention the following :-
(1) Affidavit Form (1) duly completed.
(2) Our Letter of Undertaking to pay further estate duty and interest.
(3) Copies of the Bank Statements of the deceased's current account No.411-078-9735-9 with The Chartered Bank, Hong Kong, covering the period from 1st June 1973 to 31st July 1976.
Would you please issue to us as soon as possible the Provisional Certificate of Payment of Estate Duty and the Provisional Schedule of Property
..../..
A member of Standard and Chartered Banking Group
TR 7A
6. The Part I of the Schedule 1 to Account 1, and Schedule
true and particular lists of the debts due and owing from the deceased at the time of his death contracted in the Colony to persons resident therein or charged on property situate within the Colony, together with the names and addresses of the several persons to whom they are respectively due and the descriptions and amounts of such debts.
* Delete whichever is inapplicable.

With seventeen children from two wives, and his favouritism for sons, the death of Bunnan was always going to lead to a messy struggle for his inheritance.

Bunnan's eldest son got his company, his second wife got most of his remaining assets including his offices, warehouses, properties, stocks and cash. 84 Robinson road with 24 flats also created lots of conflict. The flats were supposed to be divided equally between his six sons, but his daughters found out about the arrangement and at his deathbed begged on their knees for him to reconsider.

The relationship between the siblings, always fragile, came close to breaking point. Following his death, the two sets of children from his two wives ceased all communication, even though many of them lived in the same building.

擁有兩個妻子和她們生的十七個兒女，再加上家族重男輕女的傳統，賓南的死毫無疑問為家族帶來爭奪遺產的混亂局面。

賓南的長子得到了他的公司，他的第二任妻子得到了他剩餘的大部分資產，包括辦公室、倉庫、物業、股票和現金等等。羅便臣道84號的二十四套公寓也引發了不少爭執。這二十四套公寓本應該平均分配給他的六個兒子，但他的女兒們在他死前發現了這個安排，在賓南臨終前跪在他病床邊懇求他重新考慮。

兄弟姐妹之間一直脆弱的關係在這時已臨近破裂。

在賓南死後，兩邊的兒女之間停止了所有接觸，儘管他們之中的許多人依然住在同一棟樓裡。

Before his death, Bunnan lived on the top floor of 84 Robinson Road with his second wife. After his passing, many of his belongings representative of his life with his first wife were put into storage. Including the photo album taken at his 59th birthday party, which took place in the basement, in front of the bamboo bush. The second wife was not invited.

賓南死前和他的第二任妻子住在羅便臣道84號的頂樓。他去世後，許多他與第一任妻子生活時的留下的物品被封存了起來，包括他五十九歲生日派對時在竹叢前拍攝的照片。第二個妻子並沒有被邀請參加那次的派對。

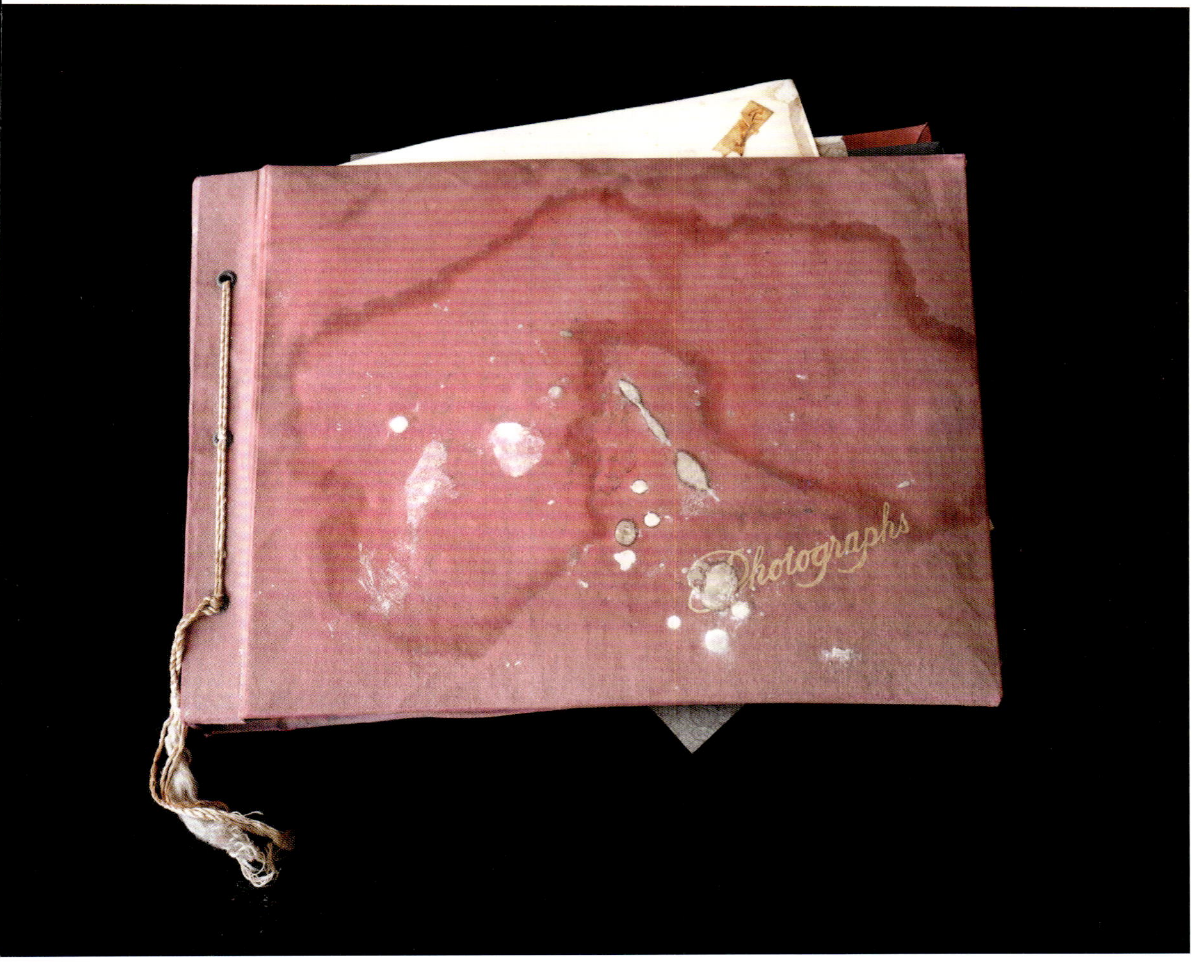
Photographs

「個老頭子都死咗，仲生嚟搏乜嘢?」

“didn’t think you’d still be trying for another boy, now that the old man is dead”

Following the death of Bunnan, only one more grandchild was born from the children with his first wife. Tai Ching and Yip Hung would have another boy in 1977, named King Fung.

Upon hearing the news, Tai Kung's wife said to Yip Hung, "I didn't think you would still be trying for another boy now that the old man is dead, who are you trying to impress?"

賓南去世後，他第一任妻子的兒女們只再生下了一個孫子。大楨和業恆卻在1977年又生了一個男孩，名叫景鋒。

大鈞的妻子聽到這個消息後，對業恆說:「個老頭子都死咗，仲生嚟搏乜嘢？」

房號/床號
Room or Bed No. 202

Name 姓名 唐景鋒
TONG KING-FUNG

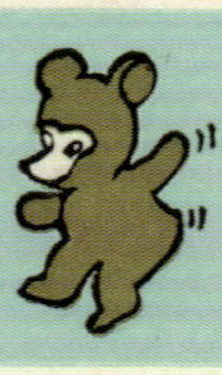

Length: 20"

It's A Boy 男孩

出生日期
Date of Birth 10-5-77

時間
Time 4 38 p

出生體重
Birth Weight 7 14/16 lb. Weight on discharge 7 14/16 -磅 lbs.

醫生/助產士
Doctor or Midwife S. C. Ng.

XVIII 阿鋒
Ah Fung

After putting up a block of flats in 1971 at 84 Robinson Road, Bunnan lived on the top floor until he died in 1976. Ah Fung grew up on the floor below, the eleventh floor. A special key was needed to go to the twelfth floor via the lift and the door leading to the stairs was always locked. Sai Mei, meaning 'small grandmother' lived up there by herself and since his father hated her, Fung saw her almost as an evil stepmother. He never went up there and as a child, the twelfth floor became his bogeyman.

1971年，賓南在羅便臣道84號蓋了一座公寓樓後，一直住在頂樓，直到1976年去世。阿鋒在十一樓長大。通過電梯到十二樓需要一把特殊鑰匙，而通往樓梯的門則總是鎖著的。細嫲（小奶奶）一個人住在那裡，由於父親恨她，阿鋒覺得她有點像個邪惡的繼母。小時候他從沒上去過十二樓，那兒對他來說就如妖窟一般。

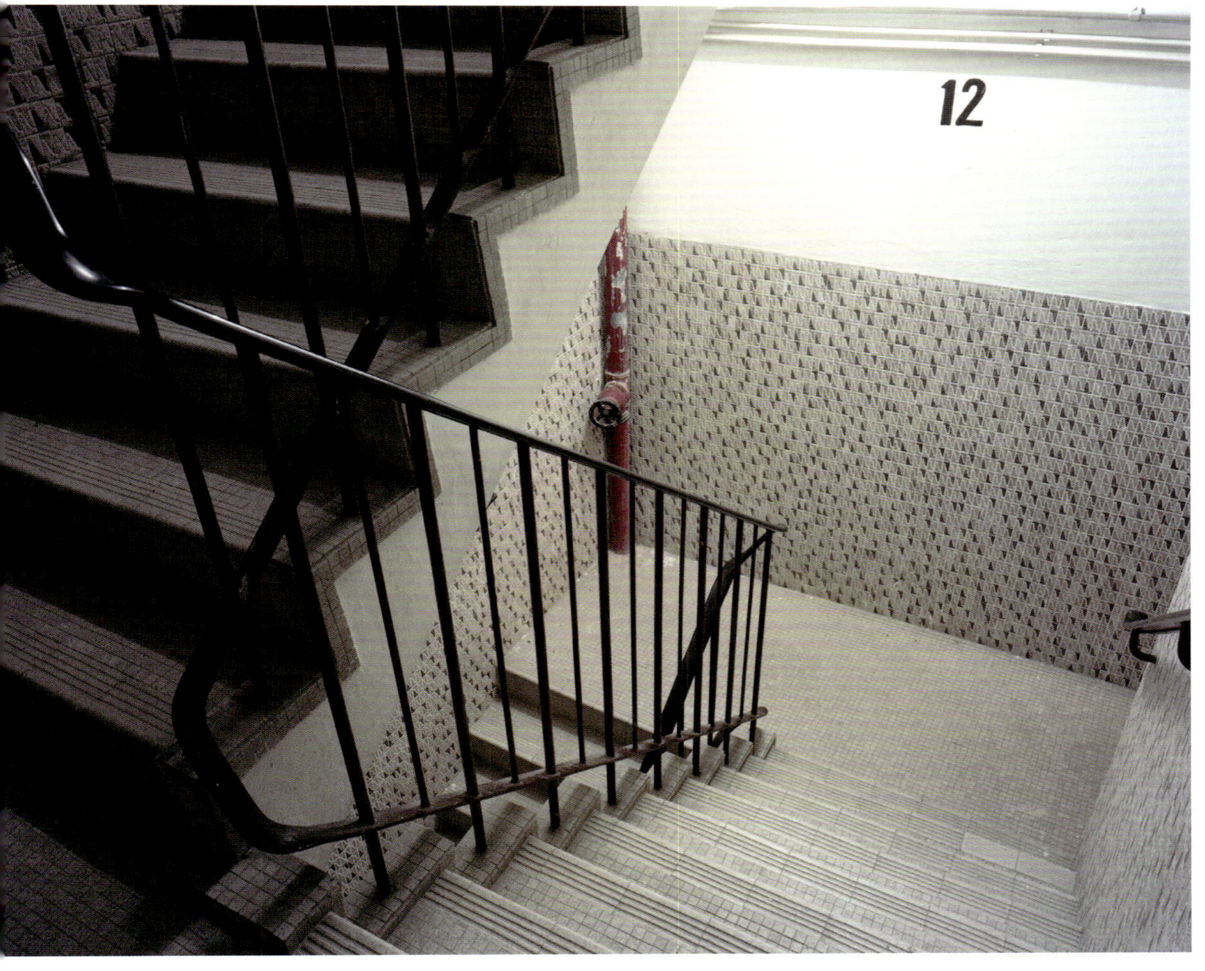
12

King Fung,

Received your letter, many thanks.

I have been in California for five months, studying in second grade. Your have much homework? Here, English is very difficult, maths is really easy. I really miss you, Lu Kin Koon, Pon Kee Yee, Lu Duk Yu, Hui Wen Chun, you are all my best friends. If you ever come to America to play, you must come to my house.

My new address is :

636 Scottsbluff Drive,
Claremont, Calif. 91711
Tel (714) 626-2910

Wishing you
A happy new year

Yel Man
Dec, 18th

景峰:

收到你的信謝謝.

我來了加州五個月, 讀二年班。

你的功課多嗎?這裏英文很深, 數學很淺. 我很想你, 盧建權, 龐建宜, 呂德雨和奚永中, 你們都是我的好朋友. 你如果來美國玩, 一定要到我家來玩.

我的新地址是:

636 SCOTTSBLUFF DRIVE
CLAREMONT, CALIF. 91711

電話 (714) 626-2910

祝你
新年快樂　　燿文上

十二月十八日

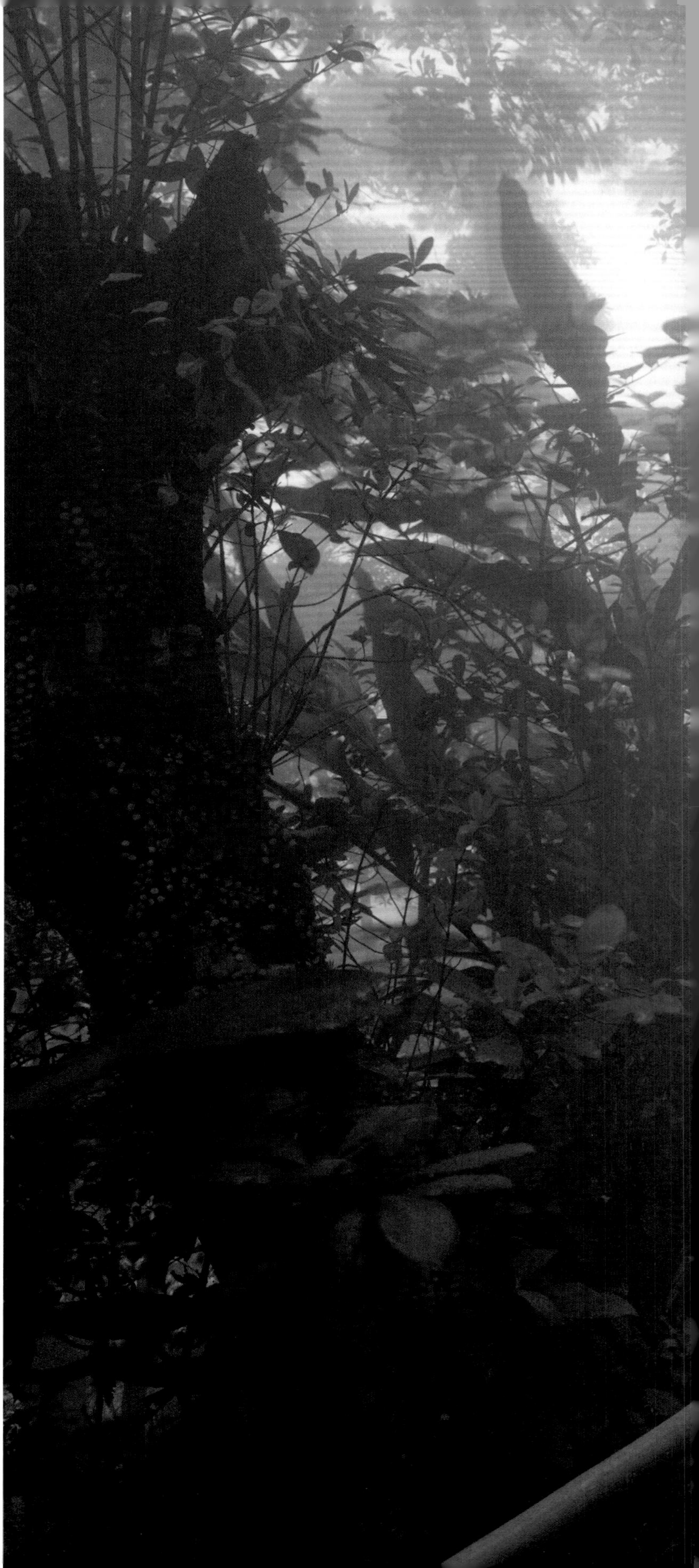

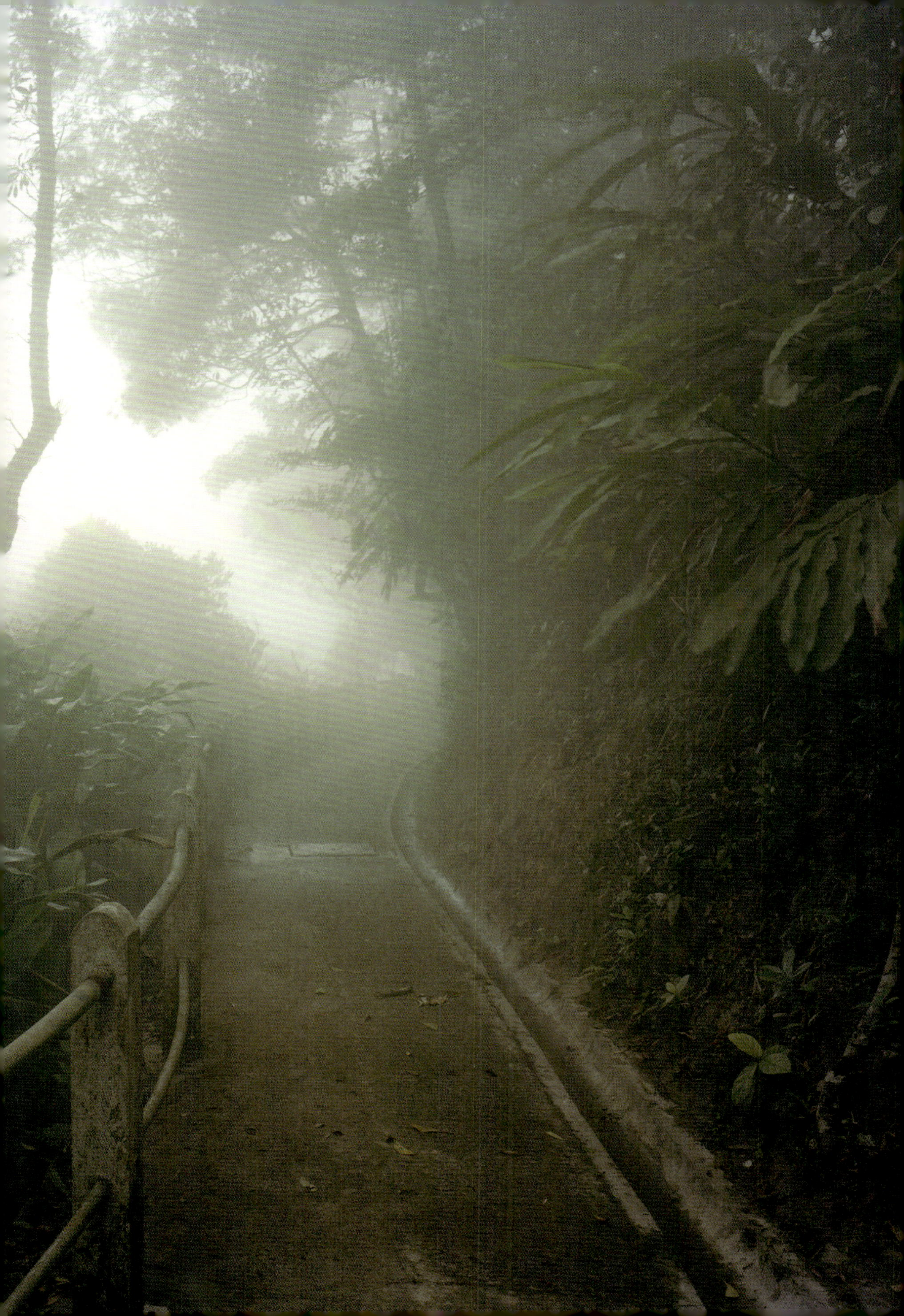

Bunnan and Co. ran an import and export company. Business flourished in the 1940s and 1950s.

From the late 1960s, however, as more and more people in Hong Kong spoke English, foreign buyers went straight to the manufacturers and cut out the middleman. Only the more conservative companies such as Woolworths still bought their stock. By the 1970s, Tai Kung, Tai Ching's brother had monopolised the company and forced everyone else out. However, he failed to adapt with the times. Whilst others had branched into manufacturing and property, he kept the old business model and the business looked doomed. Fung remembers going there as a child and even then, thinking how lame the toys were.

賓南在二十世紀四十、五十年代經營進出口貿易，生意十分紅火。

不過從二十世紀六十年代末期開始，隨著香港會英語的人數越來越多，外國買家可以直接和製造商聯繫，從而跳過中間人。只有伍爾沃斯等比較保守的公司仍在購買他們的貨物。到了二十世紀七十年代，大楨的哥哥大鈞壟斷了公司的經營，把家族其他人都趕了出去。但是，他沒有適應時代的改變。雖然其他人已經逐漸涉足製造業和房地產業，但他仍然堅持原有的商業模式，因此生意注定要失敗。阿鋒記得小時候曾經去過那裡，那時已經覺得公司裡面的玩具非常無聊。

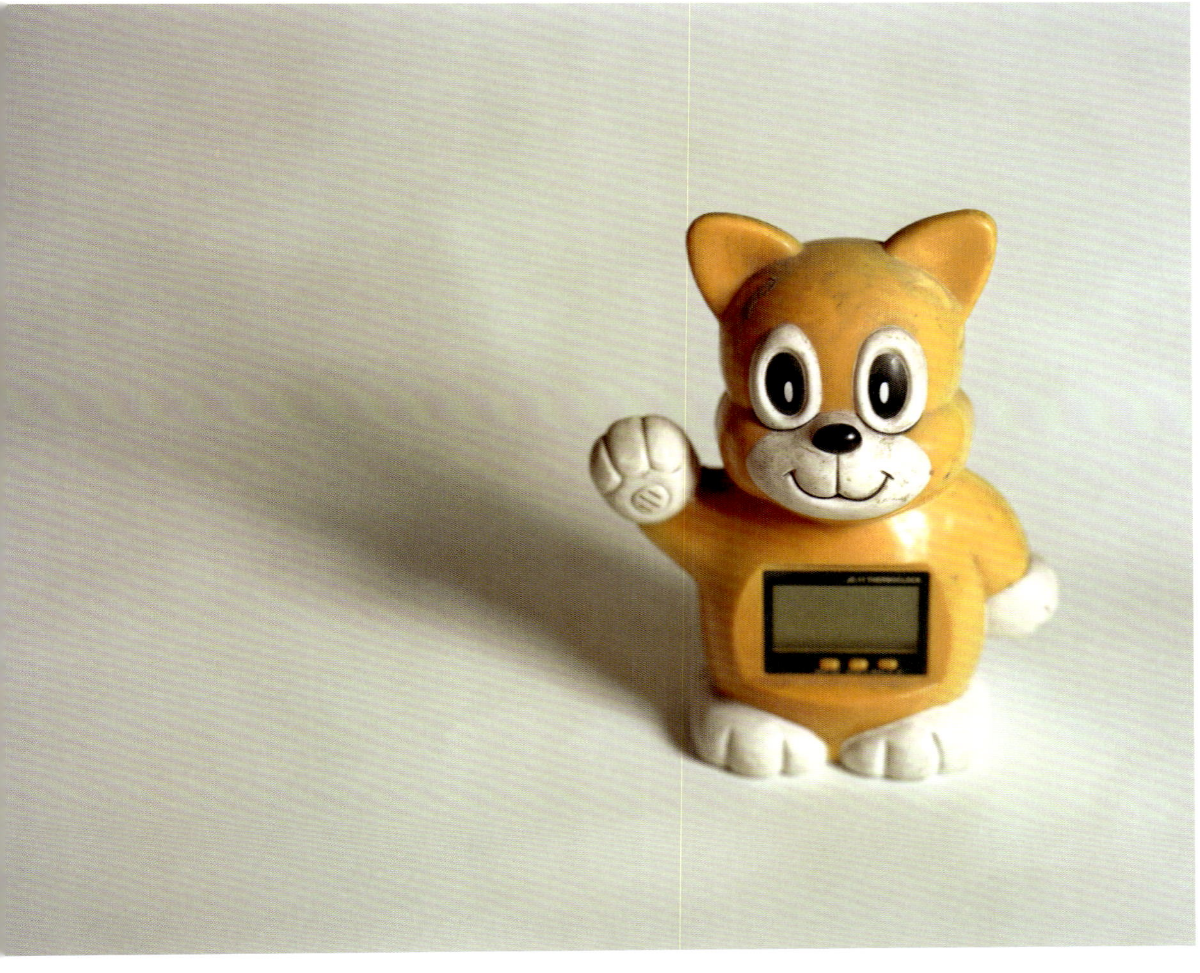

GRADE	DATE	OFFICIAL EXAMINER
9TH KUP		
8TH KUP B	11/5/85	곽 재 영 7단
7TH KUP B	14/9/85	곽 재 영 7단
6TH KUP -A	28/12/85	곽 재 영 7단
5TH KUP +B	29/3/86	곽 재 영 7단
4TH KUP +B	7/6/86	곽 재 영 7단
3RD KUP B	20/9/86	곽 재 영 7단
2ND KUP B	17/1/87	곽 재 영 8단
1ST KUP +B	11/4/87	곽 재 영 8단
1ST DAN	23/1/88	곽 재 영 8단
2ND DAN		
3RD DAN		
4TH DAN		

NO.

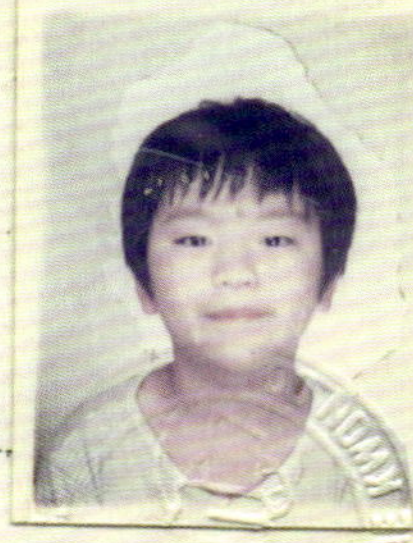

NAME 唐景鋒

ADDRESS 84, Robinson Road Flat 11A HK

DATE OF BIRTH 10 th May 1977

SCHOOL/CLUB Wan Chai

HOLDERS SIGNATURE TONG King Fung

The Hong Kong Tae Kwon-Do

Ah Fung attended Taekwondo classes from the age of eight, although his master often likened his kicking to ballet dancers. Nevertheless, he obtained his black belt at the age of ten, one of the youngest to do so in that school.

阿鋒從八歲開始就上跆拳道課，他的老師常形容他踢腿踢得像芭蕾舞演員。儘管如此，他還是在十歲時拿到黑帶，是該校最年輕的黑帶之一。

Tai Ching is a keen pianist, something that he wanted all of his children to do. All four of his children were sent to piano lessons and made to practise everyday. Growing up, Ah Fung hated it, but he especially hated his piano teacher, who used to hit him on the head when he got a note wrong. Ah Fung tried everything he could to get out of going to the lessons. For a while, he would eat the fluff off the carpet, believing the germs would make him sick.

It never worked.

大楨對鋼琴有著濃厚的興趣，他希望所有的孩子都能夠學習鋼琴。他的四個孩子全都被送去上鋼琴課，並且需要每天進行練習。阿鋒從小就不喜歡彈鋼琴，更討厭他的鋼琴老師，因為老師經常在他彈错音的時候打他的頭。阿鋒想盡一切辦法不去上課。有一段時間，他會吃地毯上的絨毛，因為相信上面的細菌會讓他得病。

他從未得逞。

XIX 星期日五點
Sunday at Five

The 1980s and 1990s in Hong Kong was a contradictory period. Skilled people began to move abroad, fearing what might happen after the handover. Yet, at the same time, the economy boomed. Skyscrapers went up all over the colony.

二十世紀八十、九十年代的香港是一個矛盾的時期，大批有良好教育背景的人對香港的前景表示擔憂，開始移民外國；與此同時，社會經濟蓬勃發展，摩天大樓遍布城市。

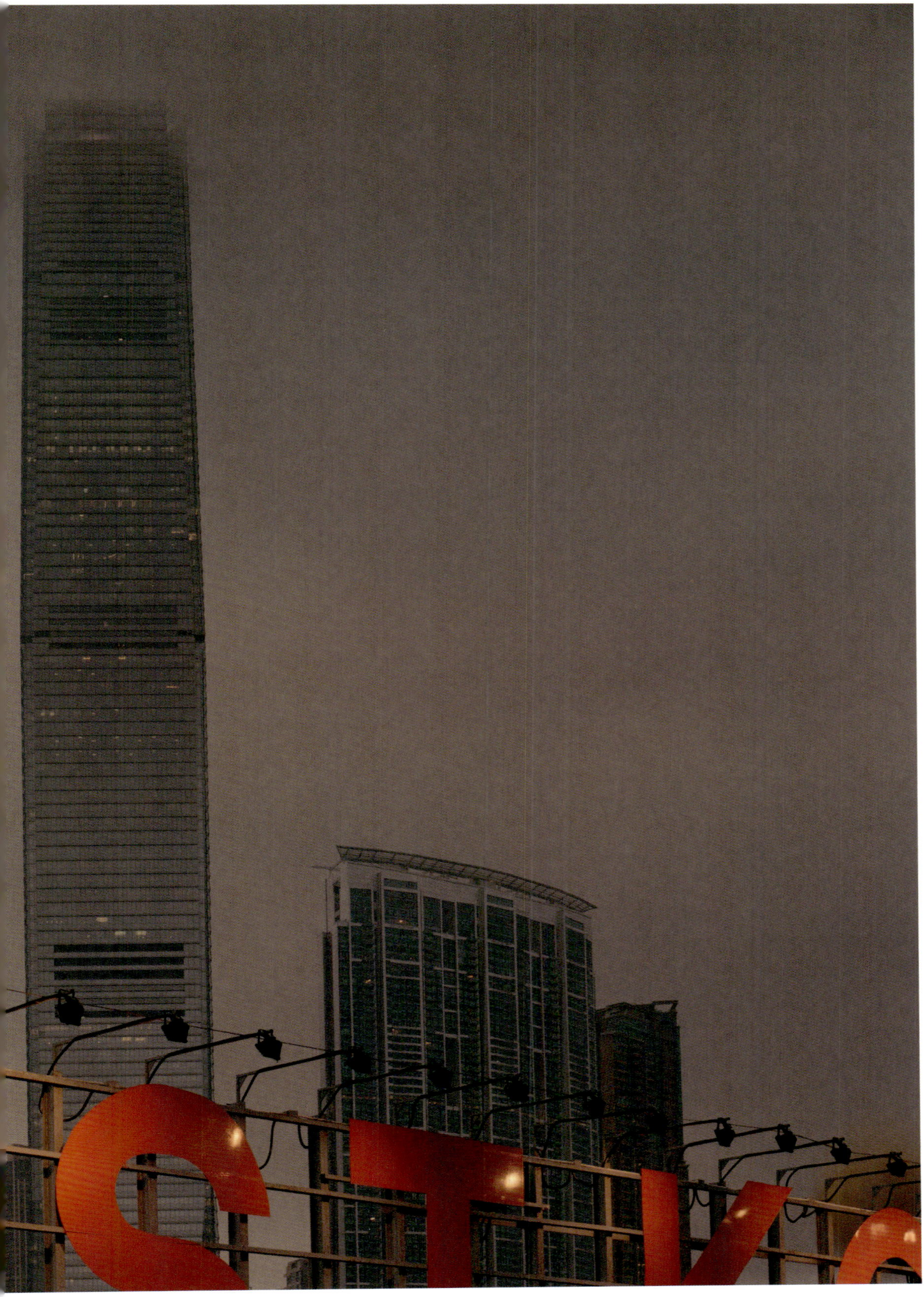

A page out of Fung's leaving book when he left Hong Kong in 1990. The uncertainty of the 1997 handover back to China loomed over everybody across all ages in Hong Kong.

阿鋒1990年離開香港時告別留言冊上的一頁。1997年香港回歸中國的不明朗因素籠罩著香港各年齡層的人。

NAME KEVIN MA

TEL 8731798

ADDRESS 23F., Room 4 ^ Flat B, Hoi Chu Court, Aberdeen. H.K.

BIRTHDAY 02 - 04 - 19

BLOOD TYPE A 型

MESSAGE

今朝雖分別，前途各自分；
但若能相會，勿當過路人。

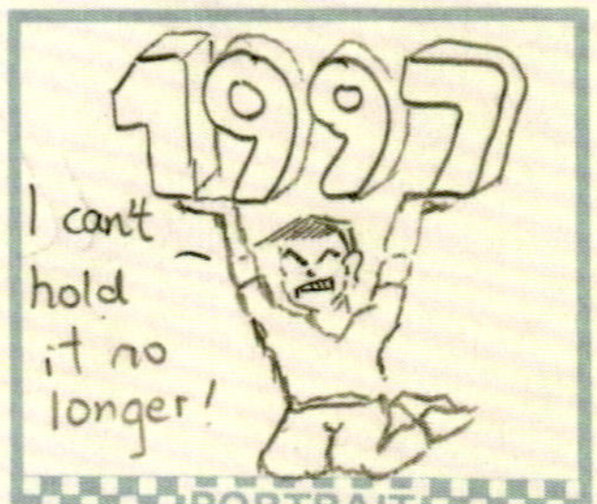

PORTRAIT

Perimeter fence at the former Hong Kong International Airport (Kai Tak Airport).

Ah Fung was sent to study in England in 1990 at the age of thirteen. His two sisters and brother were also sent to boarding schools in England when they turned thirteen. Flights to the UK tend to take off late at night, making the drive along this fence one of the last things that would be seen before being sent off to live in another country.

前香港國際機場啟德機場的圍牆。

1990年阿鋒在十三歲時被送到英國留學。他的兩個姐姐和哥哥也是在十三歲時被送到英國的寄宿學校。飛往英國的航班往往在深夜起飛，這道牆便成為他們在被送到另一個國家前最後看到的事物之一。

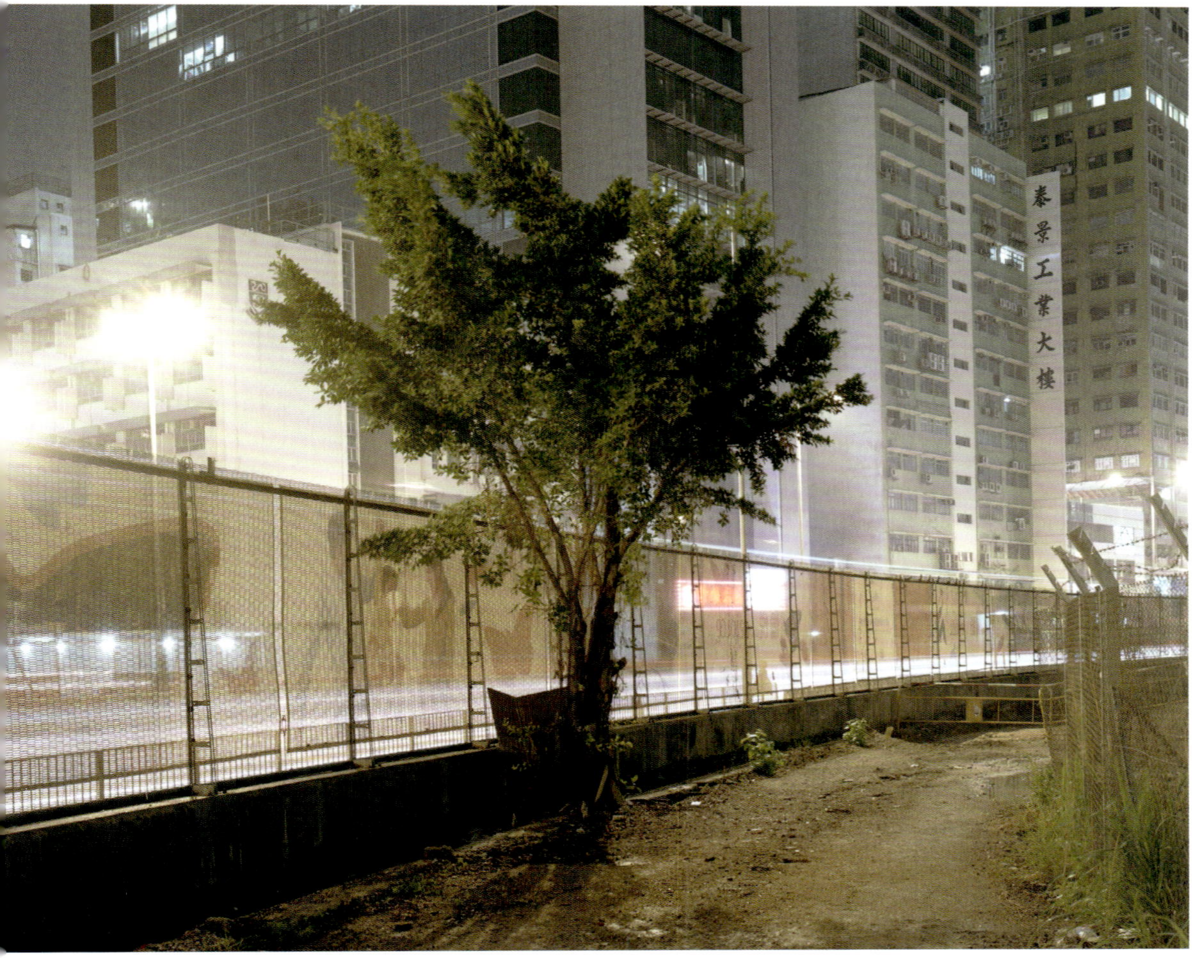
泰景工業大樓

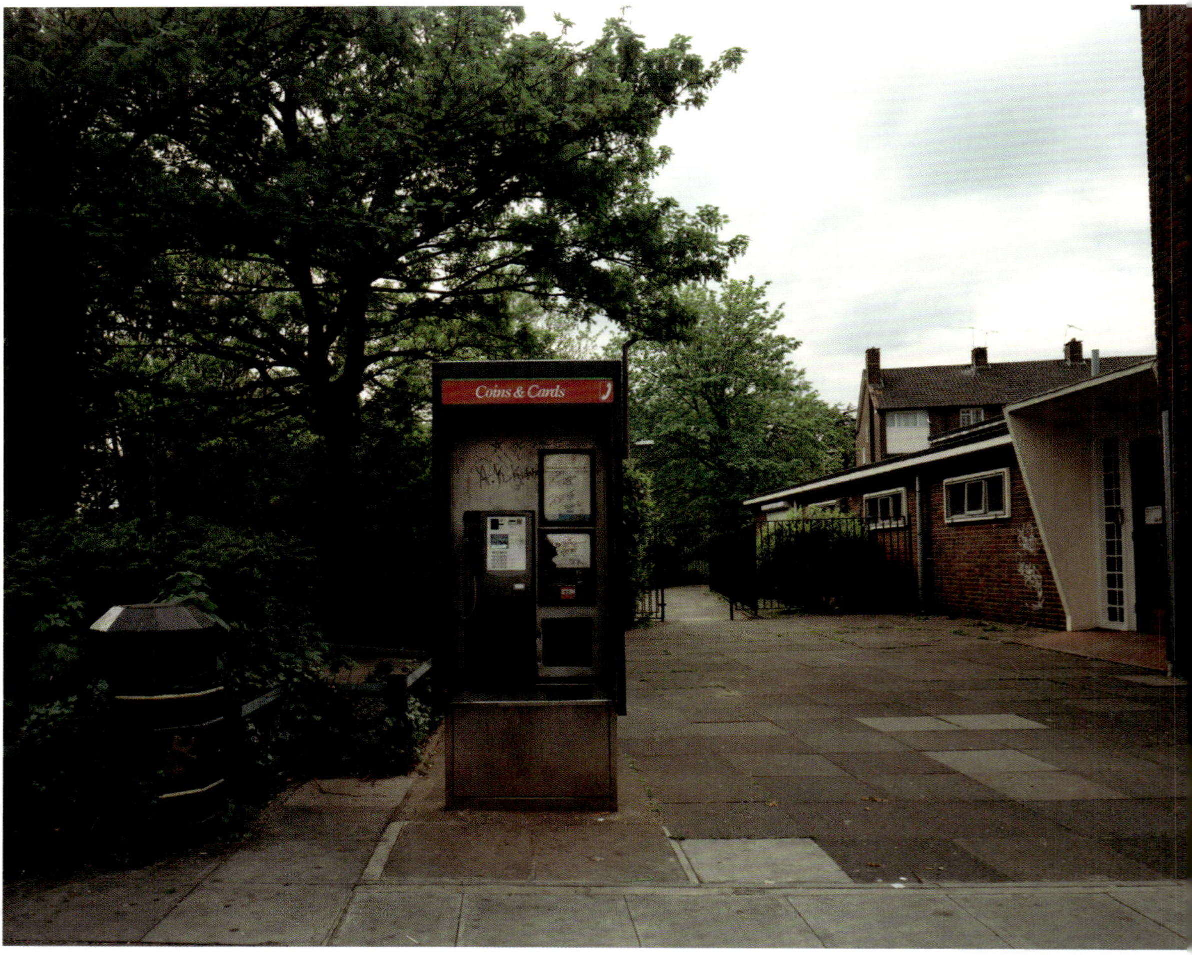
Coins & Cards

Before the days of Skype and FaceTime, Fung used to arrange for his mother to call him at a phone booth near his boarding school. Usually at 5pm on a Sunday, making it past midnight in Hong Kong and therefore a cheaper phone rate.

在還沒有Skype和FaceTime的時代，阿鋒總會讓他的母親星期天下午五點打電話給寄宿學校附近的電話亭。因為香港已經過了午夜，所以電話費會比較便宜。

At boarding school, Fung formed a band with a few of his school friends. Nirvana was one of his favourite bands and he thought he looked a bit like Kurt Cobain in this photo.

在寄宿学校上学时，阿锋曾和几个朋友一起组乐队。Nirvana是他最喜欢的乐队之一，当时的他觉得这张照片中的自己有一点像主唱柯本。

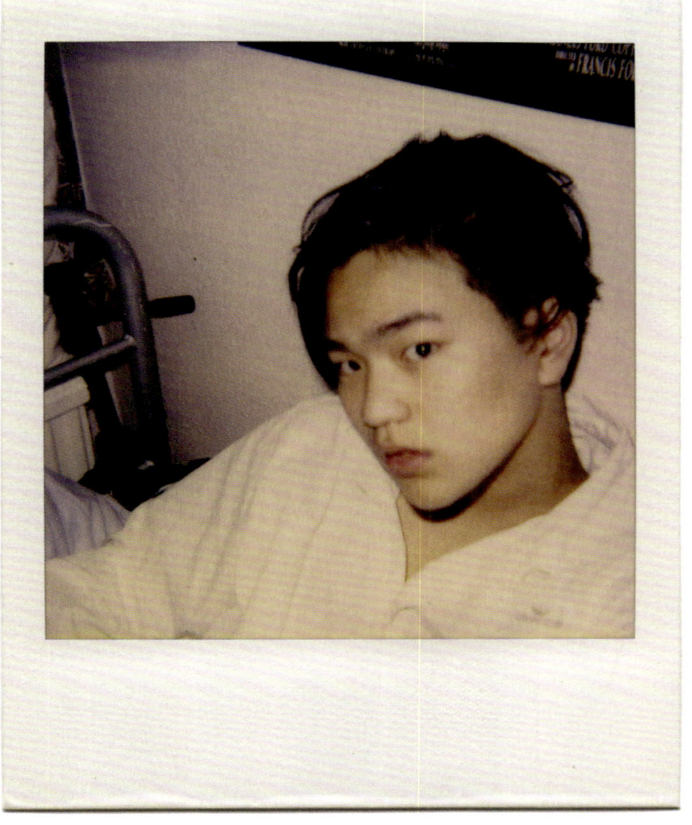

The final part of the Lantau Link opened two months before Hong Kong was to be handed back to Chinese rule. Margaret Thatcher performed the opening ceremony on the 27 April 1997. The bridge connects Hong Kong to Lantau Island, primarily to the new Hong Kong International Airport. Tai Ching and Yip Hang emigrated to England on the 28 June 1997 and one of the last things they did was to go for a drive on the bridge, partly because they feared they might never return to Hong Kong.

They moved back in February 1998.

大嶼山幹線的最後一段路在香港回歸前兩個月通車。瑪嘉烈戴卓爾夫人於1997年4月27日主持了開幕式。它連接香港和大嶼山，特別是新的香港國際機場。大楨和業恆於1997年6月28日移民英國，他們最後做的其中一件事就是開車過橋。他們曾經認為回歸後可能永遠不會再返回香港。

他們於1998年2月搬回香港。

After leaving school, Ah Fung spent two years travelling and working around the world. He spent the best part of a year as a volunteer in a mental institute for children in northern Romania, in the border town of Siret. Here he met his future wife Su, who was also working there, though they didn't actually get together for another four years, after getting back in touch a few thousands miles away in India.

阿鋒從學校畢業後，花了兩年時間環遊世界及工作。他有差不多一年時間在羅馬尼亞北部一個叫錫雷的邊境小鎮上的兒童心理研究所做志願者。在那裡他遇到了未來的妻子蘇。但在之後的四年時間裡面他們並未再見面，直到在幾千英里外的印度重聚。

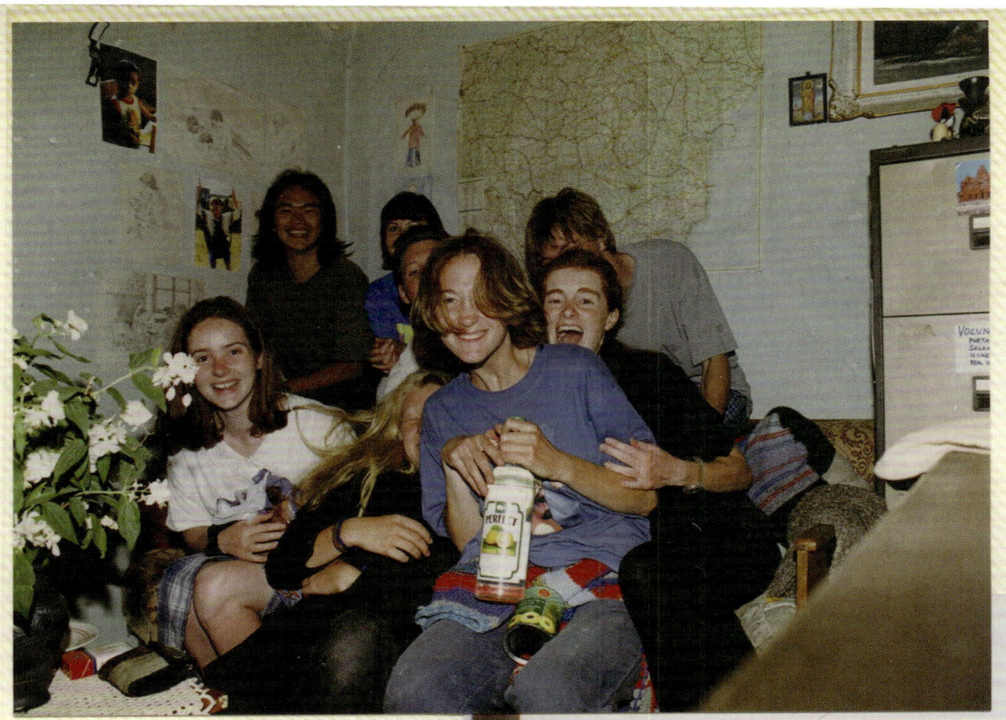

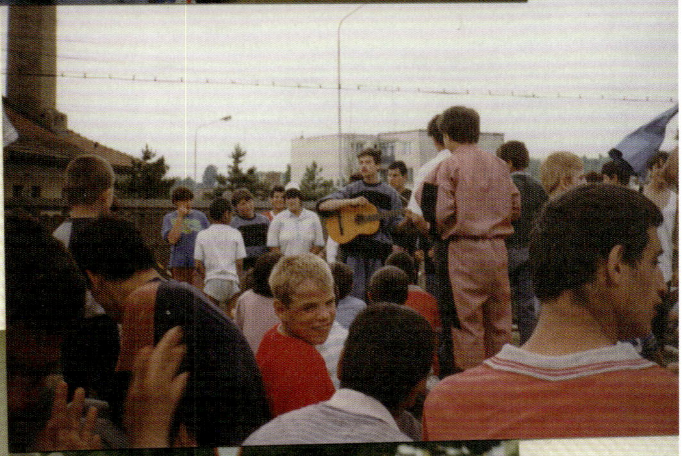

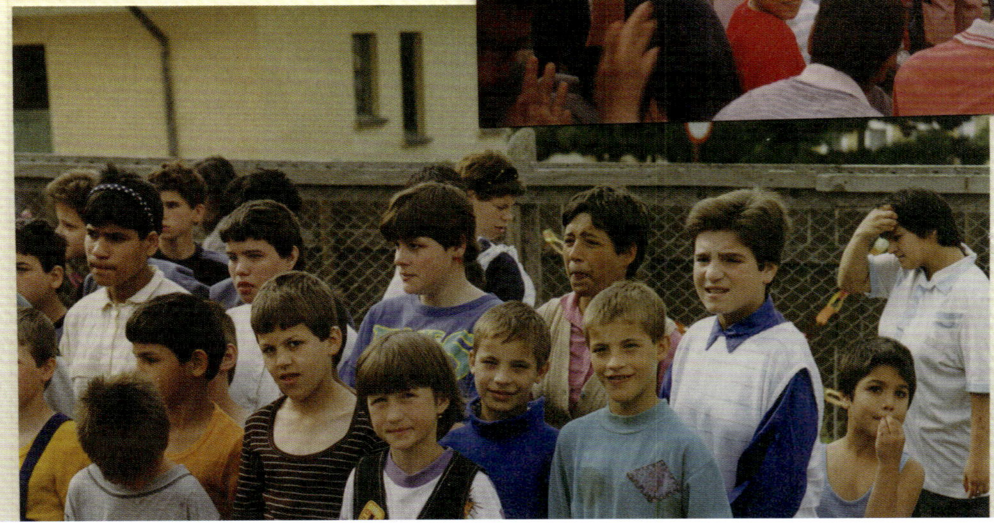

To my daughters Leia, Isla & Lyra,

This book is by no means the complete story. During the making of this project, I collected hundreds of old photographs, letters and items. They came from all over the world, surviving wars and numerous migrations across oceans and cultures. Familiar stories were retold to me by different relatives, many new ones came to light for the first time; some fasinating, some touching, some amusing and some shocking. Moving to England at the age of 13, I spent my teenage years wishing I was like everyone else, dyeing my hair, wearing coloured contact lenses, naively thinking it would help me fit in. Spending many years in my 20s travelling and working around the world, the question of culture rarely came up. It wasn't until you were born that I confronted it again. I came to the project rather unsure of my own cultural heritage but left proud to be Chinese. I hope you will grow up proud to be who you are and embrace both your heritages. I hope one day we will have time to sit down so I can retell some of the stories to you in more detail as well as the many other tales that didn't make it into the book.

Throughout my research, I was surprised by how little information/records there were on my grandmothers. Once they married into a new family, it was clear that they were no longer part of their previous family. The Wong family tree can be traced back 27 generations but only along the male lines. I don't feature on it. I can only tell you my side of the story, you should find out more about your Scottish side of the family when you get the chance.

Let me sign out with the tale of the looted stained glass screens. The photograph the follows on the next page was taken in one of the best restaurants in Guangzhou. Several relatives have told me that the stained glass screen came from the Wong's Mansion; the were looted by the communist army and many years later, resurfaced in the restaurant. Since there is no trace of the Wong's Mansion left, I was so excited when I got permission to shoot the screens. However, it took all of ten seconds for me to realize that all the screens were new and couldn't possibly have come from the Wong's Mansion. I showed the pictures to your grandmother; she is still convinced they've come from her old house.

I am sure I will be making many of the details up when it's my turn to tell you; we can start with how I met your mother :)

With all my love

獻給我的女兒子洛、子希和子月

這本書中的內容並非故事的全部，在項目的創作過程中，我收集了數百張舊照片、信件和物品。它們來自世界各地，在多次的戰爭和移居中倖存下來。不同的親戚給我講了許多熟悉的故事，我也聽到了許多全新的故事。它們有些很有趣，有些讓人感動，有些十分逗樂，有些則令人震驚。我十三歲的時候便搬到英國居住，在青少年時期，我曾希望自己能和其他人一樣，染頭髮，戴有色的隱形眼鏡，幼稚地認為這些有助於讓我融入群體。二十多歲時，儘管花了很多年的時間環遊世界，有關自身文化的問題卻從未被我重視。直到你們出生，我才必須再次面對它。在創作這個項目時，我對自己的文化背景持有相當懷疑的態度，但對自己的華人身分感到自豪。而我希望你們能以自己的身份自豪地成長，珍惜你們從父母身上傳承的文化。我希望有一天我們有時間坐下來，我可以向你們詳細地複述一些細節，以及許多其他沒有寫進書裡的故事。

在做關於這個項目的研究時，我驚訝於有關我祖母和外婆的資料和記錄非常少，一旦她們嫁出，她們就不再被視為家庭內的成員了。黃家的族譜可以追溯到二十七代之前，但卻只收錄了男性成員。在這裡，我只能告訴你們我這邊的故事，有機會的話，你們應該多了解一下蘇格蘭那一邊的家庭故事。

最後請讓我用一個彩色玻璃屏風的故事來結束。這張照片拍攝於一間在廣州非常好的餐廳。有幾個親戚告訴我，這家餐廳裡的彩色玻璃屏風來自黃家的舊宅，它們在一次洗劫後遺失，在許多年後出現這家餐廳裡。由於黃家大宅早已不見踪影，我非常興奮能獲准拍攝這些彩色玻璃。然而，只在玻璃前花了十秒鐘我便意識到，所有的這些玻璃都是新的，絕不可能來自黃家舊宅。可我給你們的奶奶看了照片後，她卻仍然相信這些玻璃是來自她的舊居。

還有太多的細節，就留到未來我再一一講訴；那時我們可以從我如何認識你們的母親開始 :)

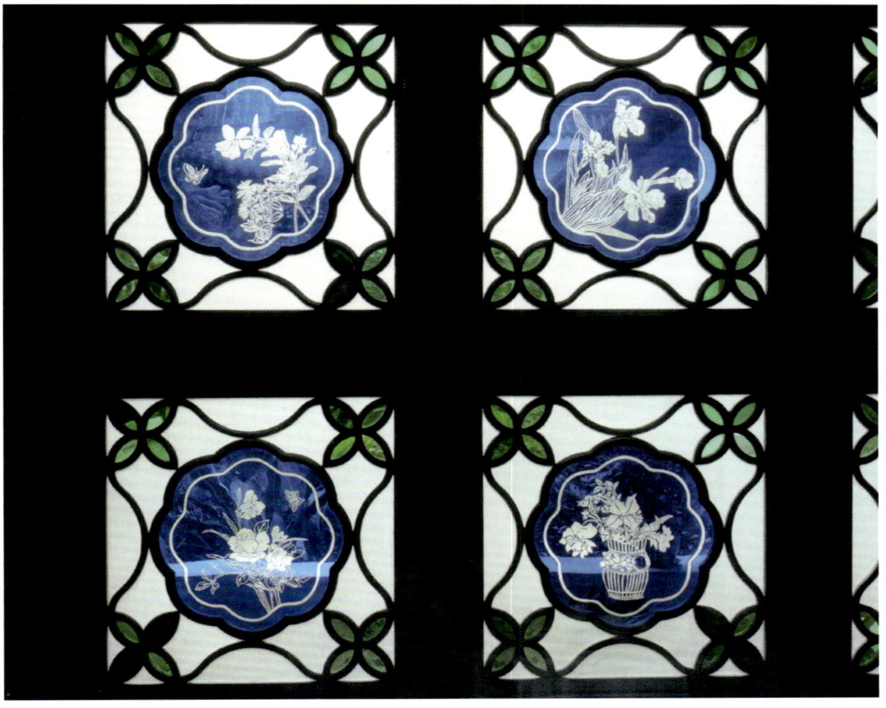

To be continued …

The Queen, the Chairman and I François Cheval

Straight from the outset, *The Queen, the Chairman and I* goes beyond the simple limits of memorial photography. It is no longer possible to envisage photographing loved ones and the reconstruction of lineage through mechanical images, without taking its contribution into account.

The book depicts a relationship to history, human journeys and the fate of a unique city, Hong Kong, interwoven to perfection. It reads like a family saga that starts with Sun Yat-sen, shifting into adventure film territory, featuring sailors, smugglers and merchants in a shady metropolis. Kurt Tong turns archive photography into a form of profound solidarity between generations. The past plays out and connects with the present through a network of threads that link each element of a reconstituted story. The narrative blends the history of the port city with the blips in the lineage. Kurt Tong has spent much of his life in England. He admits to being made of material from the past. He convokes souls that live on, while respecting tradition. These souls emerge from each face that is preserved on photographic paper. Family photography is not a succession of objective facts, it involves above all a relationship with whoever is in control. By recognising himself in previous eras, Kurt Tong makes his existence an attempt to link this present to that 'which once was'. Where exactly is his own life? By playing with these images, creating a layout, reorganising them, he makes them his own. He adopts them and configures them into a series that makes sense, that is almost obvious. A snag-free narrative.

Kurt Tong is a storyteller. Scene after scene, he exposes the stages of the fight for survival and the establishment of the family fortune, that involve social position and fate (fortuna). Between opium, trade and matrimonial alliances, a soap opera unfolds with episodes depicting the adventures of a family to which we become attached. The series doesn't need an ending in order to set off the imagination. We need to get closer, to act like a short-sighted person looking at a screen to really experience and feel the sensuality of a century that is gone and forgotten. The resulting collection of pictures, documents, letters and contemporary documentary photography exalts these interwoven portraits and fates. It is more than a genealogical extraction from oblivion, stories of life and flesh emanate from these obligatory poses. There is no symbolism here! Merely simple beings hiding their emotions, and concealing their desires, the things of life.

It is up to us to own this narrative and this imaginary world. We must work it out ourselves, putting on a *cheongsam* or a *hanfu*. We need to visit one of these dens, ignoring all of the clichés found in literature, the false and exotic imagery of these seedy places. On the contrary, swept along by Kurt Tong's narrative, we must blend into the subtle décor, where the best quality opium is for sale, where the most exquisite food is served, and get a massage. The great houses of Hong Kong and Canton initiated some of their offspring into opium, as it was seen as preferable to gambling as a vice. Financial ruin was the ultimate fear of all big families.

Trade was and is the be-all and end-all of Hong Kong. Great Britain forced the opium trade onto Imperial China using Hong Kong as a hub, as a result of the shameful Treaty of Nanking signed on August 29 1843. Cameras arrived in the luggage of British army personnel and tradespeople: "For the first decades, photography expanded with the western presence in China. Until 1890-1895 it was practised almost exclusively within treaty ports, along the China Coast and Yangtze river." [1]

By having their portraits taken in the first studios set up in Hong Kong, Kurt Tong's ancestors displayed their proximity to western modernity. They are the perfect representation of the middle class that could be termed 'comprador', local tradespeople that depended on foreign firms.

Behind its apparent neutrality, the family archive is weighed down by the history of the port. For the photographer, educated according to British culture, family photography is about self-discovery. This galaxy of patiently collected portraits is intended to offset the social and political events that the coast of Hong Kong underwent from the annexation to the day it was handed back to China in 1997. The narrator, a participant in the narrative, finds himself in the observations. He was/is a sailor, he was/is an opium smoker, he was/is a dancer…

The photographic experience of a memorial reconstruction attempts to resolve contradictions and create unity. The links that are recreated, the story that emerges, must unsettle his psyche to an extent. *The Queen, The Chairman and I* gives the personal experience only known to Kurt Tong, an illustrated form.

From curiosity to nostalgia, photography must be able to objectivise moods. To do so, the photographer does not hesitate to adapt. He resorts to craftsmanship, weaving elements together as weaving and storytelling are so similar. Perhaps he inherited the art of knots from his sailor ancestors! Life is but a series of interlacing connections. Our very nature is the result of a past that sticks desperately to our skin, the conjunction of so many determinations. But Tong wants to tell the future from these memories. By manipulating the course of things, he tries to find the cause.

Photography has a unique quality, that of being able to resolve the eye's impossibility to see itself.

It is out of the question for this descendant of sailors to be a shipwreck without memory, as a life without real or manufactured adventures would make no sense. For Tong, narration is life itself. The two terms are in no way contradictory. The irreversibility of time calls on ancient images to be the constituents of the present. *The Queen, The Chairman and I* at all times shows solidarity with its characters, of which he is the result. He does not tear himself away, as 'to be' today means also accepting a parentage that is global and total, with no denial. No matter where he lives, his attachment to tradition connects him to Hong Kong, the only city that counts.

Identification, the will to make one's present life coincide with the past, does not require going beyond anything. This is the past, this is me. It is a question of accepting a series of fates without any expurgation. The family saga forms a slow, uninterrupted movement explained only by the permanent to-and-fro of Tong's current stance, between collective past and individual present.

The texts that accompany the series continue this temporal dialectic; the past is essential to the writing while the photographs document the present, a necessary counterpoint to the subjectivity of the family archive. This coherent collection of writing and documents, of memories and contemporary images make up a determinist proposal that, in the end, asks questions of Tong's autonomy.

Here, we move away from the spontaneity of the piece, from the robust urgency. A palpable tension emerges between fantasy existence and artistic career. The urge to take over the entire family history, to set himself up as a separate individual, means that Tong, a photographer from Hong Kong, who has also lived in England, attempts to reconcile the power of fate and his freedom as a photographer. And it is Kurt Tong, the photographer, the artist, who resolves the apparent contradiction, by inventing Kurt Tong, the man. The free choice he makes about himself identifies finally with what he wants for his future.

1. Régine Thiriez, pp.78-82, 'Late Imperial China in Photography' in *A Journey through Light and Shadow*, Exhibition catalogue, Museum of Macao, June 2009.

女皇，主席與我

弗朗索·薩瓦爾

在創作的啟始，「女皇，主席與我」便跨越了紀念攝影領域的邊界。未來每當人們設想拍攝親人或通過機械影像重建血緣系譜時，它都將被當作一個必然的參考。

在書中描繪的是一段完美交織的關係，於歷史、人類旅程和香港這座獨特城市之命運間。一個家族的傳奇，以孫中山發起革命開篇，隨後在陰暗的大都會中水手、走私者和商人一一出場，引出一段段電影般的冒險故事。唐景鋒將檔案攝影轉化為鏈接家族世代間的緊密紐帶。故事被重構化作一張線索交叉的網絡，過去被翻開在其中與當下相連。敘事間港口城市的歷史與宗族的軼事被融合統一。成長於英國，唐景鋒自認構成自身存在的材料來源於過去。他尊重傳統的同時，召喚生活在其中的靈魂。這些靈魂於捕捉保存在照相紙上的每張臉孔中浮現。家庭攝影從不是一系列的客觀事實，它首先涉及到與掌控力量者間的關係。唐景鋒藉由研究過去的時代以自我審視，嘗試將自身的存在化作鏈條，將當下的與那曾經一度的認識聯繫在一起。在這網絡中他自身的生活應落何處？通過擺佈、創建佈局並重新組織，他掌控了這些圖像。它們被接收、賦予邏輯再分配而排入理所應當的全新序列。這是一次無疵的敘事。

唐景鋒是說故事的人。一幕接著一幕的是生存的掙扎和家庭財富的建立，這是關於社會地位和命運的舞台。一出描繪家族冒險經歷的肥皂劇，在鴉片、貿易和婚姻聯盟中上演，逐漸吸引著我們沉浸其中。這齣故事不需要結局讓想像繼續發散。我們需要做的是去靠得更近，像近視的人緊盯著屏幕般去真切地體驗，用感官去感受一個過去的、已然消逝的時代。這是圖片、文件、信件和當代紀實攝影的集合物，承載著交織中的肖像和命運。一切不僅僅是為了從湮沒的記憶中提取家族譜系，這些肖像人物姿態儘管古板，湧出的卻是關於生命和肉體的故事。在這裡沒有象徵主義！只有低微的生物隱藏著情感，壓抑著慾望，關於活著的種種。

我們必須主動方能掌控這一敘事，和這個想像中的世界。我們須自行尋找方法，穿上長衫或漢服。我們要去探尋一個鴉片館，忘記書本中所有的陳詞濫調，忘記虛假的異國風情影像中那些骯髒與混亂。唐景鋒的敘述將我們拉入的是與之相反的一處，這兒裝飾精美必須謹言慎行以融入，這裡出售最優質的鴉片，提供最精緻的食物，而你將享受一次按摩的服務。香港和廣州兩個大家族的後代都迷上了吸食鴉片，因作為惡行的它在當時卻被認為比賭博更為道德。家道沒落是所有大家族的終極恐懼。

貿易在過去和如今都是香港的全部和最終目標。英國迫使清政府在1843年8月29日簽署了可恥的《南京條約》，接受以香港作為中心的對華鴉片貿易。照相機也隨著英國軍隊人員和商人的行李抵達了：「在最初的十年，攝影術在中國因西方勢力的影響而被傳播開來，但直到1890至1895年前都幾乎僅在通商口岸城市，即沿海岸線和長江一帶被實踐。」[1]

通過在香港設立的第一間攝影工作室拍攝肖像，唐景鋒的祖先們展示了他們與西方現代性的接近程度。他們是中產階級的完美代表，即所謂買辦，幫助西方公司進行貿易的當地商人。

這些家族檔案在表面的中立性背後，是沉重的港口歷史。而對於在英國接受教育的攝影師來說，家庭攝影是關於自我發現的。這些被耐心收集起來的肖像們，串聯起了香港的社會和政治事件，從其被吞併到1997年回歸中國間。敘事者，敘事的參與者，在觀察中發現自我。他曾是/是一名水手，他曾是/是吸食鴉片的人，他曾是/是一位舞者……

這是用攝影去體驗的一次追憶式重構，它試圖去化解矛盾並創造統一。被重新建立的聯繫，浮現出的故事，都必須在一定程度上動搖他的心靈。「女皇，主席與我」所給出的是屬於唐景鋒的個人體驗，以影像的形式呈現。

從好奇心到懷舊，攝影定能夠將思緒客觀化。為達成這目標，攝影師毫不猶豫地去吸收新知。他訴諸於手工技藝，編織起故事的元素，因為編織的技巧和講故事是如此相似。他定是從他的水手祖先那裡繼承了結繩的藝術！生活只是一系列交織的聯繫。我們的本性源自於過去，而它緊密地依附在我們肌膚之上，由無數次的決定結合而成。但唐景鋒希望的是藉由記憶去講述未來。通過操縱事物的過程，他試圖找到原因。攝影具有的一個獨特品質是，能將雙眼所見自身的不可能性化作可能。

這位水手的後代不會成為一艘沒有記憶的沉船，如生活若離開了冒險，不論是真實的或被製造出的，都將毫無意義。對於唐景鋒來說，敘事便是生活本身。兩者的概念並不矛盾。時間的不可逆性呼喚遠古的圖像，使其成為當下的組成部分。唐景鋒作為其中角色的後代，讓「女皇，主席與我」時刻都展示出對他們的包容。他並不將自身從中割裂，因為生存在今日意味著必須接受一種全球性和整體性的傳承關係，不容任何否認。不論他居住何處，對傳統的依戀使他與香港，這座於他而言唯一重要的城市聯繫在一起。

身份是一種意願，讓當下的生活成為過去的重複，而無需去超越。過去，便是我。問題在於是否接受接踵而來的命運而不作任何廓清。家族的傳奇組作了一次緩慢而不間斷的運動，由唐景鋒永久往復於集體過去和個體當下之間的當前立場闡述。

在伴隨該系列的文本內，時間辯證法體現於動詞的形態中；過去在寫作中必不可少，而照片記錄了現在，這便是組成家庭檔案主觀性的必要對立。在這條理分明的收藏庫中是關於記憶與當代影像的寫作和文件，組成一份屬於決定論者的提案，並最終質疑唐景鋒在其中的自主權。

在此，我們擺脫了作品的自發性，和那強大的緊迫性。幻想的存在與藝術生涯間出現了明顯的張力。那去接管整個家族史、自命為一個獨立個體的衝動，意味著唐景鋒，這位來自香港居在英國的攝影師，試圖讓命運的力量和他作為一名攝影師的自由去和解。作為攝影師與藝術家的唐景鋒破解了這顯然的矛盾，通過去創造作為人的唐景鋒。那些關於他自身而被作出的自由選擇最終明確了他對自身未來的期望。

1. 狄瑞景，78-82頁，《凝擷光影》“攝影中的晚期帝國”章節，展覽目錄，澳門博物館，2009年6月。

鳴謝

正如你所想像的那樣，這個項目的完成離不開許多人的幫助。謝謝你們協助我的研究，分享自己的故事，和相信這個極其私人的故事之力量。

我想感謝：連州攝影博物館將展覽帶回中國並出版了本書。戴維·路易斯與卡羅琳·沃赫斯特對本書的大力支持，從做樣書開始到如今出版，我很榮幸能和你們一起工作。孫景怡在項目甚至還未完成前就給予我大量的信心，以及她從未間斷的支持。本·伯布里奇在我創作最迷失之時，為我指明方向。安妮·麥克尼爾幫助我整合了項目，並組織了在英國的巡展。段煜婷對我作品的無限信任。胡若灝幫助我解決了許多事情，不問大小。弗朗索·薩瓦爾為本書撰寫了深刻而富有洞察力的評論文章。黃煥延、黃煥平、黃仲麒、喬恩·利維、勞倫·海因茨、莫伊拉·林賽、帕特里克·亨利、比亞特·希捷斯卡、何伊寧、陳暢、希瑟·斯奈德、大衛·德雷克、殷家樑、尹子聰、奧德麗·瓦羅、章翔鷗、貝琳達·溫特伯恩、莉莎·博托什、傑瑪·巴尼特、安吉拉·希德、皮帕·奧爾德菲爾德、李國瑜、彭光源、達納·波帕、馬克·福克斯韋爾、保羅·麥克金、克里斯蒂·豪爾、麦顏玉、唐令詩、楊永金、莫里茨·紐姆勒、艾可·厄舜、連州攝影節的工作人員以及所有幫助過我的人們。

最後，我想感謝父母如此坦率地與我分享他們的故事，以及多年保存這些珍貴的信件和照片。

感謝我的妻子蘇多年來的堅定支持，以及我三個美麗的孩子，子洛、子希和子月，是你們讓我腳踏著實地。

ACKNOWLEDGEMENTS

As you can imagine, this project would not have been possible without help from a lot of people. Thank you to everyone who assisted with my research, gave their time to share their stories and who believed in telling such a personal story.

I would like to thank: Lianzhou Museum of Photography for bringing the project to China. Dewi Lewis and Caroline Warhurst for their support of the book from the very first dummy; I feel very privileged to be finally publishing the book with them. Carol Sun for believing in the project even before it was finished and her continuing support. Ben Burbridge for helping me to give the project a clear direction when I was at my most lost. Anne McNeill for bringing the full project together and touring it around the UK. Duan Yuting for having so much faith in my work. Hu Ruohao for always allowing me to run things by him, however small they are. François Cheval for contributing such an insightful essay. Wong Woon Yin, Wong Woon Pin, Wong Chung Kai, Jon Levy, Lauren Heinz, Moira Lindsey, Patrick Henry, Beata Cegielska, He Yining, Abby Chen, Heather Snider, David Drake, Yan Kallen, Simon Wan, Audrey Hoareau, Zhang Xiang'ou, Belinda Winterborne, Lisa Botos, Gemma Barnett, Angela Shead, Pippa Oldfield, Davina Lee, Pang Kwon Yuen, Dana Popa, Mark Foxwell, Paul McGurkin, Kristy Hall, Mak Ngan Yuk, Barbara Tong, Kelvin Yang, Moritz Neumüller, Ekow Eshun, Lianzhou Foto and everyone who gave me their time.

Lastly, I want to thank my parents for being so open in sharing stories about their lives and for keeping so many letters and photos over the years.

My wife Su for her unwavering support over the years and my three beautiful children, Leia, Islaand and Lyra, who keep me grounded.

First published in the UK in 2019 by
Dewi Lewis Publishing
8 Broomfield Road
Heaton Moor
Stockport SK4 4ND
England

www.dewilewispublishing.com

Lianzhou Museum of Photography
No.120 Zhongshan Nan Road
Lianzhou, Guangdong,
China

www.lmop.org.cn

ISBN: 978-1-911306-49-8
Design: Kurt Tong and Dewi Lewis
Translation: Kay Yang & Hu Ruohao
Proofreading: Sacha Dewavrin, en; Chen Zijian & Guo Yun, cn
Printed and bound: Yofus Co., Ltd.
Print: 1000

Celebrating 25 years Dewi Lewis Publishing

Lianzhou Museum of Photography
连州摄影博物馆